FROM FRONTIERS TO FOOTBALL

FROM FRONTIERS TO FOOTBALL

AN ALTERNATIVE HISTORY OF LATIN AMERICA SINCE 1800

Matthew Brown

REAKTION BOOKS

For Mairi, Hannah-Morag, Keir and Calum,
as you begin your journeys westwards

En memoria de Antonio Cisneros

Published by
Reaktion Books Ltd
33 Great Sutton Street
London EC1V 0DX, UK

www.reaktionbooks.co.uk

First published 2014

Printed and bound in Great Britain by
TJ International, Padstow, Cornwall

British Library Cataloguing in Publication Data

ISBN 978 1 78023 353 6

Contents

Present-day map of Latin America.

Latin America and the World: An Introduction

In August 2012, at the closing ceremony to the London Olympic Games, the singer Marisa Monte, the rapper BNegão, the footballer Pelé, the dancer Renato Sorriso, the supermodel Alessandra Ambrosio and the actor Seu Jorge led the Brazilian presentation of their country to the eyes of the world. The image that was displayed was one of cultural diversity, joy in physicality and dexterity in play. Brazil was fun, viewers were shown, at one with its history and peoples and ready to welcome the world. In return, the Brazilian authorities hoped that hundreds of thousands of sports fans would visit Rio de Janeiro in 2016 for Brazil's first staging of the Olympic Games (Latin America's first Games since Mexico City in 1970) and also for the 2014 FIFA World Cup, the first time Latin America had hosted the finals since Mexico 1986. To win the bidding process to host these international sporting competitions, Brazil presented itself as a young, upbeat country, entering the international economy at great speed, modernizing and welcoming foreign investment as part of the BRIC countries (Brazil, Russia, India and China) deemed to be at the cutting edge of global economic development in the twenty-first century.

This was not the first time that Latin America had presented itself as the next big thing, nor the first time that sporting events had been used to further economic, social or geopolitical aims in the region. This book will tell the story of Latin America's engagement with the rest of the world from 1800 to the present day, linking independence from colonial rule to the 2016 Olympics via the history of the intervening two centuries. Often Latin America's engagement with the rest of the world has been presented as a simple narrative of Latin

American victimhood. Stories today on Brazil, Mexico and other countries that are now confidently asserting themselves in the international arena suggest that these centuries of subordination are being cast aside on the basis of new democracies, optimism and sound economic management. Historians of Latin America, however, have documented so many false dawns that they offer more sceptical interpretations. In this book, I show that this scepticism is partly justified, but also that Latin America has been an integral part of the international community since its independence from colonial rule. The continent has never been solely defined by its poverty or its 'coloniality', the in-vogue phrase to describe the lingering social and cultural legacies of colonialism.

A narrative of Latin American victimhood has been popular both on the left and the right for decades. Eduardo Galeano's *Open Veins of Latin America: Five Centuries of the Pillage of a Continent* set out an incisive attack on the devastating continuities between the Spanish conquistadores, u.s. imperialists and kleptocratic military regimes of the 1960s and '70s. At the core of Galeano's argument were raw materials: the gold, silver, copper, coffee, bananas and beef exported from Latin American soil in the quickest, most direct fashion – and with as much of the profit as (in)humanly possible ending up in the pockets and bank accounts of unfeeling, unethical and immoral capitalists in Europe and the u.s. More recently, Oscar Guardiola-Rivera's meditation on the subject, *What if Latin America Ruled the World?*, has followed this interpretation of Latin American history and supplemented it with powerful and serious analysis of the environmental and social consequences of such a global system. Both argue that Latin America requires major social, political and geopolitical reform or revolution if it is no longer to be the victim of the actions of greedy, imperialist outsiders.[1]

From the opposite end of the political spectrum, other grand narratives of world history have used Latin American history to support their own theses. Latin American 'failure' is often invoked in such books to demonstrate the 'success' of other places. Niall Ferguson in *Empire* and *Colossus* does not provide any serious analysis of Latin America in his narratives of British and u.s. pre-eminence in the nineteenth and twentieth centuries respectively because the in-formal, competitive nature of the relationship with Latin America doesn't fit into his thesis about the rise and fall of empires. C. A. Bayly, in *The Birth of the Modern World*, barely engages with Latin America for more than a few pages, despite his title, and the per-ipheral place allocated to the region serves to buttress his claim that China and Southeast Asia, rather than Europe, are at the epicentre of global history. (As Charles Jones notes, 'Bayly is challengeable in almost every particular'.)[2] We might see these interpretations as evi-dence of the rather benign neglect of Latin America characteristic of a British imperial historiography that still focuses on the lands that once were painted red on the map. In *Civilization: The Six Killer Apps of Western Power* (2011), however, Ferguson goes further, using Latin America as a convenient example of a place where Western ideals and practices have failed without taking account of the broader internal historical changes that shaped Latin America's reception of these external forces.[3]

This is all far too simplistic. Latin America cannot be judged either as a utopian continent of hopes and dreams or as the pitiable victim of the machinations of evil empires. Somehow Latin America is always dismissed from historical arguments conducted outside of Latin America as being too peripheral, or at best is mentioned as an 'interesting' aside, an example of how things might have worked out in a different imperial context. In this book I step away from the squabble to look at the historical events, processes and individuals that are used to support these interpretations. This book aims to introduce the principal historical changes that occurred in Latin America's relationship with the rest of the world in the last two centuries. On this basis, I hope that you, the reader, can make up your own mind as to the role of the outside world in shaping Latin America – and Latin America's position in shaping global history. My own feeling is that Galeano and Ferguson might *both* be right: that Latin America was a victim of empire at the very same time as it was made to look peripheral to global processes.

An analysis of the evidence will allow us to explore how the region resisted victimhood, engaged with outsiders and found its own understanding of globalization. Perhaps the contemporary history of Latin America can tell us whether historical continuities are really now being overthrown, as some would have us believe. By using historical evidence, and the analysis and interpretations of historians, we can consider the extent to which Latin America has suffered from, and been shaped by, its relationship with global empires.

Where *is* Latin America?

Is Latin America anything 'more than an inaccurate but convenient label for books and maps', as the historian José Moya asks? We know that the 'idea of Latin America' – and the term 'Latin America' itself – only came about in the 1840s and '50s, dreamed up by men born in Colombia, Argentina, Chile and Mexico who had been to Paris and started to realize the extent of their shared cultures, histories and historical circumstances.[4] Brazil has had an ambivalent relationship with the term 'Latin America' ever since, at various stages of its history preferring to stress its relationship with Portugal, or with the u.s., rather than its Spanish-speaking neighbours, as Leslie Bethell has shown.[5] The Latinobarómetro survey regularly finds that around a quarter of Brazilians feel no affiliation to the idea of Latin America.[6] The professed Latin identity of these new Latin Americans was taken up by French writers and imperialists to promote Francophone culture and geopolitical influence within Latin America at the expense of the 'Anglo' United States and Great Britain. Many Latin Americans took it up for the same reason.

Whatever our quibbles about it, the term exists, for now, in the same way that 'Asia', 'Europe' and 'Africa' do, and what follows is an attempt to provide a historical introduction to that region's history and engagement with the rest of the world. Walter Mignolo and other postcolonial scholars are tempted to argue that simply using the term 'Latin America' is part of a European Enlightenment project, dating from the conquest itself, to survey, describe, name and ultimately control the region; to incorporate it within a discursive framework that understands 'Latin' America as inferior to other more successful, prosperous and supposedly hardworking regions. While I accept their point, I use the term as a practical phrase which most readers will recognize.

The academic literature written by historians of Latin America shows that the continent is united by a shared historical experience to a degree unimaginable of even apparently homogenous continents such as Africa or Europe. The principal characteristics shared by most of Latin America across its history are the relatively late arrival of *Homo sapiens* compared to other areas of the world; major transcontinental migration over time producing significant ethnic diversity, subsequently reinforced by transatlantic migration in the post-1492 period; and the shared history of Iberian colonialism and its legacies (for example, in linguistic terms, leading to the dominance of the Spanish and Portuguese languages, and culturally, the popularity and authority of the Catholic religion). All of these factors occurred before the middle of the eighteenth century. Nevertheless these legacies were shaped according to the geographical and demographical landscapes that they encountered, to the extent that Moya suggests redefining the Americas into three regions/categories according to its separate colonial legacies.[7]

This is a helpful way of thinking about the history of the western hemisphere. Rather than the binary of North against South America (Mexicans will never tire of reminding the ignorant that their country is well and truly situated in North America, contradicting the assumption by citizens of the United States that 'America' is theirs and theirs alone, which is demeaning as well as ignorant), or of Anglo- versus Latin America, Moya suggests 'a conceptual triad that fuses geographical and ethnohistorical components'. By this he means that it is useful to think of three large geographical regions in the Americas that share overlapping ethnic and/or historical characteristics. These are Indo-America, Afro-America and Euro-America.[8]

'Indo-America', or mestizo America, comprises the western highlands of the Americas, the areas where Amerindian populations were most densely populated before the Iberian conquest and which remain as the strongest representatives of the indigenous peoples of the continent today, both demographically and culturally. This means the highland areas of Mexico and through Central America – the lands of the Aztecs and Mayas and thousands of other indigenous societies, south into Andean Colombia, Ecuador, Peru, Bolivia, Paraguay and northern Chile and Argentina – broadly corresponding to the limits of the Inca empire in the fifteenth century, and today populated by several million speakers of Quichua, Aymara and Guaraní. These areas attracted the interest of colonizers in the sixteenth century because of their silver and gold mines and the availability of an indigenous population that could be harnessed for extracting the precious metals. Mexico City, Lima and Potosí were famed for their colonial opulence resulting from the forced labour of indigenous miners. After independence from colonial rule, as this book shows, these areas continued to attract interest from imperial powers who wanted to exploit the resources hidden beneath the soil – and this longstanding colonial legacy has not gone unnoticed by the people who have defended, resisted or engaged with these interlopers.

'Afro-America' occupies the tropical coastal lowlands, including the tropical islands of the Caribbean, where European conquest wiped out or advanced against indigenous societies. During the colonial period, these areas were developed for the production of tropical cash crops for export to Europe: tobacco and sugar at first and, later, bananas. In order to work the plantations that made these businesses profitable, colonial rulers resorted to the mass importation of African slaves throughout the sixteenth, seventeenth, eighteenth and nineteenth centuries through the so-called 'triangular trade'. During this Atlantic trading arrangement European merchants took their ships, loaded with brass, textiles and cheaply produced items, to exchange these products on the West African coast for human beings. Eleven million Africans were forcibly transported across the Atlantic Ocean, often in terrible conditions, and those who survived the Middle Passage were sold to plantation owners in slave markets. The ships were then loaded up with the products of the slave plantations and transported back to European ports such as Nantes, Bristol, Liverpool, London, Seville and Amsterdam, where the lucky merchants cashed in their enormous profits and started the whole enterprise again. Afro-America, in this formulation, corresponds broadly to the islands of the Caribbean, northeastern and some parts of central Brazil, parts of the south of the United States, the Caribbean coasts of Central and South America, and the Pacific coastal strips of Peru, Ecuador, Colombia, Panama and Mexico. In the colonial period, these areas had fabulously wealthy elites. The islands of Cuba, Barbados and Sainte-Domingue (later Haiti) produced the wealth that fuelled the imperial pretensions of their European masters: Spain, Great Britain and France respectively.

'Euro-America' consists of the temperate lands on the northern and southern edges of the Americas: the north of the U.S. and Canada, and the belt stretching down from São Paulo to southern Argentina and the southern half of Chile. Lacking precious metals or significant potential indigenous labour, these areas were rather neglected by the colonialists and consequently remained impoverished backwaters by the standards of the imperial jewels of Peru, Mexico, Cuba, Barbados and Sainte-Domingue.

It is useful to employ the distinction between Indo-America, Afro-America and Euro-America, forged in the experience of colonialism from 1492 to 1810, as we try to understand the historical trajectory of Latin America after independence from colonial rule. For our purposes, following the most widespread understanding, Latin America means everywhere in the Americas apart from the U.S., Canada and the British islands of the Caribbean. Haiti, which achieved its independence from France in 1804, abolishing slavery and becoming the second independent republic in the Americas, is generally included within discussions of Latin America because its nineteenth- and twentieth-century history shares greater commonalities with Central and South America than with France or the U.S. Historians do, of course, continue to debate whether any of these inclusions or exclusions make sense.

The principal hypothesis that I will advance in this book is that one of the principal historical experiences that unites Latin America from its independence to the present day is the continued presence of imperial involvement in the region, and the efforts of leaders, writers and the general population to make sense of this and deal with it as they see fit. Crucially, there was a wide variety of ways in which people thought about and engaged with the considerable foreign influences that shaped their lives. This began in colonial times, of course, and with independence and increased communication and travel speeds the region was brought more explicitly into the worldview of outsiders. Independence was to many Latin Americans a largely hypothetical construct which did not explain the continued presence of the foreign mining firms, railway builders and financial investors that held sway over their elected representatives and leaders. Others, such as Simón Bolívar and José de San Martín, saw how they could use and manipulate global powers and their representatives in order to find space for their own attempts to grab and hold on to legitimate power.

In the nineteenth and twentieth centuries, European and North American merchants, investors and travellers sought to emulate the Spanish and Portuguese success at harnessing the productive power of Latin America for their own benefit. Population growth in Europe triggered a demand for food and the temperate lands of the Southern Cone (southern Brazil, Argentina, Uruguay and Chile) were able to fill that gap, sending wheat and meat across the Atlantic. The factories that sprang up in São Paulo, Buenos Aires, Montevideo and Santiago would be filled by workers who crossed the Atlantic seeking opportunities to 'make it' in the Americas, following the same pattern, at the same time, as the migration from Europe to New York, Chicago and Philadelphia. Some 60 million Europeans crossed the Atlantic after 1492 to make new lives for themselves in the Americas, the vast majority of them enabled by the steamship technology of the nineteenth and twentieth centuries. As Moya summarizes,

the poorest colonies thus became during the nineteenth century the richest countries of the Americas and the richest regions within those countries. By the early twentieth century, per capita GDP in the United States, Canada, Argentina, Uruguay and Chile was two to six times higher than the average elsewhere in the continent. The North, the South and the East of the United States, Brazil and Argentina respectively – which had been the least developed areas of those countries before 1800 – became the wealthiest.[9]

In exploring the major ways in which Latin America's relationship with the rest of the world has been transformational, a significant avenue of investigation involves the effect that foreign investment, migration and commerce has had upon Latin American economies, cultures and politics. The temptation is to focus on Euro-America, and to look at where foreign migration and cultural transformation was most obvious. Though I acknowledge that Argentina, Brazil and Mexico were probably the countries that were the most closely tied into international economies, especially in the nineteenth century, I have deliberately tried to avoid focusing just on them. I have looked to provide illustrative cases from across the continent. At the same time I have tried to provide an introduction to the major episodes that anyone looking at Latin American and global history needs to comprehend, from railway building to the Cuban missile crisis, from Bolívar's armies to the Falklands/Malvinas War. That said, this is not a comprehensive history of Latin America – there are plenty of those already, listed in the bibliography. Because I want people reading this book to read further into the cases and episodes discussed here, I have cited primarily English (rather than Spanish or Portuguese) texts. This is not intended to demean the research of scholars who have published in English – my previous books all rely primarily on works in Spanish. Here, I have deliberately chosen to cite the most readable and accessible of these English-language books and articles; although there has been a great boom in academic publications about Latin American culture and history in the last two decades, only a fraction of them are written in clear, jargon-free language. Of course it helps to have specialist and linguistic skills if you want to understand the history of Latin America, and although many historians working these days can read in Spanish, Portuguese and academic English, and often French too, such fluency is not necessary for the general reader. Indeed, by choosing to guide readers towards English-language sources, I want to explicitly demonstrate that language is not a viable explanation for the way that global historians continue to neglect Latin America in their analyses.

Latin America and Global History

Latin America is important to our understanding of the global history of the last two centuries precisely because it was so central to the development of the historical processes that we know as 'globalization' today. Latin American declarations of independence in the 1820s were anti-colonial but they were also 'liberal' in the sense that sovereignty came to reside in the people, and legitimacy became grounded in the consent (rather than just the domination) of the governed. The French Revolution, from 1789, may have initiated this period in European history, but events and ideas in Latin America often overtook those of Europe and provided a huge swathe of republics, some liberal, some not so, that Europeans and North Americans looked to for inspiration – and often with some anxiety – during the rest of the nineteenth century. Chapter One explains how and why this happened at such a relatively early stage in Latin America: because of a participation in global processes that are often ignored or denigrated by historians more interested in other parts of the world.[10] The independence of Latin America also gave rise to a series of brand new nation-states, entities that characterized this continent much more, and much earlier, than any other region of the world.[11] The struggles, disadvantages and triumphs of Latin American state building in the face of the global imperial expansion of other powers in the second half of the nineteenth century is the subject of chapter Two. After independence, who was 'in' the nation, and who was 'outside' it? Against what backdrop were nations imagined, invented and built? How did Latin Americans experience the interventions and influences of the world empires?

This book also contains plenty of evidence of the influence that Latin America has had upon the rest of the world. It is no backwater periphery, but neither has it been only the provider of raw materials – gold, silver, sugar, coffee, rubber, oil – as some of the literature that casts the continent as a victim might have us believe. Politics and culture have seen transfers out as well as in. Scientific observation of Latin American wildlife enabled Darwin's theories about human evolution. Latin American leaders inspired others elsewhere – Benito

Mussolini was named after the Mexican president Benito Juarez, for example, and Simón Bolívar, Emiliano Zapata and Che Guevara inspired many fans and imitators worldwide. Oscar Guardiola-Rivera has suggested that economic boom and political confidence in Latin America is such that in the twenty-first century, the time might have come for the predominant direction of traffic to be reversed and for Latin America's influence upon the world to become more significant than the world's influence on Latin America. He might be right, but in the last two centuries the direction of travel has primarily been inwards, towards Latin America. This explains the much greater number of pages dedicated to exploring the nature and consequences of international relationships on Latin America and Latin Americans, rather than on Africa, Asia, North America and Europe. The most significant contributions came from Europe and North America, though the legacies of Asian and African influences are also detailed here.

The chapters of this book have been divided in order to broadly correspond to phases in the historical evolution of Latin America's relationship with the rest of the world. It first looks at the causes, processes and consequences of independence, and then focuses on the nation building programmes of 1830–70. Chapter Three examines the social and political changes that took place as a result of the continent's increasing interactions with global trade, and the surge in u.s. involvement around 1898, while chapter Four discusses the revolution in transport infrastructure around the turn of the twentieth century that tied Latin American businesses and exporters more closely to their foreign investors and markets. Chapter Five tackles the region's full incorporation into the international economy as a provider of raw materials to the industrializing countries, and the political and nationalist responses to these relationships. The sixth chapter looks at the Cold War, asking whether Latin America was an active participant in this conflict or a simple theatre for proxy wars. Chapter Seven explores the spread of globalization in the 1980s and '90s and the final chapter looks at the first decade of the twenty-first century, observing the changing relationships between empires and globalization, in particular the rise of China and 'global' culture.

A historical analysis can privilege both imperial and local explan-ations. It shows that civil wars were the arena in which national identity was disputed and negotiated by Mexicans, Colombians and Peruvians, though always within a geopolitical context of imperial powers looking on, intervening or threatening action. By the end of the twentieth century, football and popular culture had become just as important to Latin Americans' national identities as history and national elite culture. But even there we find the legacy of empire, with Venezuelan and Dominican baseball players now being snapped up to play in the U.S., and Brazilian and Argentinian youngsters travelling to join European football academies at a tender age. It might look as though everything has changed, and yet everything has stayed the same. This book hopes to provide a compelling summary of the key historical episodes in Latin America alongside a succinct analysis of the region's historical encounters with empire, blending narrative with historiographical analysis. At the beginning of the twenty-first century, is Latin America casting off empire through its sporting, economic and political innovations?

Key Concepts

Before proceeding, I want to summarize the different interpretations that have been used for this subject: from dependency theory to neo-imperialism. All of them try to pin a concept or definition upon the set of shifting historical processes and circumstances described here. 'Colonialism' is understood to describe the period of formal sovereignty asserted over the Americas by Spain and Portugal from 1492 and 1500 respectively. It entailed sending political governors, exerting economic benefits (in tax as well as precious metals) and using the force of culture (language, religion, customs) to maintain the subordination of local native traditions. Colonialism came to an end in Spanish America (except Cuba and Puerto Rico) by 1824; in Portuguese America, two years earlier. What came next has been called many things. Some see 'neo-colonialism' in the efforts of Britain and the U.S. to control the lands the Iberian powers had vacated; by 'neo-colonialism' we mean that the strength of influence was 'as good as' colonialism. Others have used the term 'informal empire' to describe how Latin American countries often behaved and felt as if they did form part of Britain's nineteenth-century empire, or the United States' twentieth-century variant, even if sovereignty was not normally formally exerted. The economic dimensions of these structurally unequal relationships were theorized in the 1960s as 'dependency' on the understanding that Latin America's economies had become dependent on the markets, investors and technologies of Europe and the U.S., and could never break that circle. The concept of the 'coloniality of power' suggests that Latin American cultures and ideologies have not been able to throw off the colonial frameworks that prevent them from asserting their own independence and sovereignty.[12] In the 1990s scholars began to lump all these economic, political and cultural inequalities together and to use Antonio Gramsci's concept of 'hegemony' to describe how one state/region/culture had held sway over others. Many followed Néstor García Canclini's work on 'hybrid' cultures, producing dense work that celebrates authenticity and originality and decries evidence of outside cultural impact. These points were well made. Hybridity characterizes many of Latin America's cultural, social and political forms. In this book it will be obvious that many of the cultural and social practices I describe – from football to salsa to magical realism to tango – were themselves 'hybrid', meaning that they were the result of encounters between cultures. Fernando Ortiz called this 'transculturation'.[13]

The historical analysis that follows attempts to show that Latin America's relationship with global empires after 1800 has been shaped by many different, shifting and competing hegemonies, be they cultural, imperial, national or economic, and variant along chords of gender, class, region and ethnicity. Of course, any attempt to provide such an analysis in 200 pages will have to miss out episodes, processes, hybridities and protagonists. I accept and regret this. My only defence is that I have selected those which I felt most significant to the theme of this book: the evolution of Latin America's relationships with the rest of the world from 1800 to the present.[14] I am by training, travel and inclination an Andeanist as much as a

Latin Americanist, and hope to have given fair and accurate coverage to each part of the region as far as possible while accepting that such a goal is impossible.

Latin America and the West

If Latin America is definitely part of global history, does it form part of the Western world? This question has always confused my students. Is Latin America part of 'the West', or not? Geographically, of course, if Latin America isn't part of a Western world divided along a meridian emanating north–south from London, Berlin, Paris, Istanbul or even St Petersburg, then one wonders where on earth it might 'fit'. But historians of other parts of the world have always been reluctant to include Latin America in 'their' West. In *Civilization*, Ferguson is resolute in including Latin America among 'the rest' rather than 'the West' due to its failures in competition, science, property ownership, medicine, consumption and work. Understanding the West in terms of cultural and economic characteristics that are unique to the United States and some areas of Northern Europe, as Ferguson does, is of course going to exclude Latin America, whose cultural and economic history have been different. But what Latin America's history shows us is that the West has never been a closed-off place or region, let alone a civilization. I hope that the examples included in this book will show that Latin America has been an interlinked part of the West since 1492, when Columbus's arrival began the exchange of products, peoples and practices that created the conditions for the ascendance of empires ruled nominally from Madrid, London, Paris and Lisbon.

Marcelo Carmagnani has argued this from the opposite direction in his *The Other West: Latin America from Invasion to Globalization* (2011).[15] He argues that the definitive 'Westernization' of Latin America occurred precisely from the mid-nineteenth century, and is still ongoing today. For Carmagnani, this was marked by 'the establishment of similar political, economic, social and cultural institutions' in both the Americas and Europe: representative democracy, the rule of law and liberal rights agendas, including citizens' and property rights – one might add the adoption of organized sport.[16] Carmagnani is at pains to demonstrate that Latin America was not 'a passive subject that merely endured Westernization', but an integral part of a historical process which brought the trajectories of Europe and all parts of the Americas closer together, eventually merging into the process often called 'globalization' today.

Carmagnani's focus on showing how Latin American history has been much the same as that of many other areas is reinforced by Charles Jones. Jones focuses in particular on the comparison with the u.s., showing how Latin America's history has followed lines not at all dissimilar to that of the u.s. in its political, economic and cultural trajectories. The differences have been in degree and extent. Jones's essay *American Civilization* (2007) shows that 'debates in the Americas about modernity, economy and civility have followed courses and flowed within quite generously set limits that are distinctively American.'[17]

Recently Latin America has been lumped in with the 'Global South' in an attempt to articulate Latin America's historical role as a recipient of the forces of European imperialism. Like the 'West', the 'Global South' attempts to distinguish between commonalities and historical difference as an ideological project. This book explores networks, exchanges and encounters of Latin America's global relationships by setting them in the context of their global, imperial histories.

Methodology: Why History?

As I said at the start of this introduction, the approach adopted in this book is determinedly historical. It tests theories about Latin American history that have been elaborated and propounded by journalists, philosophers, sociologists and economists. It is probably worth spending a little while explaining exactly what I mean by a historical approach and why it deserves the respect I accord it here.

The discipline of history allows the simultaneous adoption of multiple perspectives on the past. Rather than arguing for or against a given hypothesis, the historian absorbs herself or himself in sources that have survived from the given period and in the writings of other historians about that time. Those sources are not limited to correspondence or government files, often seen as the essential tools of the historian's trade. Indeed, in the not-so-distant past, histories of Latin America would be solely political or economic, focusing on the sources and events deemed as significant in national history: presidents, exports, legislation, warfare, revolutions. In the last twenty years the fashion for cultural history has swept over much research on Latin America. This has opened up a whole swathe of written and material culture for the historian's analysis.[18] Sources can be anything: from archaeological remains to maps and paintings, from novels to secret state telegrams, from football matches to graffiti and soap operas. These can all be evidence for a historical interpretation. In this book I use all these types of sources and more to explain the curious cultural, economic and political forces that have tied, and continue to tie, Latin America to the rest of the world over the last two centuries. Of course there are limits of time and brain cells for any one individual historian and I am tremendously indebted to the historians whose articles and monographs I draw on, cited in the references and bibliography. There are also limits on the number of examples, dates and names that can be usefully included in a short, introductory book like this without overload. I have deliberately decided not to try to cover each country in the depth it deserves, and indeed I have not attempted to mention every significant episode or individual. Some of those whose significance is unquestionable, but don't appear here, include Faustino Asprilla, Paulo Coelho, Garrincha, Gilberto Gil, Nicolás Maduro, Carlos Menem, Carmen Miranda, Gabriela Mistral, Raul Prebisch, Ayrton Senna and Carlos Slim. Instead I have chosen a very broad narrative, interspersing it with more detailed discussions of particular texts or events which can provide a degree of light to shine upon the bigger picture. Hence the approach adopted here is rather less like a conscientious survey of the land and more like a mosaic, a collection of details which are intended, when one steps back from them, to reveal a shape and a texture which might not be appreciated close up.

My very broad approach to what constitutes a historical source, and to which subjects might usefully be considered as the object of historical investigation, allows this book to range beyond the relatively narrow interpretations of Galeano, Guardiola-Rivera, Jones, Carmagnani and Ferguson, who focus, understandably and sometimes persuasively, on the political, economic, diplomatic and financial links which tied (and tie) Latin America to global empires in the past. These writers often spend relatively little time on culture, on the everyday processes, customs and traditions that bind the economic and political factors into people's lives; for that reason, any historical approach that disregards culture is, for me, neglecting an essential tool of analysis. That is why there is just as much discussion in this book of football as there is of frontiers. That is why you will find discussion of the laying of railway lines alongside analysis of novels. And that is why there is more discussion of Shakira and Diego Maradona than of any minister of finance or ambassador. I have tried to tie cultural discussion into economic analysis. Often I jump between the two and allow the reader to decide upon the significance of the links between them. There are many ways to analyse the history of Latin America: this account of the multiple external connections is one alternative, one way of engaging and understanding rather than standing and shouting.

I imagine that academic specialists in particular periods and places in Latin America will find much to disagree with and debate here. But my intended audience are first-timers, primarily outsiders who are beginning to study or planning to visit Latin America for the first time, perhaps with a view to maximizing their enjoyment of the 2014 World Cup in Brazil, or the 2016 Olympic Games in Rio de Janeiro. The interpretation may also be of interest to Latin Americans who are new to the historical relationship of their continent with the rest of the world. I have included within the text a number of boxes guiding the reader to some of the major historical figures without whom the last two centuries of Latin American history cannot be understood. Armed with these facts, and guided by the historical analysis that follows, every reader can feel ready to wade into the debate about history that is central to much of the culture, politics and everyday life of Latin America.

ONE

Goodbye, Colonial Worlds: Independence

Latin America wrested itself free of colonial rule after 1808. The process was often bloody, drawn-out and contentious. By 1826 the vast majority of the American continental landmass was independent, an almost unimaginable state of affairs for those Latin Americans who had heard of the brutal repression of the Túpac Amaru uprising back in 1781. The only exceptions, by 1830, were those Caribbean islands whose imperial masters clung tightly to them (in the Spanish case, these were Cuba and Puerto Rico). On the American mainland there were the French, British and Dutch strongholds in Guyana, and the British held on to their slice of Honduras in Central America (today Belize) and to Canada in North America. The map of the Americas had been painted in resounding, vibrant republican colours that made the world look very different.

The independence of Latin American countries from colonial rule has long been studied in markedly national terms. Historians of Colombia studied the factors that led to their independence from Spain with little communication with historians in neighbouring Ecuador, who looked inwards rather than outwards in search of explanation. Historians in Spain, by contrast, chose not to study these massive colonial defeats in any detail at all. Since the 1960s historians have come to analyse the processes of independence within bigger pictures. They have asked to what extent independence formed part of a broader fracturing of the Atlantic world, related to events in North America in 1776 and France in 1789, that we might call an Age of Revolutions. The growing interest of British historians in Latin America has led to more research on the influence of the

British empire in encouraging, shaping and even permitting the independence of Spain and Portugal's American colonies. The international geopolitics of Latin American independence have now come to occupy centre stage in historians' interpretations.[1]

After the Battle of Trafalgar in 1805, the British Royal Navy was the principal maritime force in the world. Drunk on their newly acquired prestige and glory, some of its commanders chanced their luck on the conquest of Latin America. Rear Admiral Sir Home Popham's audacious invasion and capture of Buenos Aires and Montevideo in 1806–7 was not the result of direct orders from London, but his conquest of these Spanish colonies was cheered loudly at home because visions of Spanish gold whetted the British appetite for further imperial expansion. There were great celebrations when the news reached London, with trophies freshly minted and widespread belief that the entire continent and its commerce would soon fall into British hands.[2] But they had not banked on local resistance; the British invaders were quickly booted out, providing a catalyst and stimulus to nascent notions of difference and national identity to locals, who saw that their nominal Spanish 'protection' was worthless if they had to arm themselves to fight off foreign invaders.[3]

In 1807 the Royal Navy performed what was probably its most influential act in the entire process of Latin American independence. When news of Napoleon Bonaparte's decision to invade Portugal finally reached Lisbon, the Portuguese royal family was able to enact a well-prepared strategy of leaping into British ships and fleeing to Portugal's colonial possessions in Brazil. British ships escorted the royal family, their treasury, their libraries and many of their material goods across the Atlantic, depositing them safe and sound in Rio de Janeiro early in 1808. From there João VI ruled the United Kingdom of Portugal, Brazil and the Algarves. In doing so João and his British supporters were able to avoid the vacuum of legitimacy that emerged in Spain's American colonies when Napoleon's armies charged into Spain not long afterwards.

When news of Napoleon's 1808 invasion of Spain, kidnapping of Fernando VII and installation of Joseph Bonaparte (Napoleon's brother) on the Spanish throne reached the American colonies, the first reactions were confusion, insecurity and uncertainty. Each town and city reacted independently as the news arrived by ship, first in the ports like Buenos Aires or Cartagena, and later by mule to the mountainous centres such as Mexico City, Cuzco or Potosí. Most urban elites, meeting as juntas or *cabildos*, declared that they were in possession of sovereignty until Fernando VII was able to return to his rightful place on the throne. The figure of Fernando – *el deseado*, the desired one – would later come to provide a kind of veil behind which new ideas of autonomy and even independence could grow.

As Napoleon's grip on Spain strengthened from 1809–11, and news permeated the Atlantic, the Spanish American elites considered how best to protect themselves from a possible French attempt to take Spain's American colonies. Soon emissaries were racing to Great Britain in search of diplomatic, financial and military support. The most famous of these agents was Simón Bolívar, the Caracas-born landowner who travelled to London in 1810 seeking recognition of the justice of his rebellion against colonial rule. Bolívar and his companions, Andrés Bello and Luis López Méndez, promised Britain commercial advantage and undying gratitude if in return it would use its imperial power to protect Venezuela from Franco-Spanish retaliation. But, perhaps with their fingers burned from the recent ultimate failure of Popham's expeditions to Buenos Aires and Montevideo, British politicians were wary of antagonizing their Spanish allies, and Bolívar was offered nothing more than vague declarations of encouragement.

London was the revolutionary capital of the Latin American independence movements throughout the 1810s. Nearly everyone who was anyone in the continental fight for independence either lived or passed through London in these years. On Piccadilly, in bars and in the British Museum's library they imbibed a liking for British culture that would remain a reference point. For some this meant an admiration for British educational innovations such as the Lancasterian System, according to which older children, rather than teachers, took on the responsibility of teaching younger pupils. Others acquired an abiding faith in the British system of constitutional monarchy, of checks and balances, of aristocratic governance tinged and legitimated by new ideas of democracy. Bolívar himself retained a soft spot for the House of Lords, and later even modelled his own ideal constitution for Bolivia on the British system.[4]

British influence also reached Hispanic America via the constitutional convention that met in Cádiz in 1811–12, virtually the only part of mainland Spain that Napoleon did not conquer. The British not only imported food, drink and weapons into Cádiz but ferried exiled Spanish politicians into the city so that they could participate in the drawing up of a new system of political governance for the Spain that had resisted Napoleon. It should not surprise us, therefore, that the fruit of these deliberations, the Cádiz Constitution of 1812, bears the mark of Spanish liberals who had spent time in Great Britain as political exiles, and who repaid the favour by applying a British brand of liberalism to their new constitution. Cádiz was an important step towards establishing political rights and equality in Spain and in those areas of the colonies that still remained loyal (particularly Mexico, Central America and, to a lesser extent, Peru).

Back in Hispanic America, the elites were trying to work out how they might establish functioning systems of government with a recognizable legitimacy, even in the absence of colonialism and monarchical power. Neighbouring cities and regions ended up in violent conflict as they sought to establish and demarcate areas of influence that did not correspond to colonial boundaries. Inter-ethnic warfare was recurrent, especially in Mexico, where Miguel Hidalgo led an army of indigenous and mestizo farmers towards the capital with the aim of taking power and overthrowing Spanish rule. The suppression of Hidalgo's revolt, and a further rebellion that followed it, led by another priest, José María Morelos, was often brutal but failed to stub out resistance to renewed colonial rule across Mexico. Once the dreams of independence had been ignited, they proved very difficult to extinguish.

The intense violent conflict that plagued many areas in these years, particularly in the Andes, meant that clear political ideologies of independence were slow to emerge. When they did, they came out of the experience of exile. Bolívar's Jamaica letter, composed in 1815 in Kingston and addressed to a British merchant, Henry Cullen, is

South American revolutionary leader Símon Bolívar (1783–1830), known as 'The Liberator', engraving by N. M. Bate, 1819.

Simón Bolívar (born Caracas, Venezuela, 1783, died Santa Marta, Colombia, 1830) was the son of a landed, slave-owning colonial family who reached the peak of his career in 1825 after bringing off a mind-blowing military strategy via several campaigns crashing south from Venezuela through Colombia and Ecuador and into Peru. His star was so high that Upper Peru's elites elected to rename their country Bolivia, and his individual fame is so closely linked to the independence of so much of the Andes that rare is the city, town or village that does not have a Plaza Bolívar or an Avenida Bolívar. A master horseman, Bolívar was a political thinker with an eye for the long view when most other military leaders were unable to think beyond rationing and billeting troops and avoiding battle until they had found sustenance for their soldiers. Bolívar was a prodigious writer and dictator of letters who decreed in his will that all his papers be burned; his executors, who included an Irishman and a Frenchman, ignored his wishes, thus ensuring that his voice would continue to be heard down the generations. The resultant 32 volumes of collected documents include speeches, notes, acts and correspondence with widows and common soldiers, as well as international luminaries such as Jeremy Bentham, William Wilberforce, the Marquis de Lafayette and Alexander von Humboldt.

In his last years Bolívar's star waned. He preferred dictatorship to democracy, and centralism and authority to federalism and discussion (or as he saw it, anarchy). A failed assassination attempt in 1828 disillusioned him, and his worsening illness (most likely tuberculosis) sent him to Santa Marta, where he died. Many remember his final lament: 'He who serves the revolution ploughs the sea.' Bolívar wrote in 1826 that 'it seems that, if the whole world should have to choose its capital, the isthmus of Panama, located as it is in the centre of the globe, with Asia on one side and Africa and Europe on the other, would be the site chosen for this grand design.'[5]

the most celebrated attempt to catch the spirit of independence in text. In it Bolívar expressed fervently anti-colonial and anti-slavery ideas, drawing on the Enlightenment thinkers he had read in his youth. He proposed the radical notion that people born in Hispanic America were potentially the equal of those born in Spain, and dreamed of a supra-national entity, a pan-American republic that would stretch from Northern Mexico down to Patagonia. But even in his wildest dreams Bolívar retained a pragmatic edge. He acknowledged that geographical barriers – and, more importantly, the great delays in communication across the Americas – would prevent his goal from becoming a reality. He chose instead to focus on institutionalizing the revolution and crafting a sense of loyalty, or collective identity, that would bind citizens to the new states that would be created for them. He came to believe that military service could turn peasants and slaves into citizens (although they didn't always share his beliefs) and, increasingly, he believed that it was his destiny to liberate the American continent from colonial rule. Many of these ideas were shared by Bolívar's contemporaries. What set him apart was his global perspective. Bolívar focused great energy on a formal alliance with Britain, and when this was not forthcoming he proposed and engaged foreign support through loans, trade and mercenaries.[6]

What were the Causes of the Struggle for Independence?

Latin American independence was not the 'liberation' or 'emancipation' of nations struggling to wrench themselves from colonial oppression. Without the catalyst of Napoleon Bonaparte's invasion of the Iberian Peninsula in 1807–8, Bolívar may well have spent his life womanizing rather than revolutionizing, Hidalgo would have remained a humble priest with eccentric ideas, and future military rebels such as Agustín de Iturbide, José de San Martín and Andrés de Santa Cruz would most likely have served loyally in the Spanish army throughout their lives. The French invasion, however, changed everything. It forced the Portuguese evacuation to Rio, creating the first new imperial metropolis in the Americas since the Incas built Cuzco four centuries earlier. It created a vacuum of legitimacy in

Spanish America into which rushed new, revolutionary ideas. Imperial restructuring in the late eighteenth century – the Bourbon reforms – had already created an evolving sense of difference among the American-born Spaniards, what the historian David Brading called 'creole patriotism'. These ideas of separateness from Spain fused, after 1808, with a new sense of how the 'sovereignty of the people' might replace the divine right of the Spanish monarch to rule in the Americas. There was no quick switch from regal majesty to 'the majesty of the people', but rather a gradual evolution of one concept of legitimacy into another. The fire that fuelled the process of new abstract ideas becoming reality was war.[7]

Warfare across Hispanic America between 1808 and 1824 was immense in scale, entailed the largest ever military mobilization of the continent and included among its consequences the decimation of several populations, most notably in southern Mexico and Venezuela, where the death tolls ran into hundreds of thousands. Silver and gold mines, which made up a large part of the economy, fell empty and were flooded as miners were conscripted into both royalist and independent forces. Once the warfare had begun in Spanish America it took on a life of its own, expanding and intensifying upon longstanding regional and ancestral grudges. All groups used the violent conflict to seek resolution to longstanding social and economic problems. Indigenous groups in southern Andean Peru, for example, fought long and hard to defend the colonial system to the bemusement of liberal white elites in Lima, who thought the Indians' sympathy should automatically lie with the cause of 'liberty'.[8] Slaves across the continent joined the armed forces in their tens of thousands (though not in Brazil, the largest slaveholding society, which largely avoided violence in this period, and therefore, crucially, kept control of its slaves). Slaves often had little choice but to enter the service of whichever side dominated the territory where they worked, but some were able to exploit the desperation of military commanders to win promotion, status and protection for their families.[9] As the armed conflict spread from cities into the countryside, and correspondingly non-white peoples started to make up the vast majority of the armed forces of both sides, the elites started to worry about the potential consequences of the promises of 'freedom' and 'equality' which the independent armies, especially, were bandying about to recruit soldiers and donations. The possibility of a 'second Haiti' where slaves would rise up and seize power from their former masters, as had happened in the French colony of Sainte-Domingue over the past two decades, consumed the minds of slave-owners, especially around the shores of the Caribbean, where dispossessed French planters sought refuge, bearing stories of looting, rape and murder.[10] These fears about the threats to white rule, many of them exaggerated for political effect, go a long way to explaining the political negotiations that eventually ended armed warfare in Mexico and Peru, which involved white officers in the Spanish army and colonial administration 'defecting' to the independent side and then ratifying 'independence'. Agustín de Iturbide, who led Mexico's independence with his 'Plan de Iguala' in 1821, was the most prominent example; similar anxieties about slave and black mobilization in civil warfare prompted Pedro I to declare Brazilian independence in 1822 when his father returned to Portugal.

At the beginning of the Wars of Independence, fears of French invasion of the Americas served to stir creoles into political action to safeguard the power and economic interests that they were grasping in the wake of the disintegration of Spanish power. But the French armies were destroyed by fighting through the freezing Russian winter, and Spanish guerrillas thwarted French domination of the Iberian peninsula. Other foreign powers now cast their eyes towards Spain's restless colonies, wondering if some advantage might be had by intervening in the conflicts in some way. These were the United States of America and Great Britain.

Casting off Colonialism

Great Britain's invasion of Buenos Aires and Montevideo in 1806–7 was common knowledge across the continent by 1808, having been widely reported in the Spanish-language newspapers that had sprung up with the continent's first printing press (dating from the 1790s). The leaders of independence movements were fearful that the British might attempt further land grabs. At the same time, however, British friendship was essential if they wanted to trade freely – both with Britain and with each other, given British control of the seas – and so Latin American leaders attempted to ingratiate themselves with Britain. The failures of 1806–7 did not deter British politicians from flirting with the idea of launching a conquest of Mexico or South America. London playhouses often showed dramas about the con-quistadores – Cortés or Pizarro – during the 1810s, and no doubt some civil servants and junior military officers dreamed that they might undertake similarly thrilling feats in the name of the British, rather than the Spanish, Empire. Only a last-minute change of plan, based on a shift in diplomatic strategy that decided to favour the European rather than the American stage, saved Mexico from receiving the major expedition led by the Duke of Wellington, which ended up in Spain itself.[11]

Nevertheless the focus on supporting freer trade remained official British policy throughout the period. Foreign secretaries urged new independent states to lift commercial restrictions, abolish the trade in slaves where it still existed (the British parliament had declared an end to this traffic in 1807, though slavery itself persisted in British dominions until 1833) and establish stable, legitimate governments. British financial houses, in tandem with this diplomatic policy, sent agents to Latin America and received Latin American agents to negotiate immense loans that would pay for the armies needed to win independence from Spain, and to institutionalize the new states that would replace the colonial system. Loans were made to Brazil, Chile, Colombia, Mexico, Buenos Aires and Peru from a variety of invest-ment banks and agents, totalling over £21 million in the money of the day (the equivalent of at least 30 times that in 2014 values). Compared to this show of diplomatic and financial muscle, U.S. actions in Latin America during the independence period were relatively minor. U.S. representatives were sent to key ports to see if they could sneak some commercial concessions under the wing of British power, and politically active representatives occasionally got up the noses of Latin American leaders whom the North Americans considered insufficiently republican, as did Joel Poinsett in Mexico.

The British policy worked best in Brazil. While the Portuguese monarchy was still in charge, ruling largely from Rio, the British were able to extort considerable trading concessions and British merchants made considerable incursions (and profits) from trading with Brazil. When the commercial treaty between the Portuguese and British Empires was published in Rio, Brazilians noticed that it was clearly a Portuguese translation of an English original. Enjoying daily access to ministers and privileged positions in the key ports, as well as control of the shipping that linked the realm together, Britain operated hand-in-glove with the government, quickly reaching a position of pre-eminence compared to other powers. British agents were unable to shift Brazilians on the question of slavery (some historians doubt the extent to which they tried, given the profits British merchants in Brazil continued to make from the trade), but the British mark on other commercial and political developments is unmistakable. When independence was declared in 1822 the prompt arrival of the first British ambassador, Sir Robert Gordon, was a formal expression of the de facto British influence in Brazil.[12] When civil war threatened to break up the unity of the new Brazilian empire British naval forces were engaged to assert the power of central government, including Admiral Lord Cochrane, fresh from his successes in the Pacific (on which more later).

The process of independence, and Britain's role in it, was very different further north. When Simón Bolívar declared the independence of the Republic of Colombia in 1819, he claimed jurisdiction over the territories that today compose Venezuela, Ecuador, Panama and Colombia. The vast majority of that territory remained under royalist control, having been 're-conquered' for Spain by an expeditionary force led by General Pablo Morillo. Over the next two years Bolívar led his armies on a series of military campaigns that finally reversed the defeats Morillo had inflicted on them. Serving under Bolívar were several thousand European mercenaries (mainly Irish) who had been recruited in London, Dublin and Edinburgh to fight for independence. These individuals sought adventure, honour and pay, and included many politically committed volunteers who saw themselves in the vanguard of a wave of liberty that was sweeping across the world. Many others were hopeless drunks who quarrelled with Venezuelan cowboys, never learned any Spanish and were of very questionable value to Bolívar. The biggest brake on the success of the British and Irish Legions, however, was disease. Two thousand men died within months of arriving on South American shores, victims of yellow fever and malaria, to which they had no immunity. Shocked by the mortality rates of their comrades, many others deserted and returned home to tell tall stories of the dishonours to which they had been exposed. Relatively few, around 500 men, remained in Bolívar's forces throughout the conflict, though many of them rose to positions of considerable authority and power. They included General Daniel O'Leary, Bolívar's assistant and biographer, and General Francis Burdett O'Connor, who eventually settled in Bolivia.[13]

British military and naval assistance was similarly important in assisting the groups seeking independence in the Southern Cone. Aspirant soldiers who reached the River Plate in 1817, like William Miller from Kent, found that their services were no longer required. Miller raced on horseback across the pampas and over the Andes in less than a fortnight in order to enlist with San Martín's Army of the Andes, which sought to engineer victory in Chile and then to move north towards Peru. In Chile Miller was met by news of the mass arrival of British sailors, who would dominate the officer class of the Chilean navy at the request of the new Chilean government, under the command of their startling new signing, the Scottish renegade Lord Cochrane. Thousands of British sailors signed up under Cochrane and their experience – and the second-hand ships and weapons they brought with them – won some crucial naval victories against the Spanish fleet in the Pacific. The most famous was the Capture of Valdivia in 1820, in the south, where Cochrane bluffed the royalist commanders of the fort into giving up command of their cannons without firing a shot. Something similar happened on the River Plate, where William Brown founded the Argentinian Navy and Peter Campbell led the Uruguayan Navy. Cochrane experimented with rockets in naval warfare, using the most advanced technology of the time.[14] Brown and Campbell settled in the region and became national heroes because of their feats in the wars of independence, despite their foreign birth. Put simply, if the independent cause had not enjoyed a strong naval force courtesy of British subjects like Cochrane, Brown and Campbell, and the thousands who served under them, the stability of the new regimes in Santiago, Buenos Aires and Montevideo would have been sorely tested.[15]

Crucially, however, British soldiers and sailors fought in Latin America as private individuals, not in the service of the British Empire. Official support for their expeditions was always denied, even when, as one Spanish ambassador to London pointed out, they were embarking on ships moored within sight of the Houses of Parliament. British cabinet ministers valued the Spanish alliance against France too much to endanger it with visible support for rebels in the American colonies.

Few British soldiers served in the independence of Peru, though William Miller was an active participant in the south, and Francis O'Connor was the chief of staff at the Battle of Ayacucho, which sealed Peruvian independence in 1824. Alongside New Spain (Mexico), Peru had been one of the jewels of the empire, and so the elites in Lima were much more reluctant to give up on the colonial link that they had benefited from than were creoles in other, more impoverished colonies such as Venezuela or the River Plate. Brutal repression of Andean rebellions in the 1780s also served to stiffen support for the colonial regime across Peru. When Peruvian independence eventually came, it was provoked by the arrival of San Martín's army from the south. The Argentine general declared Peruvian independence in 1821 and set up camp outside Lima to wait for local elites to come out to embrace him and his cause. They never came, in the majority preferring to nail their colours to the royal standard. San Martín eventually travelled north and met Bolívar in the port of Guayaquil (now in Ecuador) to plan the independence of Peru, the last major region that stayed loyal to Spain. After a famous interview, San Martín headed for retirement in France and Bolívar led his Colombian army south to 'liberate' the reluctant Peruvians. Going was tough in the Andes and when decisive military confrontation could no longer be avoided, two armies made up primarily of Peruvians (one of 'Colombian' adherence, one of 'Spanish' allegiance) fought at Junín and then Ayacucho in late 1824. Victory for the Colombians triggered the final expulsion of the royalist officers and the dispersal of their army.

The other bastion of colonialism in Spanish America, Mexico, avoided a final military conflict through hard-nosed political negotiation among the elites in Mexico City under the careful supervision of the Catholic Church. The very first explosions of anti-colonial protest had been led by priests, and the memories of the suppression and defeat of Hidalgo and Morelos's non-white armies in 1810–15 shaped all subsequent strategies over the next decade. Mexico's shattered economy depended on British support, especially for the transport and protection of bullion as it crossed the Atlantic, but British forces were not present during the ongoing civil warfare of 1810–21 that the historian Eric Van Young described as 'the other rebellion', a popular and essentially localist uprising that promoted regional autonomy and paralleled elite moves to promote independence from Spain. When the royalist officer Agustín de Iturbide declared independence on the basis of his Plan de Iguala of 1821, with the support of 'the people, the Church, and the army', he hoped to usher in a peaceful transition to independence. But with the legitimacy of colonial rule in tatters, Mexico's new rulers experimented with many systems in order to cement the existence of their new state. Iturbide even had himself crowned emperor, but was soon exiled and then assassinated upon his return. A succession of presidents, many owing their allegiance to Masonic groups with international links, attempted to calm violence and embed stable political transitions in Mexican political culture. One of the unique ways that they did this was through the *pronunciamiento*, a recurrent proclamation of political demands that threatened violence but in fact aimed at peaceful resolution to conflict.[16]

In Central America the influence of the Cádiz constitution was felt in the resurgence of municipal councils and regional governments. Following the model traced for New Granada (Colombia), geographically isolated but neighbouring regions often resorted to violent conflict in the attempt to resolve their differences. These were temporarily papered over in 1825 with the establishment of a weak, centralized Federal Republic of Central America. Already, however, the relative poverty and factionalism of Central America, compared to Mexico, was opening space for foreign adventurers to seek power and glory. Subsequent chapters contain a litany of filibusters and imperial enclaves opening up in Nicaragua and Guatemala, for example. During the independence wars the most notorious of these adventurers was 'Sir' Gregor MacGregor, a minor member of the Scottish nobility who had married a cousin of Bolívar and raised expeditions of mercenaries to fight for independence in the Hispanic Caribbean. In 1821 MacGregor claimed control of a neglected slice of Central American coastline (now in Nicaragua), and declared the existence of the independence of the Republic of Poyais. MacGregor himself would be 'Inca' of the new territory, which he festooned with a new constitution. He offered the Poyaisian armed forces to both the Spanish and British empires (separately) to carve out further territories from indigenous peoples living in the interior. Many of MacGregor's Scottish migrants died of the diseases they encountered in low-lying areas. MacGregor was declared bankrupt in the late 1820s and spent time in debtors' prison in London.[17]

The Consequences of Independence

New states had to keep paying their huge armed forces, even once the wars of independence were over, for fear that the Spanish might return (Spain didn't recognize the loss of its colonies until the 1830s, and did occasionally entertain the possibility of re-conquest after that) or that other powers might try their luck at invasion. Another major fear that kept governments taking out loans in order to pay idle armed forces was that the politically mobilized, ethnically diverse men who made up their armies might revolt and try to take over power from the white creole leaders who saw themselves as superior. Indeed, the extent to which the leaders of Latin American societies continued to be white, male, educated and with Iberian surnames suggests to some historians that nothing really changed at all as a result of the revolutions of independence. The social order, in this view, simply had the Spanish layer sliced off the top, leaving the rest of the hierarchy unaltered.[18] However, new cabinet ministers and presidents across the continent found themselves with some radically new problems.

The vacuum of legitimacy inherited by the independent states was filled with state-construction, institutionalization and nation building. Ministries published flurries of reports with particular emphasis on the potential for tax collection and increasing exports, viewed as the potential saviours of empty treasuries. The challenge was to secure a fiscal future for states that now carried the burden of the heavy debts accrued during the independence campaigns. During the 1820s only Brazil did not default on its debts to Britain. The reason for this unique position was because Brazilian policy after independence was so closely aligned to British interests.[19]

How to Invent a Nation

Recognizing that the new Latin American nations had not preceded independence, but rather had had to be 'invented' after it, new leaders and policymakers resigned themselves to building new ones. During the day cabinet ministers like José Manuel Restrepo in Colombia attended to matters of jurisdiction and domestic policy. By night they wrote national histories in immense tomes that detailed every action of the independence wars, setting down a patriotic narrative of victory courageously plucked from the claws of corrupt colonialism in volumes that were to be passed down to eager and not-so-eager generations of schoolchildren. These narratives provided the framework for a new cult of the founding fathers, the *proceres* or *padres de la patria*, whose examples of heroism or stoicism and martyrdom – whether voluntary or at the hands of barbaric Spaniards – would guide the new nations' sense of identity.[20]

But of course memories of moustachioed men on horseback fighting the elements and withstanding enemy fire would never be enough to create fraternal nations of equals from societies with such embedded hierarchies of caste and gender. Almost immediately after independence had been achieved, civil conflicts broke out that, viewed in one light, present a picture that is not dissimilar from those of the wars of independence themselves. Many of the same individuals were involved and many of the same key territories were fought over. Many of these new 'civil' (as opposed to 'anti-colonial') wars were disputes for control of national resources (such as ports, where import/export taxes were collected, or mines, from where precious metals were extracted). These 'civil' wars, of course, provided a convenient use for all those armies that had been raised to expel Spaniards and which could not be immediately disbanded for fear of unleashing non-white, armed and militarily trained men into society.

Civil, violent conflict erupted for all kinds of reasons after independence was established. Cities proud of their pasts as legal, political and administrative centres of colonial viceroyalties or captaincy-generals, like Lima, Mexico City and Buenos Aires, defended their interests against what they saw as upstart, provincial rivals such as Cuzco, Veracruz and Córdoba. Often these interests took the form of debates over federalist or centralist political systems or between liberal or conservative political agendas. At their heart, however, was always the same conflict over the meaning of the new nations. Would they be outward-facing polities, geared to engage in foreign trade and generous and welcoming towards foreigners, or would they be more inward-looking, more tolerant of their own regional and ethnic diversities? Would they look to cut import duties and allow foreign – mainly British – goods to flood their markets? (These latter views, often baldly and pretty inaccurately described as 'liberal', were more prevalent in port cities, where foreign merchants and financiers were most likely to reside.) Or would they be more protective of established provincial economic interests, such as manufacturing and mining? (These tendencies were generally stronger in areas far from the coast.)[21]

Taken together, from the vantage point of 1830, we can see that the independence period – often picked out as a great upheaval, a magnificent and revolutionary historical process that bore little in common with the placid centuries of lingering colonialism that preceded it or the incomprehensible and pernickety civil wars that followed – actually carries many important continuities with both those eras. The most important is the relationship with the outside world. During the independence period, the contraband trade which flooded Caribbean shores up to 1808 was transformed into a newly legal commerce. But both before and after independence, this trade was centred on Great Britain and its West Indian colonies, especially Jamaica. Trade figures may well have increased because of the speculation encouraged by independence leaders, and loans rocketed in the wake of the disintegration of Iberian power in the Americas. But even these increases followed trajectories that were firmly rooted in the 1790s, and even before, as British financial and commercial power expanded across the globe while French and Spanish imperial networks fractured under the weight of warfare. What came with independence and after was certainly closer interaction with the rest of the world, especially Britain, than had previously been the case. The shifting of the imperial centres north from Lisbon and Madrid to London had considerable and significant effects, particularly in terms of trade but also relative to culture. Examples include the many editions of Walter Scott's novels that now circulated, the thousands of British, German and French travellers who sniffed around for commercial or evangelical opportunities and the similar numbers of migrants who married into Latin American societies.[22]

In December 1826 George Canning MP declared to the House of Commons that 'the nail is driven, Spanish America is free, and if we do not mismanage our affairs badly, it is ours.' Canning's bombast was appropriate to an age in which British loans to Latin America were booming, travel narratives about the continent were ever more popular and British naval power felt unassailable. But on the other side of the Atlantic the aim of inserting independent states into the global economy had begun to lose its lustre. Anti-colonial war was succeeded by civil war and political conflict was continued by recourse to violence. Before his death, in 1830, Simón Bolívar declared that the continent had 'become ungovernable for us' and that the 'only thing to do is emigrate'. Bolívar also despaired that 'European powers won't even bother to colonize us.' He was largely correct in his analysis, but he did not foresee the future of informal empire and neo-colonialism that awaited.[23]

TWO

Building Nations, Looking for Models

By 1830 the map of Latin America looked pretty much as it does today. Brazil remained an empire until 1889 but its territorial extent and unity was well established. Argentina wasn't called that yet, and still had several civil wars to endure as the provinces and Buenos Aires fought for control. Uruguay was founded in 1830 as an independent buffer zone between its neighbours to north and south. Similarly Ecuador came into being in 1830, the result of the fact that neither Colombia to the north, nor Peru to the south, were able to incorporate the region into its sphere of influence. With Bolívar's death the republic of Gran Colombia bequeathed separate republics of Colombia, Venezuela and Ecuador. Peru and Bolivia continued to flirt with the idea of reunification, which was briefly a reality under the presidency of Andrés de Santa Cruz. A united federation formally governed the region of Central America until the 1840s but in reality the administrative areas that today are republics enjoyed a large degree of autonomy.

Capital cities were usually found in the geographical centres of the new republics, often at or close to the principal port linking the country to its principal markets (as in Montevideo, Buenos Aires, Caracas–La Guaira, Lima–Callao, Santiago–Valparaíso). Those which had major topographical barriers between capitals and ports (as in Ecuador, where Guayaquil was several days distant from the Andean capital Quito, or, even more extreme, the journey separating Bogotá from Cartagena, which meant crossing Andean mountain passes on foot or on a mule before journeying down the Magdalena River to the Caribbean, sometimes taking up to two months) had particularly fractured the early lives of putative nation-states.[1]

There were two major exceptions to this harmonious image of historical continuity from colonial viceroyalties to republican states. One was Peru and Bolivia's Atacama desert, largely lost to Chile in the War of the Pacific (1879–83, discussed in the next chapter). The other was the large swathe of Mexican territory ceded to the U.S. as a result of the Mexican–American War of 1836–9 and the 'independence' of Texas in the 1840s. This spectacular loss of national territory – including the states now known as California, New Mexico and Arizona as well as Texas – marked Latin America's sense of historical identity just as dramatically as it changed the map.

In the interior of South America, after independence, nation-states also started to make serious inroads into regions that had in the late colonial period been largely left to indigenous communities. Rather than being satisfied with their maps drifting off into blank spaces at the borders of their territories (as colonial administrators had been), the new national elites wanted to extend the presence and the authority of their states into every corner, valley and woodland that corresponded to their legal jurisdiction. Theirs was a two-faced motivation. On the one hand, of course, there was the desire to maximize landholdings and extract economic benefit from agriculture and the raw materials held beneath the soil, and to prevent other powers from getting there first. But on the other, an equally important driver was the desire to incorporate indigenous communities into the nation so that they could benefit from the perceived advantages of republican life, such as citizenship, commerce and organized religion. In the south of Chile leaders in Santiago began to work towards incorporating the lands of the Mapuche into the Chilean state, something the Spanish colonial system had never managed to do due to the initial and continued resistance of the 'Araucanian warriors'. The Mapuche and other indigenous groups in Patagonia had long cultivated relationships with the residents of Chile's central valley, as well as with seafaring nations such as the British, and negotiated the fates of shipwrecks and other captives.[2] It was only in the 1880s that the increased use of physical force by the Chilean state enabled the

'Pacification' of the South and the extension of Chile's maps to make it the 'long, thin country' that parallels the southern Andes today.[3]

The same pressures, sticks and carrots were used against indigenous groups throughout the continent. In many places *resguardos* – Indian reservations – were set up to preserve indigenous autonomy and then sold off to the highest bidder in order to provide access to the property market which, it was hoped, might inspire capitalist entrepreneurship in communities which had hitherto been excluded from – or had chosen to retreat from – national markets. There were exceptions, but much of this newly available land was snapped up by capital-city-dwelling speculators, often themselves closely linked to the politicians who had changed the rules in the first place.

The role of protecting the indigenous peoples was in many areas taken by the Catholic Church. Independence from colonial rule had launched the Catholic Church in Spanish America over a precipice and into a long-lasting dilemma about its role and identity. Three hundred years of the Church's central role in colonialism – as educator, landowner and mortgage provider, to say nothing of its place as spiritual leader and provider of legitimacy to the monarch – had been broken asunder. The new republican states wanted to educate citizens in their own schools and to wrest back some power from the Church. In many of the region's nineteenth-century civil wars the place of the Church in society was one of the issues at stake, and in some it was the catalyst or driving factor. The Vatican refused to recognize the independence of the new states until well into the nineteenth century, and indeed managed to hang on to many of its privileges, especially in Colombia, Chile and Ecuador. In Cuba and Brazil, which were governed by monarchs and emperors until the end of the century, the Church's prestige remained higher for longer. The influence of the Vatican and the Catholic Church in shaping Latin American society after independence, therefore, must not be underestimated.[4]

After independence, across the continent, the new nation-states had to deal with everyday pressures from external powers who, unlike the Vatican, could send armies and navies to cement pressure. With hindsight Mexico was doubly affected because of its predatory neighbour to the north, but in the 1830s and '40s all Latin American countries feared the renewed imperialism of European or North American powers. Mexico repeatedly expelled Spanish subjects as a defensive measure, and nascent nationalists frequently raised the fear of invasions by Britons, Frenchmen, Germans or Spaniards in order to secure popular support at home. Yet if we look at what happened between 1830 and 1870, we see that the economic troubles of the new nation-states – often bumping along near bankruptcy, renegotiating credit with international banks and internal lenders – were in fact matched by the poverty of intention shown by the imperial powers.

Put simply, the European powers might have recolonized Latin America had they wanted to – had they sent sufficient armed forces and cultivated enough of a charm offensive – but they chose not to. Instead India, China, Southeast Asia, Australia and Africa received the brunt of European imperial offensives in the mid-nineteenth-century, such that Eric Hobsbawm was able to label it the Age of Empire (1848–70) regardless of the fact that in Latin America that period saw only one major imperialist continental land grab (by the French, in Mexico) which was shortlived and so resoundingly unsuccessful that it put the French off new colonial ventures in the Americas for good.

After the failures of the invasions of Buenos Aires and Montevideo back in 1806–7, the British restricted their explicit imperialism in Latin America to strategic points, the 1833 occupation of the Islas Malvinas/Falkland Islands being the most celebrated example. Historians and politicians still debate the extent of the Argentine hold on the territory in the early 1830s, and indeed point to the even earlier occupation of the islands by France in the late eighteenth century. Certainly at the time the British claim to the islands was by no means universally accepted, but because of the islands' geographical distance from the American mainland and their limited potential for providing revenue for the cash-strapped Argentinian state, quarrelling with the might of the British Empire not unsurprisingly slipped down any list of priorities.[5] To the north Britain expanded the territory of its colony in Guyana at the expense of the Venezuelan Republic. Venezuela continues to dispute the boundary in the twenty-first century (though now with the independent Republic of Guyana) just as the Argentinians do regarding the sovereignty of the Malvinas/Falklands.[6]

Alongside Britain's territorial acquisitions in Latin America in the 1830s, and indeed rather facilitated by them, came the expansion of scientific expeditions into the region as British and other European travellers followed in the footsteps of Alexander von Humboldt, seeking to bring scientific logic, observation and analysis to the natural landscape and its flora and fauna. Mary Louise Pratt argued that the male travellers formed part of a 'capitalist vanguard' who described, measured and mapped out the region all the better for its exploitation by the next generation of investors, traders, miners and speculators. (Pratt suggested, based on the study of female travellers like Maria Graham and Flora Tristán, that women travel writers had more empathy with Latin Americans and therefore did not fit into the same category.) But the most celebrated British traveller in Latin America in this period was not interested in the region's people as much as its plants and animals.

Charles Darwin travelled on the *Beagle* across the Atlantic to Brazil. After seeing Rio the ship touched at Montevideo, Buenos Aires, the Falkland Islands (only recently occupied by British agents) and Tierra del Fuego and proceeded up the Chilean Pacific coast. His most famous discoveries were in the Juan Fernández Islands (belonging to Chile) and the Ecuadorian Galápagos, where his observations of the unique turtles there gave rise, later, to his interpretations in *The Origin of Species.* Darwin's travels, and the assistance he received from Latin Americans in his research, are a good example of how, even in its tumultuous and economically difficult early republican years, Latin America continued to play a central role in global scientific discovery and the debate and dissemination of ideas.[7] Yet Darwin's Latin American guides and informants do not have the same celebrity as the famed 'discoverer' of evolution.

Overall the European powers limited the resources of their missions in Latin America, sent only cursory naval squadrons to try to put the wind up recalcitrant nationalist governments who sought to alter the terms of trade and generally did anything they possibly could do to avoid being dragged into warfare in the Americas. This often led to increased cooperation between imperial powers rather than competition between them. A good example of how this worked in practice is the case of Colonel Rupert Hand, an Irish mercenary in the service of Simón Bolívar's armies who was arrested in 1831 and imprisoned in Cartagena de Indias, charged with the murder of a Colombian general, José María Córdova. Hand claimed that he had killed Córdova in self-defence but was found guilty of homicide and sentenced to death in 1833. Hand's escape from jail was partially fortunate (it coincided with news of a political uprising reaching the port and a slave rebellion nearby) but it was also the result of coordination between the French consul, British businessmen and the u.s. representative. All of these took it on themselves to ensure Hand's escape; they were also aided by the desire of the central government in Bogotá under President Francisco de Paula Santander to avoid a diplomatic or military conflict. Eyes were averted, bribes were paid and disguises were put on, and Hand escaped to become, later in life, a respected professor of English Language in Caracas, Venezuela. A French blockade of Cartagena followed in retaliation for the arrest of its consul, but it was half-hearted and achieved nothing.[8]

Debt and Repayments

Imperial powers collaborated on a much larger scale, too. The Argentinian president Juan Manuel de Rosas pursued a protectionist, nationalist stance regarding trade imports and exports to and from the River Plate. This brought him into conflict with the British and French merchants based in Buenos Aires, who eventually persuaded their diplomatic representatives to authorize naval blockades of the port between 1838 and 1840 until unsatisfactory trade barriers (as they saw them) were removed. Ironically cooperation between imperial powers only made it easier for nation builders like Rosas to portray Europeans as one-dimensionally 'Other', and to define a national identity in opposition to these pushy outsiders with superiority complexes.[9]

The bigger picture behind the events of this period is one of economic retrenchment caused by the expense and consequences of the wars of independence, and extenuated by the ongoing need to repay foreign and domestic creditors for the loans provided during those conflicts. Political independence produced new states that were economically shackled from birth. Banks in London sent negotiators across Latin America in the 1830s, '40s and '50s, asking where their money was and expecting states to find ways to pay it back.

Loans floated in London and made to Latin American states in 1820s[10]

1822	6%	Chile	£1,000,000	Hullet Bros & Co.
1822	6%	Colombia	£2,000,000	Herring, Graham & Powles
1822	6%	Peru	£1,200,000	Thomas Kinder & Co.
1824	5%	Brazil	£1,686,200	Baylett, Farquhar & Co.; Alexander & Co.; Wilson, Shaw & Co.
1824	6%	Buenos Aires	£1,000,000	Baring Bros & Co.
1824	6%	Colombia	£4,750,000	B. A. Goldschmidt & Co.
1824	5%	Mexico	£3,200,000	B. A. Goldschmidt & Co.
1824	6%	Peru	c. £750,000	Thomas Kinder & Co. (for balance of 1822 loan)
1825	5%	Brazil	£2,000,000	Rothschild & Sons
1825	6%	Guatemala	£1,428,571	Barclay, Herring, Richardson & Co.
1825	6%	Mexico	£3,200,000	Barclay, Herring, Richardson & Co.
1825	6%	Peru	£626,000	Thomas Kinder & Co.
1829	5%	Brazil	£800,000	Rothschild & Sons; Thomas Wilson & Co.

But it wasn't just the fat cats sitting around the directors' tables who looked frustratedly across the Atlantic at debt defaults and slow repayments in the middle of the nineteenth century. A large swathe of British society developed a personal, financial interest in Mexican politics in this period precisely because their investments depended on the establishment of a strong, central government that could assure that payments would be made. (They were, to a large degree, disappointed and often impoverished as a result.[11])

The area of Latin American economic activity that most concerned Europeans in this period, however, was not debt repayment or mineral extraction but rather a longstanding trade with increasingly difficult political connotations. This was the slave trade.

The Transatlantic Slave Trade

In the late eighteenth century, free blacks and slaves in the French colony of Sainte-Domingue had united and overthrown their colonial masters, abolishing slavery and establishing Haiti, the first black republic in the new world in 1804. In 1807 Great Britain abolished the trade in slaves (but not slavery itself, which persisted in British colonies until 1833). The Haitians remained the leaders in this field. In 1816, when Simón Bolívar arrived in Haiti seeking the assistance and military support he had not found on the British island of Jamaica, he found enthusiastic back-up. The condition that Haitian President Alexandre Pétion put on his support of Bolívar's expedition was that he expected Bolívar's first action in independent Venezuela to be the abolition of slavery. This was duly carried out, although Bolívar quickly hedged it with a decree forcibly enlisting all free men into his army.[12] Most of mainland Latin America endured slavery in law in the 1840s and '50s.

Yet despite Haitian, British and republican Hispanic American abolitionism, in the mid-nineteenth century the numbers of Africans being forcibly transported across the Atlantic reached their highest levels ever. The principal markets for these new slaves were the Spanish colony of Cuba and the booming coastal plantations of imperial Brazil. In both places the maintenance of a monarchical order had enabled the survival of legal hierarchies that put whites at the top, blacks at the bottom and slaves barely considered human at all. This period saw what historian Dale Tomich has labelled 'the second slavery', the huge rise in the numbers of trafficked Africans to Cuba, Brazil and the south of the u.s. (until abolition after the civil war in the 1860s). During this period the Royal Navy had a loudly proclaimed duty to chase and intercept ships suspected of slaving and enjoyed massive resources to carry out this effort. Yet although considerable successes were made, and thousands of Africans were liberated either at home or on the holding island of St Helena, the Royal Navy's efforts did not make a serious dent in the profitability of the slave trade for Brazilian or Cuban elites.[13] Furthermore, despite British representatives being very highly regarded in Brazil in this period, to the extent that Brazil is sometimes referred to as being part of Britain's 'informal empire' during the nineteenth century, successive Brazilian governments did not bow to Britain's official abolitionist policy. Paradoxical though it may seem, maintaining slavery was a form of resistance. It provided a long history linking Latin America with Africa through migration, labour, culture and memory.[14]

Civilization and Barbarism

For many white and creole leaders in Latin America in the nineteenth century, Europe represented all that was civilized in the world. Their own countries' interiors – the plains, the mountains, the forests – were correspondingly labelled, in a now famous dichotomy, as representing all that was barbarous and uncivilized. Many extremists believed that the two types of society were locked in a fight to the death in Latin America; the fear of the entrance of the barbarians into the civilized city was only balanced by the desire to expand civilization's frontiers and conquer uncivilized lands.

The most famous description of the civilization and barbarism debate, *Facundo*, was written by the Argentinian writer and politician Domingo Sarmiento in the 1850s as a thinly veiled attack on President Juan Manuel de Rosas, whom he saw as having brought uncultured savagery into government. Sarmiento posited intellectualism, urbanism and models from the French and British Enlightenments as the principal bulwarks against Rosas's populism and the charisma he employed to attract support from illiterate peons and gauchos, whose oral culture and physicality Sarmiento was repulsed by during his brief travels through the Argentinian pampas on his way into exile in Chile.[15]

In political terms examples of attempts to civilize 'barbarous' peoples in nineteenth-century Latin America are numerous. These included road building and railway construction schemes which, it was felt, would bring nations more closely together through infrastructure revolution and allow the values of civilized society to trickle through to those peoples who had not previously been able to access them. Often, and without irony, physical force was used to spread what were thought to be 'civilized' values among peoples who were thought to be 'barbarous'. The contortions that this entailed go far beyond irony. The 'Conquest of the Desert' in Argentina began in 1872, which led to the near complete destruction of the country's indigenous population between 1879 and 1884 under President Roca and the expansion of white-owned farms, was initiated by President Domingo Sarmiento: the same man who had authored *Facundo* just two decades earlier. The domination of the national space by the white, intellectual elite was a goal that was accomplished through military conquest as well as through mapping, fencing and mountaineering. Before elite Argentinians could climb the country's mountains they had to carry out the 'erasure of native and local peoples': to forget that humans had previously climbed these summits in order to proclaim that they had conquered them for the first time, thus asserting the strength of the new nation to the world.[16]

Was Europe Always Seen as Civilized?

Some writers recognized that the civilization and barbarism debate should not be limited to national territories. The Colombian Jorge Isaacs, for example, shared many of Sarmiento's fears about the impermanence of intellectual culture in his country and worried about the ability of the Colombian state to instil loyalty and allegiance across its wide geographical extremes. Yet Isaacs recognized that these debates were now global, rather than purely national. In his novel *María* (1867), whose style drew heavily from French writers, Isaacs told a tragic love story of two cousins, Efraín and María, who are doomed never to be able to share married happiness together. The critic Doris Sommer has influentially argued that it is María's ethnicity (specifically her Jewishness, held by Sommer to symbolize ethnic difference in Colombia more widely) that prevents a happy union between the couple. Lee Skinner has argued that it is the spectre of incest (Efraín and María are second cousins) that triggers her illness and frustrates their desires. But examination of the structure of the novel demonstrates quite clearly where Isaacs believed the problem lay. The two lovers manage their ethnic difference and familial closeness in a satisfactory fashion until Efraín is sent to London, where he is to study medicine. The dirty, unhealthy, contaminated industrial environment that is the British capital contrasts sharply with the green, welcoming Cauca valley that touches the traveller through every pore, every sense, when he returns home. But by then it is too late. Efraín's departure to the centre of the modern world has triggered María's illness, and upon his eventual return he is unable to use his new, professional medical skills to revive her. *María* is thus a sad, melodramatic novel which lays the blame for Colombia's difficulties on ill-considered plans to modernize the country along European models. Isaacs's politics are notoriously difficult to pin down, as he switched between the liberals and the conservatives during his life, but with hindsight we can see him, like many Latin American intellectuals of this period, primarily as a nation builder, concerned with depicting his country's peoples, customs and landscapes and taking umbrage at the presences – directly or indirectly – of global empires within their national territories.[17]

The processes of state construction and nation building of the mid-nineteenth century might appear from some angles as having taken place in a relative geopolitical vacuum, while imperial powers were looking the other way, given historians' overriding focus on nation building and regionally specific processes in the last few decades. Indeed it is true that, compared with Africa and Asia, Latin America was relatively free of neo-colonial interventions in this period. But the effects of the power of global empires in this period are clearly visible in culture and politics as well as in international relations. A good example of the influence of French and other European politics is in the way the European Revolutions of 1848 inspired groups across Latin America to attempt or to suppress rebellions in their own backyards.[18] French movements towards democracy and popular sovereignty were hailed as a universal inspiration in Mexico,

Peru, Argentina and Colombia, though leaders were not always able to achieve the success they dreamed of.

In 1833 Great Britain assumed formal sovereignty over the Isles Malvines (claimed by the French at the end of the eighteenth century), given that the new republic based in Buenos Aires did not have the time or the resources to occupy them securely itself. The Falkland Islands were recognized as an increasingly vital imperial stepping stone, crucial to keep steamships full of coal as they crossed the Atlantic or traversed around Cape Horn. The seizure was duly noted in Buenos Aires, though it was only the more aggressive brand of nationalism that arose in the mid-twentieth century that would trigger Argentinian attempts to reclaim the islands. A decade later Britain made a subtler but more audacious land grab by expanding its territory in Guyana at the expense of the newly independent republic of Venezuela. The agent of this expansion was a Prussian, Robert Schomburgk, who spent two years in the early 1840s walking, sketching and marking out the lands around the Essequibo River, and whose actions triggered the British unilateral declaration of the new border between the republic and the empire (a shift of around 300 miles west). Venezuela could do nothing, and duly did nothing, given that its foreign minister at the time was a Scotsman, Guillermo/William Smith, and the acting British ambassador in Caracas, Daniel O'Leary, was the brother-in-law of the country's president, Carlos Soublette. Surviving archives show that the British Foreign Office put much more effort into safeguarding President Soublette's honour than it did into protecting the national sovereignty of the country he governed.[19]

While Argentina lost some symbolic islands that began to have economic worth (through oil production) only nearly 200 years later, and Venezuela lost several thousand square kilometres of rainforest with much economic potential (not to mention the thousands of Venezuelan citizens living among it), Mexico's experience at the receiving end of foreign imperialism in this period was the most severe on the continent and had the most immediate, and long-lasting, consequences.

At the beginning of this chapter I noted how the distance and communications between capital cities and principal ports played a large part in shaping regional and/or political strife in nineteenth-century Latin America. In the case of Mexico the journey between Mexico City and the port of Veracruz only entailed a few days on horseback until the construction of a railway at the end of the century. The repeated rise to power of Mexico's most famous and most derided caudillo, Antonio López de Santa Anna (who was president on fourteen separate occasions between 1832 and 1867), owed everything to his influence in Veracruz and his ability to carry patronage and soldiers with him up to the capital city. Perhaps, if Mexico had existed in a geopolitical vacuum, Santa Anna would today be remembered as the man who made the nation believe in itself and constructed institutions and a political culture that would ensure its survival, like Diego Portales in Chile.

The Growing Expansionism of the United States

Santa Anna's career, like Mexico's early nationhood, was overshadowed by the expansionist presence of the United States of America to the north. In 1823, when Santa Anna was a young officer, U.S. President James Monroe decreed that no European power would be permitted to interfere in the sovereignty of any American nation. Just thirteen years later, this doctrine was observed to the letter. Britain, France, Spain and Russia and its Holy Alliance looked on with indifference as the U.S. itself did the most to undermine Mexico's sovereignty over its northern territories. In 1836 the Mexican garrison at El Alamo, Texas, was besieged and defeated by Texan landowners and insurgents who acted in the belief that they would be supported by the U.S. federal government. Santa Anna lost a leg in the firefight, returning humiliated to Mexico City as Texas declared its independence before joining the Union soon afterwards. Worse was to come for Mexico. In 1845–8 the so-called Mexican–American War led to the wholesale defeat of the Mexican army, which was entirely unprepared for the invasion of its lands by the U.S. Mexico was left with the rump of its national territory south of the Rio Grande. Gold was discovered in California at almost exactly the same time, meaning that it was the U.S., rather than Mexico, which benefited from the rapid transport revolution and consequent industrialization catalysed by the Gold Rush. As migrants trekked west in search of the precious metals, they expanded the frontiers of the U.S. and moved its centre of gravity away from the east coast for the first time. Although attempts to construct a railway across Panama in the 1850s (to get migrants from the east to the west coast of the U.S. quicker than the conventional transcontinental trek) created what historian Aims McGuinness calls a 'path of empire', crucially, the ports of both embarkation (New York) and destination (San Francisco) were now part of the U.S. Had California still been Mexican, as it was just a decade before the discovery of gold, the Gold Rush would have been much more of a transnational phenomenon than a transcontinental one. While the U.S. hurtled on towards its own, defining civil war in the 1860s, Mexico looked in on itself, seeking resolution in Liberal–Conservative partisan factionalism and religious/spiritual/ ethnic conflict. The 'War of the Castes', which persisted in Yucatán through the second half of the century, was mainly a conflict over taxation, landownership and the reach of the Mexican state. It was also a reaction by Mexico's Maya citizens against the encroachment of outsiders upon places understood as ancestrally 'theirs'.[20]

The expansion of the U.S. westwards was often held up as an example of the country's Manifest Destiny to occupy and civilize lands inhabited by indigenous peoples or Catholic Hispanics. This process of territorial expansion during the nineteenth century stopped at the Rio Grande. Attempts to stretch the boundaries of the Union overseas were only rarely successful, as in the Philippines after 1898. But that did not mean that imperialist impulses on the part of U.S. citizens were reined in after the Mexican–American War. Dreams of incorporating Cuba were consistent among some U.S. groups throughout the century – and were shared by some Cubans, too. Some Colombians flirted with the idea of offering their state to the U.S. as a method of undermining some of the ultra-patriotic factionalism that left the country immersed in civil war. More common, but less understood, were the actions of what might be termed 'rogue adventurers', who left the U.S. looking for glory in the lands to the south, and found themselves seeking power and infringing on local and national sovereignty. As in Panama in the era of railway construction, these adventurers often happened to find themselves in places of U.S. commercial or geopolitical interest.

William Walker is the most famous of these adventurers or filibusters who tyrannized Central America in the middle of the nineteenth century. Looking to seize power from what he saw as an ineffective local government, he thought that he had the skills and the charisma to impose order and liberty upon towns and regions throughout the region. Leading private armies across Central America, overthrowing local authorities and establishing his own personal rule, Walker was an unsympathetic character and reviled by his many opponents. But he was not an anachronism: he was following an established tradition, from Gregor MacGregor in Poyais (Nicaragua) in the 1820s through to the Venezuelan-born Narciso López's attack on Cuba in the 1850s. If successful, Walker expected the rewards to be immense, in terms of both political status and financial reward. In 1856 he allied with some local rebels and installed himself as president of Nicaragua. Opinion is not divided – his reign, which reintroduced slavery and made English the official language, was a disaster. Nicaraguans saw him as the representative of Yankee imperialism, and other U.S. citizens with an interest in the region, such as Cornelius Vanderbilt, resented his incursions on their own commercial interests. He was overthrown by a large coalition in 1857. A similar attempt to rule Honduras a few years later ended with Walker's execution. At the time of writing no revisionist historian has attempted to rehabilitate Walker's memory – he is still seen pretty universally as a greedy, ambitious and violent man whose efforts ran contrary to the ideals of national sovereignty, liberty and equality that nineteenth-century Latin American states professed to hold dear.[21]

Latin America, 1830–70: The Victim of Continued (Neo)Colonialism?

In many works denouncing the neo-colonial nature of Latin America's first half-century of independence, the War of the Triple Alliance is held up as the smoking gun. In the version of history told by

Eduardo Galeano, in the mid-1860s Britain encouraged nationalism and warmongering in Paraguay, Brazil, Argentina and Uruguay, leading directly to a war in which Paraguay was all but destroyed by the Triple Alliance. In this interpretation Paraguay had followed an independent course since the departure of the Spanish colonialists, taking advantage of its relative geographical isolation in the centre of South America and developing an autarchic, nationalist and protectionist economy that, when the British eventually learned of it, triggered an irrational desire to destroy an alternative model to its own free-trading liberal capitalism. Wary of expending unnecessary resources on such relative small fry, British banks and diplomats leaned on Paraguay's Atlantic neighbours to teach the regional upstarts a lesson when President Francisco Solano López declared war in 1868.

The war, certainly, was a disaster for Paraguay. Its economy was ruined and one in ten of its population (one in five males) was killed. Hundreds of thousands of lives were lost as well as swathes of national territory. Nevertheless the surviving archives demonstrate British indifference towards the conflict rather than any active encouragement of the participants on either side. Certainly Brazil and Argentina hoped that their actions would be approved of in London, and Paraguay's armed forces were stocked with British advisers and physicians (and the First Lady, Eliza Lynch, was a francophile Irishwoman who delighted in holding dinner parties for European visitors). British personnel, weapons and credit were everywhere in the War of the Triple Alliance – as they were across much of Latin America in the mid-nineteenth century, from railway construction in Argentina to breweries in Mexico. But it is going too far to imagine that the British engineered this devastating conflict for their own benefit.[22] It is instead an excellent example of the depth to which foreign – primarily but not exclusively British – influence had embedded itself in Latin America in the 50 years since independence. Furthermore this international war served to catalyse the formation of nationalist sentiment both in defeated Paraguay and in victorious Brazil, Argentina and Uruguay.[23] As the next half-century went on to demonstrate, nationalism in Latin America and continued imperial presences on the continent were intimately related.

THREE

Raw Materials,
Raw Wounds

L atin America's full incorporation into the global economy took place from around 1870 to 1890. The continent now became absolutely tied into global commercial and financial networks, compared to the (relative) autonomy it had enjoyed in the preceding half-century. The late nineteenth century saw the quantity of trade, especially exports, increase dramatically. It witnessed the beginnings of industrialization in certain urban centres and the boom of European and U.S. investment in railway construction, rubber, copper, bananas and, increasingly, oil. All these factors fed into one another. In response to major industrialization and the corresponding escalation of demand for materials in Europe and North America, Latin America grew into a role of providing materials extracted 'raw' from the ground or the trees to be transported to other continents, which would produce 'manufactured' items, adding value to the 'raw materials' and gaining the principal share of the profit from the final sale, often back to Latin America itself.[1]

Galeano argued in *The Open Veins of Latin America* that this period represented a definitive return to colonialism, albeit this time with Britain and the U.S. taking the Iberian empires' positions as imperial masters. The Uruguayan president Julio Herrera y Obes said in 1890 that his job was 'like being the manager of a great ranch, whose board of directors is in London'.[2] Economists, historians and social scientists came to talk of this as a period of Latin American 'dependency' upon European and North American markets and sales, a relationship which locked Latin America into a 'structural' subordination from which it could not break out. By exporting its raw materials and buying in cheap manufactured goods from Europe and the United States, Latin America was unable to start its own manufacturing industries as it was forever kept in a position of competitive disadvantage with regard to the economies which had industrialized first.[3] This chapter examines the last three decades of the nineteenth century, ending with the events that definitely heralded the increasingly predatory role of u.s. influence in Latin America: the Spanish–American War and the independence of Cuba (from Spain) in 1898 and the independence of Panama (from Colombia) in 1903.

Galeano equated British and North American economic dominance in Latin America with a neo-colonialism which featured human rights abuses as serious as those of the era of Spanish colonialism. Reports from the booming rubber industry, discussed below, certainly demonstrated that. But, at the same time, profound cultural changes were occurring across the continent and nationalism was catalysed by the presence of different, foreign peoples, especially when they seemed to be benefiting economically more than local peoples. Yet, at first sight paradoxically, the boom in foreign investment and the increase in European and Asian migration to the region was accompanied by the adoption of many European cultural modes and leisure activities, especially the growth of football. This chapter explains the international economic, social, cultural and political processes in this age of empires and nationalisms.

The War of the Pacific, 1879–83

Conflict over potentially lucrative products and export trades sometimes spilled over into international warfare. The War of the Pacific demonstrates many of the competing processes at stake here. Ostensibly it pitted Chile against an alliance of Peru and Bolivia. The Chileans sought to expand their territory northwards into the lands of nations its white elite considered ethnically inferior, and Bolivia lost its only seaboard (which it has never forgotten, and for which it continues to fund a navy). On an economic level it was a competition over the increasingly valuable nitrate-producing coastal areas and islands, as the three countries fought over which of them would bene-fit most from the sodium nitrate deposits in the Atacama Desert. These, like the guano, or seagull droppings, high in nitrates, that were exported to Europe for use as fertilizer until chemical advances stymied the trade in the early twentieth century. The scramble for Peruvian nitrates had environmental, economic and political con-sequences across the world, from Pacific atolls to the headquarters of Unilever. Financially all sides sought credit from international financiers in order to raise and ration their armies, leading to allega-tions that Britain and France were fighting a proxy war via chequebook as they sought hegemony in the Andes.

The effects of the War of the Pacific have been much debated by historians. Florencia Mallon, drawing on local archives in the Andes, argued that indigenous Peruvians in the southern highlands were radicalized by the experience of being recruited into, and fighting in, a national army which existed in order to preserve the national territory. Heraclio Bonilla, in contrast, argued that any new con-sciousness on their part must have been resolutely false, rather than national, because of their continuing subordination within the nation and the ongoing condescension and exclusion practised by the white, coastal elites. Historians have tended to side with Mallon in recent years as they have delved further into municipal and regional archives and sought to recover the voices of subaltern and subordi-nated peoples from history. The War of the Pacific, which made national heroes in Peru and Chile respectively of the descendants of European migrants such as Miguel Grau and Arturo Prats, demon-strates how global empires impacted upon Latin America at many different levels in the late nineteenth century.[4]

At that time Latin America pursued its own arms race to mirror that pursued with greater intent between Great Britain and Germany, which is generally held to be one of the causes of the First World War. Marcelo Carmagnani makes a good case that the Chilean and Peruvian purchases of British ships 'led to the outbreak' of the War of the Pacific. He shows how the regular 'military missions' sent from Europe to Latin America in this period had significant consequences. Britain, France, Germany and Italy all wanted to sell military materiel to Latin America and to train military officers and commanders so that they would come to share a military ethos with their trainers – which in the long term would lead to alliances, assistance and further arms sales, all perceived as being good things for everyone concerned.[5] The effective role of Prussia/Germany in training and advising Latin American armies in this period can still be seen today in the prevalence of German-style military uniforms for the soldiers guarding presidential palaces in Latin America, from Lima to Bogotá.

The Height of British Informal Empire?
The Baring Crisis, 1890

This was, without doubt, the British period of Latin American history. It has been estimated that between 1865 and 1913 British trade with Latin America tripled, leaving competitors flailing and Latin Americans acutely aware of which nation was the preeminent economic and political power in the Atlantic.[6] Britain's strongest – and most asymmetrical – relationship was with Argentina, which was often treated as if it was a member of the empire in terms of commerce and whose landowning and trading elite derived enormous benefit from the link to London. Close ties to Britain did not necessarily translate into horizontal, fraternal comradeship. In the Baring Crisis of 1890 Barings Bank in London was nearly bankrupted, being saved only by assurances given by the Bank of England and other international financial institutions. Barings had invested heavily in Argentina and the bank's near collapse brought the Argentinian economy to its knees. The Argentinian president of the day, Carlos Pellegrini, had in his youth attended Harrow public school near London, one of the most exclusive institutions in Britain. Pellegrini took political decisions in Argentina that saved Britain's financial sector and crippled his own country in the short term while retaining Britain's goodwill in the medium term. This is as good an illustration as any of the nature of Britain's 'informal empire' in Argentina at the turn of the century.[7] The crisis also affected Brazil and Uruguay, both countries where Barings had been substantially exposed. For all the transnational properties of international finance, and its ability to invest capital and withdraw it much more quickly in the age of the telegram than in that of the steamship, finance and capital still had centres where they felt more at home. Those centres remained in Europe and in North America, meaning that Latin America remained at risk of a flight of capital in the event of economic crisis triggered elsewhere.[8]

Nationalist 'Regenerations' and the Hispanic Past

As the communication revolution brought the rest of the world into closer contact with Latin American cities, and brought hundreds of thousands of migrants across the Atlantic, newly fortified nationalist movements sought to promote idealized, sometimes nostalgic versions of what national cultures should be, or might once have been before the arrival of modern ways and customs. Nationalist movements were often mirrored by ideologies that harked back to the good old days of the Hispanic colonial past. Spanish traditions, often reviled in the decades after independence, sometimes came back into fashion when they came to symbolize order, hierarchy and stability during times of civil war, upheaval or uncertainty. In Colombia the so-called 'regeneration' was led by elites who spent their spare time working on Spanish grammar rather than social policy, and for whom Spanish philosophers and artists were models for emulation. Hispanic moves to establish a pan-continental and transatlantic 'Day of the [Hispanic] Race' were popular in Mexico and elsewhere. Often, of course, attempts to revive Hispanic legacies led to further exclusion for minority groups (as ever, the indigenous and Afro-American) but also cemented the unfavourable social positions of mestizo or mixed-race people.

Moves to reunite the 'Hispanic' sectors of society in Latin America can be seen, with hindsight, as a countercurrent to the increasingly popular calls for a continent-wide, 'Latin' American identity which began in the mid-nineteenth century. Historians used to believe that the first use of the term 'Latin America' was employed by French intellectuals hoping to gain geopolitical advantage through their military operations in Mexico in the 1850s. 'Latin' America, it was thought, enabled the French to distinguish themselves (as a 'Latin'

race) from their British, German and U.S. rivals for imperial hegemony in the Americas. But scholars have recovered evidence to show
that in fact it was Latin Americans themselves, such as Justo Aro-
semena and Francisco Bilbao, who first coined the term as they sought
a positive basis for continental unions (while also keeping an eye on
potential U.S. incursions). Regardless of the etymological origins of
the phrase, important though they are, in mid-century these were
only the concerns of a narrow intellectual elite, heavily influenced
by their travels in France, the UK and the U.S. But as the presence of
the global empires became heavier after 1870, especially through the
boom in commerce, a sense of common 'Latin' Americanness, in
opposition to other generic identities ('European', 'North American'
or 'Anglo-American'), began to put down stronger roots.

Uniting Nations against External Threats

Nationalists were pushed by a perceived need to create a shared
national collective identity which would support a nation-state – in
crude terms, to ensure that citizens paid their taxes and would enlist
into the national army in times of national insecurity. The elites
employed nationalism to counteract their financial weakness and
their military defencelessness in the face of foreign threats. The fear
that social diversity would exacerbate weaknesses that would bend
towards external threats appeared to be borne out by U.S. encroach-
ments into Mexican territory and Colombia's loss of Panama. But
there was also a desire to create genuinely national markets for
manufacture and agriculture in recognition that the international
economy would never look out for the interior national provinces
that would otherwise be bypassed by the dependency between
exporting region and importing country.

At the end of the 1800s, free market and controlled labour
economies finally established themselves in the Atlantic, with the
abolition of slavery in Spain's remaining colonies – particularly Cuba
(in 1886) and Brazil (in 1888). This was not a natural consequence
of 'freer' trade or British benevolence. Great Britain's abolition in
1807 of their own Atlantic trade in slaves in fact made little dent in

the numbers of Africans being forcibly transported across the Atlantic. C. A. Bayly remarks that this period was in fact 'slavery's Indian summer', especially in Cuba and Brazil, where 'a reinvigorated Roman Catholic hierarchy continued to vigorously justify it with Aristotle's arguments, even though this subsequently became increasingly embarrassing for the Vatican'.[9] The victory of the North in the u.s. Civil War in the 1860s ended slavery in the u.s., and though its defenders did not give up the ghost, by the 1880s it was clear that a system of forced labour was no longer politically tenable. These were political rather than economic decisions. The numbers show that importing slaves had continued to bring economic profit to landowners in Brazil and Cuba throughout the second half of the nineteenth century. The elites postponed the freedom of the people they still saw as their property, and the delays were so long that alternative strategies of exploitation were developed. Very few slave owners experienced downward social mobility as a result of abolition. Railways were built and plantations were worked and crops harvested by the poor African American descendants of slaves, as well as by newly arrived Asian 'coolies' and Irish navvies.

Infrastructure and Modernization

Increasing international trade coupled with technological advances in communication and transport meant that national governments came to focus, at the end of the nineteenth century, on making their national territories appear safe for foreign investment – a trend that remains familiar in contemporary Latin American history. This meant improving transport infrastructure to reduce costs, developing urban centres so that the representatives of international trade would be comfortable in their posts, and ensuring that the majority of the population remained as quiet and loyal to the state as possible. The epitome of the success of this brand of 'modernization' was Porfirio Díaz in Mexico.

Porfirio Díaz's efforts to modernize Mexico relied on a similar way of thinking about 'improving' nations to other rulers across the continent such as Roca in Argentina, Eloy Alfaro in Ecuador or

Rafael Núñez in Colombia. A population that could become some-how whiter, cleaner and more energetic at work would be modern. Communities that did not fit into those categories would be sidelined to the peripheries of the nation or, in the worst examples, subjected to violence in order to force them to change or simply maintain their subordination. How to improve the physical and mental health of their citizens was a concern of many Latin American governments in the late nineteenth century. Improvements to sanitation and precarious national health and education services were made in this period. Alongside these practical changes like street gutters, sewers and urban health clinics came the growing appreciation of the potential value of organized team sports, both for improving masculinity and physical health, and for promoting an image of the nation abroad.

The Origins of Football in Latin America

The tensions between looking at outside models for inspiration and improvement, and seeking authenticity and meaning within local, indigenous cultures, become clearer if we look at the origins of the sport of football in Latin America. Here, as in the study of Latin American novels or poetry, questions of art, beauty and Euro-centrism arise. The origins of football in the Americas were part of a global process that followed European migrants drawn across lands and oceans by commercial enterprise, and was booted along by colonized peoples seeking avenues for achieving equality with their imperial or financial masters.[10] The case of Brazil illustrates a wider point for Latin America, showing how financial, commercial and cultural changes were part of one interlocking relationship between Brazil and Europe, especially Britain.

There is general acceptance across the football-playing world that the British (often, mistakenly, the English) were responsible for disseminating the rules and customs of the game that we now know and love. In Britain, at least, historians sense that football was one benevolent consequence of informal empire, which seems to have suited the growth of football rather more than did formal empire, in

José de la Cruz Porfirio Díaz Mori (1830–1915), 29th President of Mexico.

Porfirio Díaz (1830–1915) was the long-serving Mexican head of state (1876–1911) who presided over the country's full incorporation into the international economy, promoting foreign exploitation of oil deposits and mines, railway construction and the Paris-style urban renewal of major cities. Under Díaz manufacturing and industry in Mexico underwent a series of spectacular booms, dramatically increasing the wealth of the country, most especially for the social and economic elites, who benefited most of all. A mestizo soldier from rural Oaxaca who rose through the military ranks to seize power in a way that his ethnicity would have made impossible through civilian channels, Díaz is remembered not as an example of republican social mobility but as the old president whose refusal to leave office bottled up various social and economic tensions which exploded when he was finally removed. Like his contemporary Otto von Bismarck in Prussia, Díaz governed through a mixture of carrot and stick – *pan y palo*, bread and stick in Spanish – combining populist, personalist and paternalist gestures towards the poor in a manner reminiscent of the Catholic monarchs of colonial times, with strict authoritarian rule and the repression of political opponents. It was Díaz's indifference to the workings of democracy – electoral fraud was widespread and results manipulated at whim – that eventually triggered his downfall when a middle-class rebel, Francisco Madero, vowed to topple him by whatever means necessary. This catalysed the large-scale, urban and rural, class-based and ethnic-tinged Mexican Revolution. Perhaps inevitably Díaz died in exile in the city of Paris, which he had thought so modern and so civilized, while Mexico was torn apart through violent civil war.

The famous lament 'Poor Mexico: so far from God, and so close to the United States' is often attributed to Díaz. In 1880 he did say: 'if, from one end of the Republic to the other, the train, with its powerful voice awakens and mobilises all Mexicans, then my desires will have been satisfied.'[11]

which games such as cricket and rugby flourished better. Brazil is a good example of a country where early British attempts to play cricket were superseded by football. When the numbers of British expatriates were still relatively small, in the mid-nineteenth century, they often played cricket among themselves. From the late 1860s, as British trade and investment rose in Latin America (particularly in Brazil, Argentina, Chile and Uruguay), many more thousands of British men took up opportunities in the fields of railways, banking, ports and tramways. These individuals often set up schools and sports clubs, and more migrants followed to teach or administer them. Football therefore spread most quickly 'in the South American countries most subject to British economic and cultural influence', where the number of British migrants were greatest. Within two generations, however, by 1916, the game had been effectively 'creolized', taken over from the British by the 'respectable classes of South America', and then 'popularized' as local working-class men embraced the game as their own.[12] The British catalysed South American football first through education, with the likes of the schoolteacher Alexander Watson Hutton making the game popular in Buenos Aires, and the Instituto Presberitiano Mackenzie in Santos, the port neighbouring São Paulo which later was home to twentieth-century football's major star, Pelé. A second vector of the game's spread worked through investment and trade connections (that is, sailors and railwaymen looking for leisure activities) and a third was touring sides such as the Corinthinans, Southampton or Swindon. The sociologist Richard Giullianoti also takes as a given the 'intense cultural receptivity of South American peoples towards football': certainly one contribution to the game's growing popularity must be the fact that elite Latin Americans valued imports partly because of their foreign origins.[13]

Global historians of football's origins tend to agree with Giullanoti when he talks of 'football's global diffusion . . . trade connections, rather than imperial links, were the most propitious outlets'.[14] Where formal empire was strongest, rugby and cricket took hold because they were more rule-driven, more formal. Where informal empire was strongest, informal games like football grew organically. But how did they grow? What effect did football have on social, economic and urban development? The so-called 'founder' of football in Brazil, Charles Miller, was born in São Paulo, so the case of that city can serve as a useful example to illustrate some of these points.

Charles Miller was the son of a Scottish engineer and a Brazilian woman of English heritage. At the age of nine he was sent to be educated in Hampshire. He returned with the rules established by the English Football Association, two balls and enthusiasm for the game. Miller was born in Bras, a typical industrial São Paulo neighbourhood, not far from the train station. On his return from England in 1894 Charles Miller recruited players among the members of the São Paulo Athletic Club, which had been founded by the English community in 1888, the employees of the São Paulo Railway, where he worked, the gas company and the London Bank. From 1895 Miller organized 'official' football matches under the rules of the English Football Association, with British, German, Italian and Brazilian players. These matches did not take place in a geopolitical vacuum.[15] Miller later went on to be the British Consul in São Paulo.

1898: End of Empire, Beginning of Something New

The São Paulo Athletic Club celebrates its foundation on the same day in 1888 that the law to formally abolish slavery was passed in Brazil. This coincidence draws attention to a change in the way national economies and societies would be imagined in the twentieth century – based on greater freedom of movement and labour, with organized sport as a release for workers from the strictures and pressures of industrialized work, and as a way for nations to project themselves on the international stage. The 'foreign' origins of sports like football, baseball or cycling were quickly sidelined as the sports were used to present apparently uniquely Brazilian, Chilean or Colombian ways of playing, ways of being. This is because the period of the late nineteenth century that saw the flourishing of national organized sports also witnessed a growing pattern of emergent U.S. power along much of the Caribbean coastline, and news of U.S. aggression spread anxiety about national survival across the continent.

Cuba was a key location. Between 1868 and 1878 Cubans had fought their first war of independence against Spanish colonial rule. The rebels were led by some free blacks, including Antonio Maceo, though slave fighters were split between the rebel cause and fighting on the side of their masters. Sensing how much its economy depended upon the profits of slave-produced sugar in Cuba, the Spanish authorities resolved to fight to the death in Cuba, sending experienced veterans to the island to lead the repression and shunning reconciliation in favour of forcing the rebels into submission by any means possible. But a generation later, several things had changed. First, the abolition of slavery by Spain in 1886 severed the principal economic tie that had bound the Cuban landowning and slave-owning elites to the mother country. Without slavery, many thought, they may as well seek their own autonomy rather than continually looking deferentially across the Atlantic. Second, the u.s. was now flexing its muscles much more aggressively in the Caribbean, and many Cubans hoped that the u.s. would protect its liberties and repulse the attacks of tyrannical, monarchical Spain. In 1895 some Cuban exiles, including the writer José Martí, returned to Cuba from the u.s. Martí was killed by loyalists in his first and last military engagement, but the new – and final – war of independence (1895–8) continued. In 1898 the uss *Maine*, anchored in Havana harbour, was spectacularly blown up. u.s. naval leaders cried that the Spanish or Cubans had deliberately attacked them in order to force them into the war. Others, at the time and since, have speculated that the u.s. firebombed their own ship in order to provide an excuse to fight Spain and steal its colonies. Another explanation is the ship was simply poorly constructed and that it overheated and triggered the combustion of its own ammunition store.[16] The Spanish army and navy were quickly overcome and within six months Cuba was independent. But immediately Cuba's national sovereignty did not have an easy ride. The Platt Amendment, passed in the u.s. Congress in 1901 and integrated into the Cuban constitution in 1902, specified that although Cuba was independent from Spain, the part played by u.s. forces in the liberation should be repaid by the u.s. continuing to enjoy a veto over any act of parliament passed in Cuba. If this was not neo-colonialism or 'informal' empire, critics have thought, then a better example would be hard to find. As a result of the Spanish–American War of 1898 Cuba fell into the grasp of the u.s., and the Philippines became a formal colony of the u.s. and Puerto Rico's status was only slightly more ambiguous. In Spain the events of 1898 were deemed so significant that they spawned an entire intellectual 'generation' whose intense disillusion and despair at the loss of the remnants of empire was matched by their intense exasperation and lack of ideas as to how to get Spain out of its cycle of decline and back to the great power status they desired.

The rising power of the u.s., the lengthening 'shadow of the eagle' in the Americas, produced a variety of responses in Latin America. José Martí's evangelization for 'Our America' was one attempt to draw up a cultural blueprint of the differences between North and South America. In 1902 the Uruguayan writer José Enrique Rodó published *Ariel*, his own attempt to think through the links and divergences between what he saw as the two cultures, territorially separated, which shaped the Americas.

Rodó presented the u.s. as Caliban, the barbaric, uncultured beast in Shakespeare's *The Tempest* who is driven only by pursuing his own interests. The relationship between Caliban and Ariel, located by Shakespeare in the Caribbean, has a varied global history of its own.[17] For Rodó, the u.s. ('Anglo-America') was far too rational, too Protestant, pursuing work and profit to the detriment of its spiritual happiness. In contrast, Hispanic America was united by its spiritual dimension, by its appreciation of aesthetics, beauty and balance rather than short-term benefit or pleasure. Rodó urged the youth of Latin America to stay true to their identities and to turn away from the easy but temporary pleasures of bourgeois rational-ism. *Ariel* became a crucial rallying cry for Latin Americanism in the twentieth century. Crucially in it the u.s. became associated not with modernism, civilization and progress but with a *lack* of morals, with misplaced ideals, corruption and barbarism. Latin America would from now on increasingly measure its sense of worth and success against the great power from the North rather than the global empires emanating from Europe.

José Martí (1853–1895) was the first Latin American to capture in print the impending shadow that was about to be cast over the continent by the burgeoning imperial power of the United States. The newspaper articles he wrote in New York sketched the growing self-awareness and difference of the Latin American exile in the 1880s and '90s. From a spellbound admirer of the U.S. system he became a staunch Cuban nationalist, and called for the island's people to grasp and exercise their national sovereignty. His *Nuestra América* (1895) was embraced by anti-imperialists across Latin America. Unlike Simón Bolívar, to whom he has often been linked as an intellectual descendant with shared revolutionary, anti-imperialist ideals, Martí did not combine ability with the pen with skill with the sword. He returned to Cuba and fought for national independence against Spain in the war that would give Cuba its sovereignty, only for it to be immediately subsumed within U.S. dominance. Martí died in his first and only military action at the Battle of Dos Ríos in May 1895. Even before independence was won three years later, Martí had become a national martyr, and the Cuban Revolution of 1959 embraced his memory as one of the key national heroes upon whose legacy the revolution and its antiimperialism would be constructed.[18]

Martí wrote: 'The North had been unjust and greedy. It has thought more about assuring the fortune of a few than about creating a nation for the good of all; it has brought to the new American land all the hatreds and all the problems of the old monarchies.'[19]

José Martí (1853–1895).

In Venezuela the great powers united in an attempt to force this hitherto most unassuming of Latin American countries to toe the line. Between 1901 and 1902 a naval blockade of Venezuela's ports was enforced by a combined fleet of U.S., British, German and Italian ships, which aimed at seeing that Venezuela, at the time in the midst of a presidential succession, would continue to honour contracts beneficial to foreign interests. One of the key Venezuelan protagonists of this crisis, which acted as a rallying cry to solidarity across the continent, was President Cipriano Castro, who famously declared that 'the insolent sole of the foreigner's boots must be expelled from our country'. Latin American governments, now united by telegraph cables and increasingly anxious about their sovereignty, having observed the fates of Cuba and Panama in recent years, now repeated their call for non-intervention by foreign powers in a nation-state's affairs. The Argentinian foreign minister Luis Drago issued a memorandum to Washington repeating that 'the public debt could not be a reason for armed intervention, nor for occupying the territory of American nations.'[20] Public support made the Drago memorandum the International Relations equivalent of Rodó's literary statement in *Ariel*: a widely recognized declaration of Latin American independence and peacefulness in opposition to perceived U.S. ambition and aggression. The 'bullish' U.S. response to Drago, in 1904, was the Roosevelt Corollary, in which the U.S. attempted to appear in line with the American states' policy on non-intervention, assuring *itself* the sole right and duty to intervene in the sovereignty of American states.[21] This was the precedent that would be invoked later in the century when the U.S. felt the need to intervene militarily in Central America.

Panama, 1903

The dream of opening a canal through Central America, linking Atlantic and Pacific trade routes, had occupied imperial thinkers in Spain, France and Great Britain since the sixteenth century. Disease, technological failure and engineering mishaps had undermined all attempts to make this dream a reality. In the mid-nineteenth century a French scheme succeeded in excavating vast tonnes of earth but could not get near to completing this massive job. By the end of the century the U.S. had asserted itself as a major transcontinental republic, and now had most to gain from a canal cut through the American landmass. Given the success of the railway constructed through Panama in the 1850s and '60s, this northernmost slice of Colombian territory appeared to offer an obvious location for a new attempt at canal construction. In 1899 Colombian Liberals launched an ill-fated rebellion against a Conservative government that had entrenched itself in power with a centralist constitution in 1886 and which was in the process of 'regenerating' the country along what it saw as traditional lines of order, hierarchy and the Catholic religion. The two sides were evenly matched, and the War of One Thousand Days had begun. Several hundred thousand Colombians died in this conflict, which was immortalized in García Márquez's novel *Cien años de soledad / One Hundred Years of Solitude* as epitomizing the senseless, partisan violence that had besmirched the country's history since independence:

> one night [Colonel Aureliano Buendía] asked Colonel Gerineldo Márquez:
> 'Tell me something, old friend: why are you fighting?'
> 'What other reason could there be?' [he] answered. 'For the great Liberal party.'
> 'You're lucky because you know why,' he answered. 'As far as I'm concerned, I've come to realize only just now that I'm fighting because of pride.'[22]

With the two sides collapsing into one another's arms in 1902, peace talks were brought about on the USS *Wisconsin*, anchored off Colombia's Caribbean coast. The most significant consequence of the war was not the many deaths, nor the way in which it cemented the Conservatives in power against a weakened opposition for another three decades. Instead it was the independence of Panama, the province that had long hankered to free itself of the burden of forming part of the Colombian state, especially since the building of the transcontinental railway, which put it, in the words of historian Aims McGuinness, in the 'path of empire'. In 1902–3 U.S. agents supported Panamanian independence on the condition that Panamanians facilitated the construction of a canal across Panama in fulfilment of the dreams of a long train of adventurers and speculators. Tens of thousands of labourers flooded across the Caribbean to work on the project, many of them from Barbados, Jamaica and other British colonies; several thousand of them died, most from tropical disease. The Canal opened to transoceanic traffic in 1914, and in the post-First World War years would be a huge spur to international trade and migration. The establishment of a Panama Canal Zone, to be administered by the U.S. authorities, was an effective form of U.S. neo-colonial rule by another name. Colombians never forgot the loss of Panama – though the reparations of over U.S.$20 million into the Colombian Bank of the Republic certainly helped to assuage the immediate pain.[23] News of the role of U.S. agents in lobbying for and facilitating Panamanian independence from Colombia, and the concessions regarding the Canal Zone that were granted in return, spread across Latin America and shaped the way that states engaged with foreign powers in the period leading up to the First World War.

The Mexican Revolution

Continent-wide Latin Americanism, such as that imagined by José Enrique Rodó, began to blossom alongside newly attractive forms of nationalism. Continentalism and nationalism were far from mutually exclusive – indeed, they often fed off each other. The early twentieth century witnessed a series of social and political upheavals in which nationalist claims crashed against embedded corporate privilege (particularly that of the armed forces or the Catholic Church), foreign interests and ideas that promoted democratic cultures and widening electoral franchises.

In Mexico these all came together at a time when U.S. economic involvement in the nascent oil industry was increasingly commented upon, and when Porfirio Díaz's rule of over three decades had become stale and oppressive to many citizens. His brand of popular, corruptly democratic longevity had to end some time, of course, and when it did the lack of an obvious successor combined with structural economic and social processes to unleash a period of unprecedented bloodshed, civil war and revolution. Famine in the country, anti-foreigner anger in oil-producing areas, populist posturing and committed social and military organization on the state's frontiers created wave after wave of rebellion and counter-revolution, multiple assassinations of political leaders and much national soul-searching. Trade unionists, anarchists, socialists and communists exploited the deep-seated inequalities that had been exacerbated by the quick pace of urbanization. Workers' strikes in oil-producing areas in 1915, 1916 and 1917 had a massive effect. When the violence was finally ended, from around 1921, the result was proclaimed to have been a national revolution, the Mexican Revolution, which would now be governed by an Institutional Revolutionary Party, the PRI. During the eleven years that the Mexican Revolution took to conclude, the rest of the world had witnessed the entire First World War and the Treaty of Versailles, with its pledge of support for national self-determination, as well as the Bolshevik Revolution and Atatürk's revolution in Turkey. The rapidity and all-consuming nature of events in Mexico over a decade meant that it seemed logical to conclude that it had been an eminently national event.[24]

Latin Americans were not invited and therefore not present in the most significant debates at Versailles to feed into the post-war settlement in 1919, but they were among the most enthusiastic supporters of the League of Nations, the international body which was to regulate relations between states, encourage social and economic progress and mediate in disputes over territory and sovereignty. In this Latin America was most clearly set apart from the U.S., which was influential at Versailles but whose congress and senate refused to ratify bills authorizing the U.S. to participate.[25] As the world order was reconfigured in the decade after the First World War, Latin America's position remained ambiguous. Three major political and geopolitical upheavals had cleaved Latin American sovereignty apart in the first decade of the twentieth century: first, the 1901 Platt Amendment for newly independent Cuba did not correlate with ideas of self-determination advanced for other peoples at Versailles. Second, the creation of the Panama Canal Zone in what had been the territory of Colombia produced a physical boundary – the water of the canal – which ripped open the American landmass and laid down a symbolic marker of power. Finally, the beginnings of the Mexican Revolution in 1910 were witness to the growing strains on Latin American societies that were being forced by the economic and social changes of the communications and transport revolutions.

FOUR

New Exchanges, New Markets

The first decades of the twentieth century were a period of spectacular technological change in Latin America. The rapid expansion of telegraph communications revolutionized the spread of news: cables between diplomatic embassies brought international relations much more under the control of imperial centres rather than consular outposts. The massive construction of railways, ports and airports was a supremely visible example of the arrival of new peoples and new products into the continent – and also a useful indicator of the increasing efficiency of exporters in getting their goods to market. These technological changes in Latin America's relationship to the world brought into sharp relief the fact that the region's political leaders often played a subordinate role to stronger states such as Germany, Great Britain and the u.s. Cultural reactions to imperial presence were also shared much more quickly through the expansion of newspapers and the speed of communications. A new type of relationship between Latin America and the world arose as a result of the encounters that took place between travellers, ideas and places.

Railways

Railway construction expanded exponentially across Latin America, and the phenomenon was particularly acute in Argentina, where British companies competed to build potentially lucrative routes linking the cattle-ranching regions of the interior with Buenos Aires and the Atlantic ports. The construction of railway networks developed along the same lines, and faultlines, as the nineteenth-century nations they were supposed to guide to prosperity. Argentina's railways were like the tentacles of an octopus whose heart was in Buenos Aires – lines that did not begin or end at the capital were rare indeed. By contrast Colombia's railways were always regional, reflecting the geographical difficulties – the Andes – that separated provinces and prevented the development of a cohesive sense of national identity.[1] In Argentina nation builders welcomed the railways in order to create a shared national territory and communication between its citizens. Juan Bautista Alberdi wrote in 1914 that 'the railways will bring about the unity of the Argentine Republic better than any number of Congresses.'[2] In Colombia railways symbolize the inability of this technology to fully overcome the topographical obstacles that divide its peoples.

Railways, track length, in thousands of kilometres[3]

	1870	1900	1913	1929	1940	1950	1970	1995
Argentina	7.3	168	335	375	413	429	399	358
Brazil	7.5	153	246	320	343	367	318	304
Colombia	0.3	6	11	26	33	35	34	21
Mexico	3.5	136	205	232	230	233	245	266
Venezuela	0.1	9	9	10	10	10	2	6

The table above demonstrates the rapid expansion of the railway network in key exporting countries between 1870 and 1913. After that date the increase levelled off. While Venezuela is a smaller country than the others featured, its relative lack of railways is accounted for by the fact that its primary export product in this period, oil, had no need for railways to facilitate its export – unlike meats or coffee. Railways made a big difference to the amounts of those products that could be exported and, crucially, to the speed at which this could be done. Colombia's network was limited by the geographical obstacles (mountains and jungle) that prevented the railways from extending quickly beyond particular plains and valleys. In Mexico the railway infrastructure was designed as much with internal trade and communication in mind as export opportunities.[4] Railways were generally welcomed by nation builders as a means of communication that would bring together the sometimes disparate peoples that found themselves as citizens of the same republic.

Cables and Communications

Technological change, almost always brought from outside the region, revolutionized social life in Latin America. The telegraph cables laid across the Atlantic Ocean sea bed first carried messages in 1904, linking foreign diplomats and company representatives back to head offices in London or Paris in a way that cut a swathe through the local autonomy that clerks and consuls had enjoyed since independence. Before that, from the 1860s, submarine cables had joined coastal ports such as Recife and Rio, revolutionizing communication, which had previously been reliant on winds. The telegraph, and the European and u.s. companies that laid the wires, did more than anything else to tie Latin America into the global order at the beginning of the twentieth century.[5] The historians of communication Dwayne Wisbeck and Robert Pike have shown, through their analysis of the cable companies' archives, that disputes and negotiations between French, British, u.s. and German firms 'continued to contain a complex admixture of collaboration, competition, competition, and conflict, self-interest and opportunism, private enterprise and state intervention'.[6] Cartels, consortia and desperate attempts to preserve and protect privileged market positions were the order of the day, in which geopolitics and ideologies of empire and free trade were mixed.

Other technological innovations, like the railway and the reloading rifle, made conflicts bloodier in Latin America, just as they did in Europe. The War of One Thousand Days in Colombia featured the Battle of Palonegro in May 1900, which saw scenes of carnage almost on the scale of the events at the Somme a decade later.[7] The aeroplane had limited impact in Latin America before the 1920s, but radio was by then already establishing itself as a crucial element in tying together nations, broadcasting national news, folkloric music and, increasingly, soap operas that would unite citizens – even illiterate ones who had been excluded from accessing the previous medium of communication, the newspaper – across geographical boundaries. Facing competition from foreign music styles, such as jazz, Latin American radio producers appealed to their audiences through an anti-elitist marketing of authenticity and common experience.[8] Sport became another fundamental part of the nation building process as football matches and cycling races were broadcast to avid fans huddled around radios.[9]

Big infrastructure projects catalysed further industrialization in this period, particularly in Brazil, Mexico and Argentina. Meat processing plants sprang up around the River Plate to get beef ready for transatlantic export. The discovery of oil triggered the first forays into refinement in Venezuela and Mexico, often in partnership with foreign companies such as Shell or Exxon.[10] Sometimes, as in Porfírian Mexico, foreign investment became the stimulus for nationalism. But the big factories set up with the help of foreign investment provided work, organization and wages for large parts of the urban population, so they were often welcomed.[11] Elsewhere, as in Venezuela, the majority response was to seek to emulate the economic successes and cultural innovations of those foreigners who came to work in or with these new big industries. Venezuela's love affair with whisky dates from this period; so do most of Latin America's golf courses, first established to service the leisure time of expatriate North Americans and Europeans in capital cities. In Buenos Aires the Jockey Club was formed as a place for the new, modern elite to enjoy leisure and do business. Members of the Jockey Club became 'the intermediar[ies] for foreign (especially British) capital, and brought [Argentina] into the new global order through the industrialisation of farming, and the export of cattle and agrarian products'. Clubs like this – often called country clubs – across the continent became quickly equipped with their own cable addresses, which were recorded in the traveller's guides and explorers' handbooks of the time.[12]

Networks in the Sky: Early Aviation

Aeroplanes made the world feel smaller for those who travelled in them, and pulled Latin American countries closer to each other, when that mode of transport spread from the 1920s. The aviation historian Dan Hagedorn has recently drawn together all of the personal, amateur and professional research into the history of air flight in Latin America, a subject which until now was almost unknown outside of specialist aeroplane-buff circles, and certainly was seldom considered by historians of Latin America. Hagedorn begins his story with the first attempts at flight in Latin America by French adventurers such as M. Latet, who flew and crashed a hot air balloon in Buenos Aires in the early 1860s, but also by locally born enthusiasts such as the Peruvian Apolinar Zeballos, who flew 500 m above the central plaza of La Paz, Bolivia, in 1872.[13] The story of Latin America and aviation reveals much about the Latin American's relationship with the world in the first half of the twentieth century.

Two Latin Americans were global pioneers of human flight. Alberto Santos-Dumont was a Brazilian inventor and flier whose spectacular achievements, alongside those of the much more celebrated Wright brothers, proved beyond doubt that humans could control the flight of heavier-than-air machines. Many of his flights were made in France, but his influence and reputation back home became enormous. Jorge Chávez Dartnell, a Peruvian by birth, became the first person to pilot an aeroplane across the Alps on 23 September 1910. Chávez died of the injuries incurred when he crashlanded at an aerodrome near Milan. In 1914 Jorge Newbery, the foremost Argentinian promoter of flying, was killed in an accident. It should come as no surprise that all three of these pioneers of such an expensive pastime bore surnames indicating European heritage, but this should not detract from the great influence that Latin Americans had on aviation innovation in the early years. Latin Americans flew as combat pilots in the First World War, like the Venezuelan Carlos Meyer Baldó, who volunteered for the German Air Service. Brazilian navy officers travelled to Britain to be trained as pilots and saw service in the last months of the conflict.[14]

Aviation in Latin America, like football, began as the hobby of the elites and was quickly taken over by internationalizing influences and geopolitics. The rapid growth in successful aviation experiments in the first decade of the twentieth century meant that air combat was an important new element in the First World War. Air combat in Latin America itself was shaped by European, rather than U.S., influences. In 1918 Chile took delivery of twelve Bristol M.1C fighter aircraft from the UK, the beginning of a long tradition of air-arms purchases that continues to the present day. One of those planes was the first to fly over the Andes, piloted by Lt Armando Cortínez Mujica on 5 April that year – not coincidentally the anniversary of the famous battle of Maipú from the independence wars a century earlier.[15] The major powers of the time all wished to control the growing industry and savvy Latin Americans played them off against each other. The Venezuelan dictator Juan Vicente Gómez invited pitches from several promoters of Italian, French, U.S. and British aviation schemes before plumping, in 1920, for the French.[16]

Weapon sales, from guns to ships to aircraft, might at first glance seem to demonstrate that Latin America was the unwilling victim of European ambition and imperialism. Desperate to catch up with the major powers, Latin Americans had no choice but to buy weapons from the major industrial centres of those same imperial powers, thereby supporting the economic growth and further expansion of the empires that they purchased from. And of course, the ships and guns that Chileans and Argentinians bought were often second-hand for reasons of economy – meaning that in the event of a military conflict with one of the major powers, one could be sure which side would have the most developed, most destructive weapons. Yet although as a broad brush treatment this narrative has some allure, in the detail we can see that things were much more complicated and that Latin Americans were much more closely involved in the development of military technology and its use in their region and beyond than this narrative would suggest. The example of Jorge Chávez, the Peruvian who was the first man to fly a plane over the Alps but has been all but forgotten by Anglophone histories, epitomizes this relationship.

Exposing Human Rights Abuses against Indigenous Peoples to the Outside World

Technological change also affected the ways in which the struggle for equality in Latin America was reported globally. The development of regular, campaigning news magazines across the world created a market for denunciations of corruption and exploitation. Latin America, with its history of the 'Black Legend' of Spanish cruelty during the colonial period (historians have disputed the extent to which Spanish colonialism could be judged as any worse than British or French colonialism in the Americas, but the mud stuck) was an ideal arena for campaigners seeking to uncover stories of exploitation. A good example of the way these campaigns could turn from hunch to research to revelation is provided by the story of the diplomat and campaigner Roger Casement, who in 1910 exposed the shocking reality of the rubber business in the Putumayo region of Peru and Colombia. There was a huge demand for rubber in Europe for the manufacture of tyres, boots and sundry materials. Casement was an Irish-born British diplomat who had previously won fame by documenting atrocities in the Belgian Congo, meaning that he has been dubbed, posthumously, the world's first human rights activist. Seeking a new challenge, Casement accepted an invitation by the UK Foreign Office to investigate local allegations against the Peruvian Amazon Company, led by Julio César Arana. Peruvian newspapers and U.S. journals had alleged that indigenous workers were kept in chains, branded and routinely tortured in order to make them produce the required amount of rubber per day at their plantations deep in the Amazon rainforest. Alleged abuses against British citizens – who were in the most part black migrants from Barbados – provided the trigger that allowed the Foreign Office to intervene by sending Casement. His report of 1912, scrupulously detailed and handled with obsessive care, became a global news sensation. Coupled with the rise in productivity of Southeast Asian rubber plantations, Casement's exposure sounded the death knell for Arana's company and its violent labour exploitation methods.

But Casement's time as an imperial, humanitarian hero (he was knighted in 1912) was brief. The First World War persuaded him to travel to Germany to seek practical support for an Irish national uprising. When this did not happen he was captured and imprisoned in the Tower of London as a traitor. As part of a politicized campaign to undermine Casement's good reputation, his 'black diaries' detailing his sexual fantasies were released to the press. He was executed with little opposition in 1916. The independent Republic of Ireland adopted Casement as a national martyr in the 1920s. It took much longer for Latin Americans to recognize the role that Casement had played in opposing violence and injustice in the region; the Peruvian novelist Mario Vargas Llosa published a book about Casement, *El sueño del celta / The Dream of the Celt*, in 2010. Casement's story, and the way he approached Latin America, epitomizes many of the key themes of this book. As a British imperial agent Casement often exoticized Latin Americans, lusted after them and pitied them, and 'suffered' his travels in the continent in order to further the greater good of civilization. He exposed the inequalities inherent in the production of raw materials which were transported away from Latin America as quickly as possible, and whose profits were employed to feather the nests and massage the reputations of a business elite which thought little of the harm it inflicted on indigenous and Afro-American communities who benefited little from the heightened foreign presence in Latin America in this period.[17] Casement did much to create the image of Latin America in the rest of world as a place where the poor and darker skinned were systematically abused and cynically exploited by a small elite motivated solely by financial gain, to be had through the export of raw materials.

At the same time that Roger Casement was exploring the Putumayo region, looking for evidence of abuses against indigenous labourers in the rubber-producing forests, another English speaker with a similar worldview was also on the move in Peru, also concerned with indigenous societies. But this man – Hiram Bingham – was looking for traces of the past in the present, and would play a major role in bringing one of the continent's major tourist attractions to international attention.

Exposing Latin American History

Casement used the printed word, drawing on copious annotation of interviews and diary notes, to make Arana's abuses known to the world, and particularly his international investors. Another technological development of the period, the photograph, was used by his contemporary Hiram Bingham (1875–1956) to create another of the rest of the world's key images of Latin America: the lost city of an indigenous culture hidden away within mountainous jungle.

Bingham, a professor from Yale University, was seeking the lost city of the Incas, conducting major expeditions in the southern Peruvian Andes, examining archaeological sites and talking to local people. He travelled with the support of *National Geographic* magazine and was armed with a wealth of cameras, films and photographic equipment to record their discoveries and also, crucially, to present their successes and achievements to a readership back home that was clamouring for exotic discoveries from adventurous archaeologists. (Bingham's research in Peru was broadly contemporaneous with Howard Carter's digs in Egypt, which eventually yielded the tomb of Tutankhamen in 1922.[18]) Bingham's accounts of his discoveries throughout the Incas' Sacred Valley, culminating at Machu Picchu, were published in *National Geographic* accompanied by stunning photos of the natural beauty of the surrounding mountainous jungle and the improbable ruins perched on the mountaintop.[19] Bingham's enthusiastic and almost spiritual prose created a longlasting legend that he had 'discovered' the ruins. Describing his passage through Urubamba valley, he wrote:

> In the variety of its charms and the power of its spell, I know of no place in the world which can compare with it. Not only has it great snow peaks looming above the clouds more than two miles overhead; gigantic precipices of many-colored granite rising sheer for thousands of feet above the foaming, glistening, roaring rapids; it has also, in striking contrast, orchids and tree ferns, the delectable beauty of luxurious vegetation, and the mysterious witchery of the jungle. One is drawn irresistibly

onward by ever-recurring surprises through a deep, winding gorge, turning and twisting past overhanging cliffs or incredible height. Above all, there is the fascination of finding here and there under the swaying vines, or perched on top of a beetling crag, the rugged masonry of a bygone race; and of trying to understand the bewildering romance of the ancient builders who ages ago sought refuge in a region which appears to have been expressly designed by Nature as a sanctuary for the oppressed, a place where they might fearlessly and patiently give expression to their passion for walls of enduring beauty.[20]

On the ruins at Machu Picchu he gushed with praise for the masonry, stonework, imagination and creativity of the builders of that 'bygone race', erasing any possible link between the inhabitants of the area who had helped him to the ruins and those who had built them centuries earlier. His published travel account was full of references to how Peruvians seemed to lack the get-up-and-go required to make new archaeological discoveries for their own sake rather than for profit. Bingham was the only man, his account implied, who was up to the job.

Nothing could have been further from the truth, of course. Two local farmers were living in the ruins when Bingham arrived, using the ancient terraces for their crops. One of his own companions on the expedition declined to follow him up the final hill 'because he had been here before'. Etchings found on the site show that local officials had visited in the last decade, and historical records suggested that other travellers had also been there or nearby. But Bingham was certainly the first to realize the international potential of the ruins, and to have the resources and the technology to maximize the impact by telling stories about Latin American history through the archaeology of the ruins.[21] In subsequent trips between 1912 and 1915 he relied on local Peruvian *huaqueros* (literally, grave-robbers) to collect up relics, bones, animals and other remains. These were transported back to Yale where they could become sources for the use of science and the pursuit of universal knowledge.[22] Bingham's work, like that of Roger Casement at the same time, became part of the way in which

Europeans and North Americans sought to make sense of Latin America, a region which had been tied into their worlds during the past half-century. Outsiders could try to understand the region through archaeology – presenting great, now dead, civilizations – or human rights, through which the indigenous peoples were to be pitied and assisted in their efforts to overcome exploitation. Both played into the hands of imperial worldviews which saw Latin America, like Africa, as a place to be civilized through migration, commerce and enlightenment.

Civilization, Barbarism and Eurocentrism

Cable communication and photography meant that images of Latin America could, by the beginning of the twentieth century, be rushed around the world much more quickly than in the age of steam or sail. Control of those images tended to lie with Europeans or North Americans who had the technology, such as Casement and Bingham. Latin Americans responded to these changes in the media through which the world viewed them by elaborating new ways of thinking about themselves and their peoples.

The first decades of the twentieth century were the years when the civilization–barbarism debate was transformed from a city–countryside dichotomy into something much more complicated. As hundreds and thousands of country dwellers flooded into towns and cities, seeking employment and better living standards, they brought their traditions and cultures with them, together with the expectation that the nation-states they had been taught to love from afar would reward them with rights and respect now they lived within a stone's throw or two from congresses and senates. Urban 'citizens' and rural 'peasants' now came to have new identities, often understood by the continent's Marxists as 'elite' and 'working class'. Many countries undertook racist *blanqueamiento* ('whitening') programmes in order to avoid what elites saw as the terrible prospect of darker-skinned populations gaining power either demographically or politically. Proponents of *mestizaje* (mixing) argued that a mestizo nation (rather than one that celebrated its ethnic differences and diversity) would be more stable and ordered. But they often assumed, implicitly as well as explicitly, that *mestizaje* would lead to 'superior' white peoples imposing their cultures and characteristics upon 'weaker' black and indigenous populations. As the continent urbanized rapidly after 1900 (first in Argentina and Brazil, later in Mexico, Peru, Colombia and Venezuela) these ethnic differences could no longer be understood as somehow 'regional'. With people of all ethnicities and classes living alongside one another within huge urban centres, ethnic melting pots facilitated demographic change that affected the very national identities that elites had sought to construct in defence of the status quo. At the same time as existing cities expanded, however, growing populations were continuing to push against the frontiers of their country's borders. White and mestizo settlers pressed into the Amazon in this period,

Immigration to Argentina, 1861–1930[23]

Years	Entries	Departures
1861–1870	159,570	82,976
1871–1880	260,885	175,763
1881–1890	841,122	203,455
1891–1900	648,326	328,444
1901–1910	1,746,104	643,881
1911–1920	1,204,919	935,825
1921–1930	1,397,415	519,445
Total	6,278,341	2,898,689

Population of Buenos Aires born abroad, 1855–1936[24]

Year	Total Population	Percentage Born Abroad
1855	91,395	36
1869	177,787	52
1887	433,373	53
1895	663,854	52
1904	950,891	45
1909	1,231,698	46
1914	1,575,814	51
1936	2,415,142	36

clearing trees and laying roads, and agriculturalists moved into mountain areas to plant and cultivate coffee. Indigenous communities with long claims to these lands were pushed from their territories, often violently.[25]

The major migrant groups overall were Spaniards and Italians.[26] In particular locations, however, groups with distinctive identities were able to travel and recollect themselves in the New World. Examples include the Japanese migrants to Brazil, the Welsh settlements in Patagonia, the Chinese communities established in Mexico and in Lima, Peru – establishing the long tradition of Sino-Peruvian restaurants, *chifas* – and German villages in the south of Chile. In some cases these became mass migrations, such as the Indian 'coolie' labourers brought by British ships to produce Peruvian guano in the 1880s, the Lebanese and Palestinian migrants to Caribbean Colombia, Venezuela and Chile after the First World War, and the Jewish diaspora that spread across Latin America, especially Argentina.[27] Transatlantic population movements created a new dimension in Latin American populations, which often looked back home in search of identity or commerce.

Looking for Origins

In response to the growing acknowledgement of the external powers that were lurking at the door of national cultures and territories, the 1920s, '30s and '40s witnessed a golden age of Latin American cultural production. The search for new myths of national origin was crucial. After the Mexican Revolution nationalists reacted against the previous regime's Hispanism, for example. José Vasconcelos, Minister of Education in Mexico, proclaimed the country a celebration of *mestizaje* where African, Asian, European and indigenous American ethnicities were fused together to form a superior, 'cosmic' race. Rather than a multiculturalism of celebrated diversity, the idea of a cosmic race commended miscegenation, which would lead to the blurring of ethnicities and the creation of a superior, purified people who would be neither black, indigenous nor European, but a blend of the 'best bits' of each.[28]

Leaders sought to ground their new revolutionary nation in the popular groups which, they felt, had done so much to win the victory against Díaz and his reactionary forces. Emiliano Zapata became a national icon. Muralists including Diego Rivera constructed images of a united nation fighting together, which were plastered across public spaces and seared into the collective memory. These images were spread globally by newspapers and colour magazines, making Mexico a crucial port of call for would-be revolutionaries such as Fidel Castro and Ernesto Guevara, and for revolutionary exiles such as the Russian revolutionary Leon Trotsky, who was killed with an ice axe in the back by an assassin hired by Stalinist agents in 1940. Trotsky had been a house guest of the artists Frida Kahlo and Diego Rivera, whose works later did so much to define Mexico for external audiences. Trotsky's murder in Mexico is another good demonstration of the role that Latin America often plays in global processes, seemingly remaining on the periphery even while it is at the centre of major international events.[29]

Some of the great works of written and visual culture of these years were *costumbrismo* – literally, cultural chronicles – in that emphasis was placed on the recording of the customs, dialects and traditions of a rural way of life that the authors – generally urban, white members of the elite – saw as slipping away under the forces of modernity and in need of being preserved for posterity. Anyone learning Spanish who wants to improve their vocabulary relating to horses, leather and various types of stirrups and reins need look no further than Ricardo Güiraldes's *Don Segundo Sombra* (1926), for example, a great novel of the Argentinian pampas that uses minutely detailed descriptions to evoke the culture of the gaucho, the South American cowboy.[30]

Indigenismo was a phenomenon not entirely separate from the *costumbrismo* movement in that its authors feared that indigenous culture was being eroded and wanted to celebrate it and preserve it on paper for future generations. The works of Diego Rivera in Mexico and José María Arguedas in Peru, for example, display indigenous culture as spiritual and worthy of respect in contrast to the actions of Hispanic societies linked to international business and commerce.

Perhaps the most extreme example from this period is the Ecuadorian writer Jorge Icaza, whose novel *Huasipungo* (1934) rages against the barbarities committed against Quichua/Kichwa-speaking indigenous people in his country. The tragedies of the book are triggered by a foreign company that wants to build a road through indigenous territory in order to maximize profits from its timber concession further up the Andes. The controller of the project, the North American Mr Chapy, is an infrequent presence in the novel, but it is left resoundingly clear that the demands and expectations of the foreigners are making things worse for Ecuadorians, rather than better.[31]

Rather than celebrating indigenous culture like other *indigenistas*, however, Icaza describes in horrific detail the brutalized, even animalized lives which are suffered by indigenous peoples as a result of the callous, profiteering and self-centred actions of white Ecuadorian elites. The female protagonist of the novel, Cunshi, is victimized in every possible way: she is raped and abused by representatives of municipal power, the Catholic Church and capital city businessmen. She is even beaten up by her own husband, Andrés, who is nevertheless shown to love her. When Cunshi dies Andrés is driven to lead a futile rebellion against power, leading his fellow *huasipungeros* into a hail of bullets in the defence of their rights and culture. *Huasipungo* is a depressing book. Icaza intended readers to read it and get very, very angry, and to change the power structures that still left indigenous peoples at the bottom of the pile more than a century after independence from colonial rule. It is still an *indigenista* novel despite the lack of romance: Icaza gives over several pages to transcribing Quichua/Kichwa-language conversations between his indigenous characters, showing clearly his belief that they merited equality – on the page and consequently in society – with Spanish-speaking Ecuadorians and their North American financial masters.

The tensions between internationally connected, smart, urban, literary elites and the rural provinces they sought to control were the subject of Rómulo Gallegos's novel *Doña Bárbara* (1929). In it the European-educated lawyer Santos Luzardo intends to bring enlightenment and prosperity to the Venezuelan llanos (plains) he inherits from his abstentee-landlord father. But Luzardo comes up against the conservatism and inertia of rural life, all described in loving, *costumbrismo* detail by an all-seeing narrator. The personification of rural primitiveness is the eponymous heroine. Sensuous, spiritual and superstitious, Bárbara is also shrewd, deceitful, manipulative and apparently without principles in the pursuit of her interests. No wonder the novel was adapted into such a successful transatlantic soap opera in the early twenty-first century – it is full of melodrama, confrontation and seduction (all shown much more explicitly in the *telenovela* than in the novel, of course).[32]

At the centre of the novel is a North American immigrant referred to without much subtlety as Mr Danger. Whisky-drinking, rifle-toting, unscrupulous and exuding profiteering evil, Mr Danger serves to scare (and sometimes bully) both Santos and Bárbara into safeguarding his interests regardless of their real patriotic desires. In this sense Mr Danger is the perfect fictional representative of the threat of u.s. imperialism and economic hegemony in the first half of the twentieth century. For this reason (and because of the popularity of *Doña Bárbara*, a constant bestseller in Venezuela) he became the symbolic alter ego in the region of the apparently friendly Uncle Sam figure – so much so that Hugo Chávez had come, by 2004, to refer regularly to President George W. Bush as Mr Danger, a joke that he enjoyed all the more because it featured a cultural reference that the u.s. president did not understand.[33]

Unlike *Huasipungo*, however, *Doña Bárbara* does not end with the death of the workers, indigenous peoples or other subalterns described in its pages. As Doris Sommer argued in *Foundational Fictions*, Gallegos produced a positive, forward-looking vision for Venezuela based upon the love affair and then marriage between Santos Luzardo and Marisela, Doña Bárbara's daughter (who was born after Bárbara was raped and left by a man she had once loved). Santos teaches Marisela to use cutlery, read and write. In no uncertain terms he civilizes her and prepares her for the role of serving him in his patriotic duties of landowning and practice of the law. But he also recognizes the limits of his attempts to tame the plains and gives freedom and responsibility to the men who had remained loyal to him and his family during the decades of conflict. Mr Danger, recognizing that these lands no longer hold the prospect of profit for him, disappears from the story before it reaches its final pages, irrelevant to the future of the nation whose progress, it appears, he had been holding back.[34]

It would be easy to see the victory of Santos Luzardo over both Mr Danger and Doña Bárbara as evidence for the Eurocentrism of its author and the Venezuelan culture it came out of. Santos Luzardo, at the beginning of the novel, seems as though he would feel more at home in a Parisian salon than on the Venezuelan plains. His lawyerly, literate and intellectual manner often seems at odds with the mass of the people he is supposedly called to govern. Fernando Coronil calls this attitude 'Occidentalism', a counterpoint to the 'Orientalism' more famously described by Edward Said, in which the geopolitics of knowledge were applied to Arab countries.

Postcolonial scholars have demonstrated how novels, poetry and travel writing became part of imperial projects emanating from London, Paris and Berlin during this period. Latin Americanists have reflected on the consequences of this set-up for ways of thinking about Latin American societies. Sociologists like Aníbal Quijano call this the 'coloniality of power', in which the people with power in Latin America come to be white, male and Hispanic, and to come to see their role as to further assert a Europeanized culture over the brown, female or other subaltern peoples who lived on the land. The self-perpetuating nature of this relationship over 200 years of independence, Quijano argues, demonstrates that power itself in Latin America has been 'colonized', and that social and economic revolution are still required to overthrow these outdated ways of thinking. Gallegos did not advocate this in *Doña Bárbara*: instead the victory of Luzardo was achieved through moderation, cultural understanding and love for a beautiful woman.[35]

Many leaders, intellectuals and politicians hoped that Latin America would be able to stay true to its roots while moving towards European ideals of modernity and economic progress. Santos Luzardo's marriage to Marisela in *Doña Bárbara* was supposed to symbolize relinquishing violence and embracing love, respect and union. This was the ideal. But in reality in the interwar period –

meaning, between the European wars that became global wars – the European economic penetration of Latin America became further embedded, and more and more Latin Americans noticed and began to resent their country's dependency upon foreign markets. Furthermore culture was shaped as much by Eurocentrism and empire as was commerce. This was the period when the majority of quipus were taken from the Andes by collectors and archaeologists and deposited in museums and stores in Germany, the U.S. and Great Britain, for example. Quipus were the knotted ropes that acted as a means of keeping records for the Incas: today over half of the surviving quipus are held outside Peru, the country where most of the examples were found by early twentieth-century collectors.[36]

In this period, too, British adventurers sought to turn another of the myths of the colonial period into profit for risk-takers. The legend of El Dorado – the Golden One – had motivated conquistadores and colonizers throughout the sixteenth to eighteenth centuries as they sought to find the indigenous civilization that was reputed to worship its gods by covering a leader in gold plate, upon which he would jump into a lake to be symbolically cleansed by its natural waters. Eventually the site of El Dorado was agreed to be Laguna Guatevita, not too far from Bogotá in Colombia. Encouraged by findings of golden figures, British speculators paid for the lake to be drained. This they did, eventually, by making an enormous cutting through the mountainous crater that held the lake. The water seeped away, leaving not the wondrous treasures they had hoped for, but thick, sticky, brown mud. Some of the mud covered pottery, and the team was reputed to have packed away its materials in disappointment.[37] Nevertheless, examples of Colombian Chibcha gold still found their way to London for auction, and the collections of many university and national libraries hold the gold and silver of Latin American indigenous civilizations that they acquired in the first half of the twentieth century. The age of commercial expansion and imperial presence had direct cultural consequences. Bingham and other famous explorers created a market for indigenous artefacts abroad that has never abated.

The communications revolution of the early twentieth century made commerce quicker and facilitated the spreading and embedding of images of Latin America in the rest of the world. Tropes of poor, exploited indigenous peoples, and of sublime ruins accessible only to the most adventurous and resourceful foreigners, continue to dominate the ways in which many outsiders view the continent. The volume of trade increased thanks to the new railway lines and steamship connections, and the ties of dependency that sprang from export-oriented economies stamped their mark on Latin American cultures, politics and societies.

FIVE

Beneath a New Empire

Technological change powered the revolution in commerce and migration between Europe and Latin America after the First World War. Bigger, faster ships transported more and more migrants, and telegraph cables sent news of safe arrivals – of peoples and of products – that encouraged more travellers and business people to try their luck. Nevertheless, despite the continued close ties between Europe and Latin America, after 1930 the influence of the United States rose, reflecting its increasing share of commerce. The shadow of the u.s. continued to expand beyond the Second World War, and the beginning of the Cold War. This chapter traces how and why this happened.

Moving on from its interventions in Cuba and Panama between 1895 and 1903, the United States asserted its growing power in Central America and the Caribbean after the First World War, while other, older imperial powers shifted their resources elsewhere, to Africa, Asia and within Europe. The Latin American nation-states, now a century old, found themselves competing with a new imperial power which claimed to be like them – modern, republican, new – but that appeared to many to be better, more prosperous and more stable. At the same time much respect and admiration remained for the European powers. Nevertheless many Latin Americans felt a renewed desire to base their identities and their allegiances upon cultures that had grown up closer to home: the continent's indigenous peoples and the mixed race peoples who were coming to be ever more important both demographically and politically.

The first half of the twentieth century found the Latin American elites caught between empires and its own indigenous peoples, with a prevalent tension between the attempt to reconcile revitalized respect for indigenous cultures and a continued desire to be part of the European or 'international' world order. The continent's future relationship with the rest of the world was fought over through military campaigns, political debates and through culture – for example, music, sports, dress, films and books.

Addicted to Trade? Coffee Dependency and Rubber Booms

The early twentieth century witnessed multiple booms in Latin America exports. Colombia's 'coffee boom' of 1880–1920 made it the world's premier supplier of coffee (though Brazil soon vied with it for this title) and brought new wealth into the middling, provincial sectors that dominated production in the Andes. Coffee beans grow best at an altitude of between 1,400 m and 1,800 m in the tropics, and Colombia's unique topography, with its fractured Andean chains, made it perfectly suited to grow a lot of this crop.[1] Other products also now came from Latin America to the world markets: Chile's northern deserts were opened up for international mining concerns, and in 1915 the enormous Chiquicamata copper mine was opened, owned by the u.s. Guggenheim brothers under the umbrella of the Chilean Exploration Company. In this period Latin American states became financially dependent upon the receipts taken at the customs houses in its ports, as the table below demonstrates. The high percentages shown here demonstrate the extent to which these national economies were vulnerable to variations in foreign trade, and largely owed their solvency to international customs incomes.

In 1910, for example, nearly 90 per cent of Chilean state revenues came from customs charged on foreign trade. The disruption caused by the fall in demand for some products during the First World War, however, was counteracted by the surge in demand for the country's major export, copper. We can see that as nation-states became established (by 1950) they were slowly able to reduce their reliance on customs duties, but their dependence on this form of state funding continued well into the twentieth century. It was only in 1970, for example, that Colombia raised more than half of its income through

Customs receipts as a percentage of total state income[2]

	1910	1930	1950
Argentina	54.9%	45.1%	5.8%
Brazil	54.4%	38.0%	9.5%
Chile	89.0%	43.7%	20.0%
Colombia	77.9%	45.3%	19.2%
Peru	45.8%	30.7%	39.7%

collecting income tax, and even this can be partially explained by the fall in the price of coffee (and hence customs duties) in that period. As a rule international exports of primary materials remained crucial to Latin American economies throughout the twentieth century.[3]

In economic terms, one of the major export booms of this period was rubber. Brazil, Colombia and Peru were the main beneficiaries; most famously the opera house built at Manaus in the Amazon jungle from the profits of rubber stands as a perfect example as to how indigenous and slave labour was used to extract raw materials in order to create wealth for multinational corporations and for new states, which invested the profits in symbolic gestures aimed at demonstrating the European, modern, civilized natures of their nations. The table below demonstrates how, in certain periods, particular countries became absolutely identified with one export product, and were dependent upon it to maintain their income.

The figures and progressions presented on pp. 102–3 demonstrate much about the course of Latin American history. In Venezuela the transition from a marginal coffee economy (coffee made up 42 per cent of export income for Venezuela in 1920) to a major oil economy (oil provided 82 per cent of export income in 1930) was breathtakingly rapid. The figures demonstrate the startling extent to which both Brazil and Colombia relied on coffee as their principal export product throughout the century, with it only seldom accounting for less than 50 per cent of the national income from exports. We can also see the way in which exports of wheat, meat and wool made Argentina (like Uruguay) a society that exported animal-related products, varying across the century (note the increase in meat exports as refrigeration technology was improved). In contrast we can see the gradually rising importance of revenues provided by copper in Chile until it assumed the primary position from 1940, reflecting the diminishing import-ance of the nitrate section as synthetic nitrates were developed elsewhere as a result of research carried out during the First World War. Finally the table shows us the absolute reliance upon tin mining in Bolivia throughout the central years of the century, contributing to the success of the 1952 revolution led by leaders of miners unions and mining interests.[4] Dependency on limited numbers of export products, often located in strategic geographical areas of a country, produced direct political consequences.

Overturning Dependency: Economic Nationalism

By the middle of the twentieth century natural resources had become key tools for nationalists seeking practical advantage as well as rhetorical flourish in their attacks on foreigners. In 1938 the presi-dent of Mexico, Lázaro Cárdenas, nationalized all the oil firms in the country. This caused dismay and disarray for those businesses, particularly Standard Oil, but helped Mexicans feel in control of their resources and was as important an act symbolically as it was economically.[5] The revolution of 1952 in Bolivia attempted a similar result, though in the Bolivian case there was a substantial class element too, absent in Cárdenas's nationalization of oil, given that Mexico had already had its revolution from 1910. In Bolivia the revolution aimed to take political and economic power out of the hands of both foreign interests *and* local elites: tin and its profits symbolized both.[6]

There were many Latin Americans who were committed to expos-ing the abuses and hypocrisy of the rubber industry at the same time as Roger Casement was gaining fame for his denunciations of abuse, discussed in the previous chapter. José Eustacio Rivera linked the extraction of raw materials to the dehumanizing of Latin America's environment and its inhabitants. Writing his major novel *La vorágine/ The Vortex* in Colombia in the 1920s, in the wake of the humiliating loss of Panama and in the midst of export booms in two major prod-ucts, coffee and rubber, Rivera surveyed the national territory and

Principal commodities exported as a percentage of income from exports[7]

	1900	1910	1920	1930	1940
Argentina	Wool (24)	Wheat (23)	Wheat (24)	Meat (23)	Wheat (19)
	Wheat (19)	Wool (15)	Meat (18)	Wheat (16)	Meat (18)
Bolivia	Silver (39)	Tin (54)	Tin (68)	Tin (84)	Tin (80)
	Tin (27)	Rub (16)	Silver (11)	Cop (4)	Silver (6)
Brazil	Coff (57)	Coff (51)	Coff (55)	Coff (68)	Coff (34)
	Rub (20)	Rub (31)	Cacao (4)	Cot (3)	Cot (18)
Chile	Nit (65)	Nit (67)	Nit (54)	Nit (43)	Cop (57)
	Cop (14)	Cop (7)	Cop (12)	Cop (37)	Nit (19)
Colombia	Coff (49)	Coff (39)	Coff (62)	Coff (64)	Coff (62)
	Gold (17)	Gold (16)	Gold (13)	Oil (22)	Oil (29)
Cuba	Sug (61)	Sug (70)	Sug (87)	Sug (68)	Sug (70)
	Tob (23)	Tob (24)	Tob (10)	Tob (17)	Tob (8)
Mexico	Silv (44)	Silv (28)	Oil (67)	Silv (15)	Silv (14)
	Cop (8)	Gold (16)	Silv (17)	Oil (14)	Zinc (13)
Peru	Sug (25)	Cop (20)	Sug (35)	Oil (33)	Oil (26)
	Silv (18)	Sug (19)	Cot (26)	Cop (21)	Cot (21)
Venezuela	Coff (43)	Coff (53)	Coff (42)	Oil (82)	Oil (88)
	Cacao (20)	Cacao (18)	Cacao (18)	Coff (10)	Coff (3)

Alum = Aluminium, Anti = Antinomy, Coff = Coffee, Cop = Copper, Cot = Cotton,

looked for unifying features, customs and ideals. His protagonist, Arturo Cova, is a romantic urbanite and poet who flees Bogotá with his new love, Alicia, hoping to find work and peace first in the eastern llanos (plains) and then, in both hope and desperation, in the Amazonian jungle. Cova joins many economic migrants in their journey to the informal rubber plantations that sprouted up through the region in the early twentieth century. Like them, Cova finds a hellish mixture of isolation, physical brutality, hunger, illness and disillusion. Also like them, he is unable to save enough money to leave the jungle and return to Alicia and his imagined future life as a writer. The novel ends with Cova and his companions being

	1950	1960	1970	1980	1990
Argentina	Wheat (17)	Meat (22)	Meat (25)	Meat (13)	Meat (7)
	Meat (15)	Wool (14)	Wheat (6)	Wheat (10)	Wheat (6)
Bolivia	Tin (67)	Tin (66)	Tin (50)	Tin (43)	Gas (26)
	Lead (9)	Lead (7)	Anti (16)	Gas (25)	Zinc (16)
Brazil	Coff (62)	Coff (55)	Coff (32)	Soya (12)	Soya (9)
	Cocoa (7)	Cocoa (6)	Iron (7)	Coff (10)	Iron (6)
Chile	Cop (52)	Cop (67)	Cop (79)	Cop (46)	Cop (46)
	Nit (22)	Nit (7)	Iron (4)	Iron (4)	Fish (4)
Colombia	Coff (72)	Coff (75)	Coff (59)	Coff (54)	Oil (23)
	Oil (16)	Oil (18)	Oil (11)	Oil (4)	Coff (21)
Cuba	Sug (82)	Sug (73)	Sug (75)	Sug (82)	Sug (74)
	Tob (5)	Tob (8)	Tob (4)	Nick (5)	Nick (7)
Mexico	Cot (17)	Cot (23)	Cot (8)	Oil (65)	Oil (32)
	Lead (12)	Coff (9)	Coff (5)	Coff (4)	Coff (2)
Peru	Cot (34)	Cot (18)	Fish (27)	Oil (20)	Cop (18)
	Sug (15)	Cop (17)	Cop (25)	Cop (18)	Fish (13)
Venezuela	Oil (94)	Oil (88)	Oil (87)	Oil (90)	Oil (79)
	Coff (1)	Iron (6)	Iron (6)	Iron (2)	Alum (4)

Nit = Nitrates, Rub = Rubber, Silv = Silver, Sug = Sugar, Tob = Tobacco

'devoured' by the jungle. The heavy implication here is that nature has defeated man's attempts to harness and exploit it; that market-driven exploitation creates only suffering, not prosperity, for Latin Americans, who work to create wealth that is enjoyed only overseas.

It was not only in the imaginations of local writers that U.S. commercial interests were involved in the heart of Latin America. Examples of speculative ventures are legion. The most famous is the attempt by Henry Ford to build a rubber production and tyre manu-facturing plant in the heart of the Brazilian rainforest in order to limit the costs of his Ford Motor Company and assert control over as much of the car production process as possible. There was also a significant humanitarian motivation, in the hope and expectation that the venture would bring work and working culture to Amazonian Brazilians. Fordlandia, as it was and is still known, was launched in 1928. Local difficulties in communication and health combined with changes in the global market and technological innovations (the invention of synthetic rubber) to undermine it. The plant suffered from its dependency upon importing materials into the Brazilian interior, and also from the cultural and linguistic differences between Brazilians and the North Americans who came to live and work at Fordlandia.

> Most never really mastered Portuguese, beyond learning how to conjugate a few verbs. A joke among Brazilians who lived on the plantations went: 'What do the Americans learn how to say after their first year in the Amazon?' 'Uma cerveja'. A beer. 'And after two years?' 'Duas cervejas'.[8]

The automobile industry was transformative in Brazil, and its networks careered across the continent. Venancio Coñuepán, Chile's most important Mapuche political leader of the 1940s and '50s, worked as a manager for Ford Motors in Temuco before taking on political leadership roles. The site of Fordlandia was abandoned at the end of the Second World War, but its ruins remain as a poignant symbol, not just of failed attempts to dominate the jungle as in *The Vortex*, but of the inapplicability of Northern, Anglo business culture to ways of working in the South.

Population Growth and Urbanization

This table shows the rapid extent of population growth in Latin America in the twentieth century as a result of a combination of improved health and sanitation systems, mass immigration and reduced civilian involvement in civil warfare. The exceptions to this pattern are clear: Mexico, whose population decreased between 1910 and 1920 as a result of the revolutionary warfare; and Venezuela, which received comparatively little new immigration

Population (in millions) of selected countries[9]

	1900	1910	1920	1930	1940	1950	1960	1970	1980	1990
Argentina	4.6	6.8	8.9	11.9	14.1	17.2	20.6	24.0	28.1	32.5
Brazil	18.0	22.2	27.3	33.6	41.5	53.4	72.6	95.8	121.3	148.5
Chile	3.0	3.4	3.8	4.4	5.1	6.1	7.6	9.5	11.1	13.1
Colombia	4.0	4.9	6.2	7.9	9.2	11.9	15.9	21.4	26.5	32.3
Cuba	1.6	2.3	2.9	3.6	4.4	5.5	7.0	8.6	9.6	10.6
Guatemala	0.9	1.1	1.3	1.8	2.2	2.8	3.8	5.3	7.3	9.2
Mexico	13.6	15.0	14.9	17.2	20.4	27.7	36.9	50.6	67.6	83.2
Peru	3.8	4.0	4.4	5.0	5.8	6.9	8.7	11.4	15.2	19.5
Uruguay	0.9	1.1	1.5	1.7	2.0	2.2	2.5	2.7	2.9	3.1
Venezuela	2.5	2.8	3.0	3.3	3.8	5.1	7.6	10.7	15.1	19.5

until after the Second World War. During the first two decades of the new century, Brazil's population increased by over 9 million new citizens. Latin America's population boomed between the two world wars. Between 1900 and 1950 the populations of Mexico, Venezuela, Colombia, Chile, Uruguay and Cuba all doubled. In the same period the population of Brazil nearly tripled and the population of Argentina quadrupled. The comparatively fast expansion in the population of both Brazil and Argentina was a result of their commercial prosperity in the period as well the hundreds of thousands of immigrants who arrived (the two factors were of course interlinked). Uruguay was able to construct the world's first ever welfare state in these years, benefiting from the high prices of its exports and drawing on a rich body of thought about how to create a stable society and ensure equality among its citizens, 'pioneering welfare capitalism'.[10]

Urbanization

The explosion in population created the conditions for the beginning of the immense urbanization and rural–urban migration that continue to the present day. São Paulo is a good example. The massive urban growth of São Paulo at the dawn of the twentieth century was built upon and beyond existing spatial identities that were closely linked to categories of social class, the general rule being that low incomes were predominant in the east and north sectors, alongside floodplains and factories, and that high-income families dominated in the southwest and far from the industrial plants. A similar spatial segregation can be found in most Latin American cities that expanded rapidly at this time. In the wake of a first wave of chaotic and unplanned growth, in 1912 the City of São Paulo Improvements and Freehold Land Company Ltd (also known as Companhia City) was established as a joint initiative of Brazilian and British investors that aimed to recreate in São Paulo the model of the *cidade-jardim* (garden city). The company commissioned the British architects Barry Parker and Raymond Unwin to design Jardim America, the first garden district development in São Paulo, followed by Alto da Lapa (1921), Pacaembu (1925) and Alto de Pinheiros (1925). These developments were all connected to the tramway system and pro-vided with water and energy services, characterizing a particular partnership of private and public sectors and local and external finance.[11] On the other side of the Santos–Jundiai railway, beyond the floodplains of Varzea do Carmo, there were lower, flat lands which were more likely to be flooded and therefore considered un-healthy. These were the neighbourhoods of Bras, Belem and Mooca, where most industry was located due to the physical characteristics of the terrain and the proximity to the railway network. These areas were chosen for the first popular low-income developments that later expanded along the floodplains of Tiete river into the districts of Bom Retiro, Barra Funda and Lapa.

The sudden population growth with the arrival of immigrants led to high demand for housing, usually met by private investors. One type of housing provision was *vilas operarias* (workers' villages), enclosed communal housing areas built to accommodate industrial employees and their families. Overseas ideas, such those of the British reformer and socialist utopian Robert Owen, inspired these developments. Some villages, such as Vila María Zélia and Vila Economizadora, were model cities on a small scale, with their own schools, health centres, churches and leisure facilities.[12] People started playing football everywhere in these new developments. Football responded to the growth in the urban population, and provided a space for new immigrants to give meaning to their lives and create communities around shared physical endeavours.

During the 1920s the construction of the first skyscrapers imposed a new pattern over this design, with high densities in the city core and an outer sprawl of housing districts. By 1930 city planners had drawn up the Plano de Avenidas, the first master plan for express avenues and roads crossing the urban area, originally based on designs developed by Barry Parker, the British architect who also helped draw up the plans of Companhia City.[13] In São Paulo the creation of jobs and business opportunities attracted an unprecedented flow of immigrants. The emergent metropolis incorporated different ways of life: the numerous Europeans coming mainly from Portugal, Spain, Italy and Germany were followed by Japanese, Syrians, Lebanese and Turkish migrants, composing a mixed local workforce mainly in the fields of manufacturing and small retail business. This foreign group of urban workers shared the same challenges as the locals: of surviving in a strange, severely industrialized and, in a way, anarchic environment, looking for social integration and also for entertainment amid the mixture of languages and cultures.

Public spaces and outdoor activities made an important contribution in connecting this new cosmopolitan society in São Paulo, as they did in Barranquilla, Buenos Aires or Guayaquil. Football is popularly believed to have played a significant role in bringing different cultures together, including the many European immigrants who arrived in São Paulo at the end of the nineteenth century, especially Italians, who formed their own club, Palestra Italia (now Palmeiras). The sport thrived in the context of an emergent multi-ethnic society and later became a trademark of Brazilian cultural identity. The proliferation of grounds and club associations followed the fast pace of urban expansion. The coverage that football received from the media in the 1900s reveals how this sport was incorporated into the local culture, playing an important role in connecting the emergent cosmopolitan society while preserving loyalties from 'back home' in loyalties to clubs like Palmeiras or Palestino in Chile.

Sporting Cultures

Football prospered as the dominant sport in most South American countries. The reason often given is that it was cheap to play and easy to organize an informal match in public spaces, unlike more complicated games or those which required specialized equipment. The arrival of international sport in Latin America, and the rapid increases in the speed of communication technology (especially railways and steamships), enabled the establishment of national leagues and, soon after, international tournaments. In Latin America these changes took place at the same time as the growth in nationalism and the spread of urbanization, so sport acquired a special, central place in the construction of national identities and in the ways that Latin American countries represented themselves to the world. Football was the principal sport which played this role, but it was far from the only one. In Argentina football grew alongside polo, which remained an elite but popular sport throughout the twentieth century out of its base at the Hurlingham club in Buenos Aires, founded in 1888 and named after its equivalent in southwest London. (Argentina won Olympic gold medals at polo at the 1924 and 1936 Olympic Games.[14]) In Colombia, bicycle racing, like coffee cultivation, fitted the national topography perfectly. In Costa Rica, coffee farmers brought a love of football back from business trips to Europe. Venezuela, where u.s. influence in the oil industry produced a baseball-dominated sporting culture. Panama, which had separated from Colombia only in 1903, received a flood of u.s. workers for the construction and operation of the Canal (after 1914). Baseball in Panama therefore became a double-edged weapon of culture. In good times it was used by u.s. visitors and local people alike as a way of demonstrating Panama's modernity and its equality with the u.s. In times of economic or political downturn, like the 1950s, baseball became a focus for anti-u.s. feeling.[15]

In the 1910s and '20s these sports were progressively 'creolized', meaning that the British, Italian and Germans who had been the first players started to be outnumbered on the field by the Brazilians, Argentinians and Uruguayans who had at first watched them from the sidelines. The first players became referees as their knees started to fail them, and then moved on to serve as club directors. In 1930 the Argentine Football Association voted to rename itself the Asociación Argentina de Football, and the whistle was blown on European dominance of Latin American football. In subsequent decades, the white 'creoles' who had taken over the leadership of football would themselves have to struggle for power on the pitch and in the boardroom with another social group that embraced the game: the poor, who were white, black or brown.

'Cultural Browning'

The 1920s and '30s were a period of 'cultural browning' across Latin America, as the historian George Reid Andrews has shown in his study *Afro-Latin America, 1800–2000*. During the economic downturns of the 1930s, part of the Great Depression originated in the United States, Latin American cities faced major economic problems and unemployment rose, threatening and in some cases producing social unrest. Cuba and São Paulo both ended the policy of offering subsidies to European immigrants, and most countries put restrictions on immigration in order to preserve jobs for nationals who were already in situ. The cultural phenomenon of *indigenismo* dates from this period, when white intellectuals from the cities such as José Carlos Mariátegui and Jorge Icaza started to look for inspiration for their essays, novels, poetry and paintings in their country's indigenous past (and sometimes its indigenous presents, too). From these decades, also, came the first moves to capture and popularize African American music. In Peru, for example, the Grammy Award-winning singer Susana Baca (who found fame in the 1990s) relied on the compilations and endeavours of artists from this period who inspired her mentor, Chabuca Granda.

Reid Andrews argues that around 1930 most Latin American nations realized that elite attempts to 'transform Latin America into Europe' had failed.

These failures opened the way for new experiments in economic modernization and industrialization, in new forms of mass-based political participation and citizenship (political 'browning'), and in the construction of new national identities that, instead of denying and seeking to obliterate the region's history of racial mixing, embraced it as the essence of being Latin American (cultural 'browning').

Each of these three experiments was connected to, and reinforced, the other two. Each was linked as well to the continuing process of race mixture and demographic 'browning' that has taken place in the region since 1930, though, as the table below shows, politics and demography were not inextricably linked.

Racial composition (in percentages) in Brazil[16]

	Mulattoes	Blacks	Whites	Other	Total (m)
1890	32.4	14.6	44.0	9.0	14.3
1940	21.2	14.6	63.5	0.7	41.2
1950	26.5	11.0	61.7	0.8	51.9
1980	38.9	5.9	54.2	1.0	119.0
1991	42.4	5.0	41.6	1.0	146.8
2000	38.9	6.1	53.4	1.6	169.8

Racial composition (in percentages) in Cuba[17]

	Mulattoes	Blacks	Whites	Other	Total (m)
1899	17.2	14.9	66.9	0.9	1.6
1931	16.2	11.0	72.1	0.6	4.0
1943	15.5	9.7	74.4	0.4	4.8
1953	14.5	12.4	72.8	0.3	5.8
1981	21.9	12.0	66.0	0.1	9.7

As elites came to see traditions, customs and opportunities that they valued in the Afro and indigenous populations, nation building attempts took on a much more horizontal, rather than top-down, nature. In Cuba in 1931 mulattoes and blacks made up 27 per cent of the population. According to the census in Brazil in 1940 the figure was 35 per cent. Such a substantial part of the population could only be excluded entirely from the national self-image for so long, and half a century after the abolition of slavery, the slow process of eradicating this painful colonial legacy was begun. It would be a long time before the rest of the world started to recognize this process of change: British and North American writers continued to see the indigenous and African heritages of Latin America as part of prehistory, rather than as things to be celebrated and valued in the present: one example is Arthur Conan Doyle's *The Lost World* (1912), set in an imaginary Latin American plateau visited by a party of explorers led by Professor George Edward Challenger. Indigenous societies are the background to a novel mainly concerned with the imperial adventurers, as Kevin Foster has shown: 'by turns suave, savage and coldly scientific, the adventurers are fitting emblems of their society and the brutality that bristles beneath its civilised exterior.'[18]

In 1949 the Cuban writer Alejo Carpentier published *The Kingdom of this World*, a book about the Haitian Revolution of the early nineteenth century and the destruction of slavery by the men and women who laboured under its chains. The novel has remained famous in literary circles as the place where, in a prologue, Carpentier elaborated his theory of *lo real maravilloso*, known in English as magical realism, which presented Caribbean and Latin American reality as being deeper, broader and less tangible than reality in other areas of the world. The style had many adherents, including Gabriel García Márquez, Carlos Fuentes and Mario Vargas Llosa, all of whom were inspired by Carpentier's technique and vision. But *The Kingdom of this World* was also significant because of its subject-matter, the struggle of black Haitians to overcome the exploitation that had been their curse since the beginning of French colonialism in the island. Carpentier was fascinated by the voodoo religion of many Haitians. This had survived the passage from Africa and offered a culture and language which slaves could use to communicate with each other, planning revolution or offering solidarity, as they resisted colonialism and their white masters. Though its exoticism partly explains the novel's popularity abroad, *The Kingdom of this World* represents precisely the moment of 'cultural browning' described by Reid Andrews. It was published at the moment when white, educated elite writers reached out to black culture for the first time, sensing that what whites, blacks, mulattoes and mestizos shared as Latin Americans was greater than that which divided them, or the external threats that opposed them.[19]

Between Cities and Indians

In the period between 1860 and 1950 Latin Americans often still looked towards Europe and the u.s. with respect and awe, but they were becoming increasingly aware of the political nature of their difference and the need for international equality. The contradictory tensions that this created, inherent in the attempt to look outward and inward at the same time, with the same eyes, were best evoked by Jorge Luis Borges (born Buenos Aires, 1899). His stories have been translated into many languages worldwide.

In the short story 'El Sur' ('The South') Borges describes a journey taken by Juan Dahlmann from the city of his native Buenos Aires south into the rural pampas, where he encounters gauchos who appear entirely alien to the bookish, intellectual, civilized (as he sees it) society he inhabits in the capital. Dahlmann is first introduced to the reader as the grandson of Johannes Dahlmann, an evangelical pastor who migrated to Argentina from Germany in 1871. The protagonist of the story, Juan, can therefore be taken to be broadly representative of the waves of European migration to Argentina (from Spain and Italy, as well as Germany) that occurred in the late nineteenth and early twentieth centuries. Juan feels himself to be 'profoundly Argentinian' and, when he takes a train journey out of Buenos Aires into the interior, he finds himself being drawn towards a gaucho culture that he does not understand but which, he senses, forms part of his soul. Looking out of the train window, 'the solitude was perfect and perhaps hostile, and Dahlmann suspected that he was travelling into the past and not only to the South'. Eventually he disembarks at an unknown stop, and walks ten blocks to a bar-cum-shop where he hopes to find a vehicle that will take him to a familiar home. He walks slowly, breathing in the country air and enjoying the 'little adventure' of entering the unknown. In the bar he orders food and sits down, whereupon some local lads turn from their noisy, drunken entertainment and throw crumbs of bread at him. Dahlmann ignores them until he is threatened, and when he attempts to leave an old gaucho intervenes. The 'dark, small, dry man, who looked he came from out of time, in eternity' threw him a dagger. Borges writes:

It was as if The South had decided that Dahlmann would accept the duel. Dahlmann bent down to pick up the dagger and he felt two things. First, that this almost instinctive act meant that he would have to fight. Second, that the weapon, in his weak hand, would not help him to defend himself, but it would justify them to kill him.

In these brief moments, Dahlmann comes to recognize that he has found his Argentinian destiny here, in a dive bar in the pampas, among people he would never have recognized as his equals in Buenos Aires.

They left the bar, and although in Dahlmann there was no hope, neither was there fear. He felt, as they passed outside, that dying in a knife fight, in the open air and giving himself up to it, would have been a liberation for him, a source of happiness and joy, back on his first night in the sanatorium when they first injected him. He felt that if, back then, he had been able to choose or dream his death, this is the death that he would have chosen or dreamed.

The story ends with Dahlmann gripping the knife handle and striding outside towards his destiny. The last line of the story is the only one in the present tense; this switch underlines Borges's point about the way in which Latin American histories provide the background to contemporary debates, about how the unknowability and unpredictability of the future serves as a spur to the curiosity and ambition of nation builders. As always with Borges, an undercurrent of ambiguity allows the reader to surmise that the whole story might just have been Dahlmann's dream about what his destiny might have been if he had been able to leave hospital or his administrative job in the capital. For Borges, dreaming a future based on diverse pasts was as significant, if not more so, than practical attempts to move beyond those histories.[20]

Authentic Unions of Sport and Nation?

As nations asserted their independence and their sovereignty, sport and popular culture increasingly became the reference points for assertions of identity and community. Brazil is again a good example of how this happened. In 1889 Brazil had finally made the transition from empire to republic, the principle of hereditary power for a European family exhausted and destroyed by the abolition of slavery and the opening up of citizenship to people of African birth and heritage. The new authorities demanded a new identity that could encompass all the people, who were now citizens of a republic rather than subjects of a monarch.

To mark the birth of the new republic, the standard-issue symbols of nationhood needed to be established. A wonderful example of the power and prestige of the United States at the end of the nineteenth century is the fact that the most popular proposal for the newly designed flag of Brazil was modelled on the Stars and Stripes of the U.S. The Stripes would be gold and green, and the top-left quadrant would feature green stars on a golden background to evoke the federal states, just as they did in the U.S. But at the last minute Congress decided that it was insufficiently independent to copy another nation's flag in this way (despite the precedent set by half of Europe and Hispanic America, nations that had modelled their flags on the French red, white and blue Tricolour half a century earlier). Brazilians, it was decided, would have an entirely original flag with a blue diamond against a green and gold background, and at its centre a view of the Rio night sky captured on Independence Day. The unique configuration of the southern constellations proudly placed the flag, and the nation, in its own geographical location.[21]

The design of the Brazilian flag grew out of and reflected a new sense of the cultural and ethnic uniqueness of the Brazilian population. With the abolition of slavery, and the creation of a republic,

Brazilians were able to compare and contrast themselves – often favourably – with other republics in the hemisphere. The idea of 'racial democracy' developed to become absolutely central to Brazilians' sense of self. In 1933 Gilberto Freyre published his analysis, *Masters and Slaves*, which revelled in the physicality, sensuousness and equality that he believed was a consequence of Brazil's unique colonial and early independent society. Under racial democracy Brazilians would be valued for their individuality and competence regardless of ethnicity.[22] These years also saw the increasing celebration of samba, the uniquely Brazilian style of dance and music that was paraded through cities at the time of Carnival. Carnival, since the medieval period a time when social hierarchies were briefly overturned, with rich and poor confounded and occupying each other's status, became an 'invented tradition' of the Brazilian nation. It would be a moment of joy to the soundtrack of samba, demonstrating Brazilians' unity and their love of and talent for rhythm, sensuality and physicality; it would draw on Iberian customs and African traditions, merging them together into something that would be Brazilian culture.[23] Samba was a particular way of moving to music, and at the same time a somehow particularly Brazilian way of moving and touching a football was becoming key to making this national identity.

In 1938 Brazil's national *seleçãao* reached the semi-finals of the FIFA World Cup in France. This represented a crucial breakthrough for Brazilians seeking to assert their unique national heritage and potential on the international stage. Freyre, the sociologist turned analyst of all aspects of the nation, its culture and society, reflected in an interview that

> Our style of playing football seems to contrast to the European style because of a set of characteristics such as surprise, craftiness, shrewdness, readiness, and I shall even say individual brilliance and spontaneity, all of which express our 'mulattoism' ... Our passes ... our tricks ... that something which is related to dance, to capoeira, mark the Brazilian style of football, which rounds and sweetens the game the British invented, the game

which they and other Europeans play in such an acute and angular way – all this seems to express . . . the flamboyant and at the same time shrewd mulattoism, which can today be detected in every true affirmation of Brazil.[24]

President Getúlio Vargas secured the rights to hold the next World Cup, scheduled for 1942, in Brazil. International war intervened, meaning that the tournament could only take place in 1950. Industralization and urbanization had accelerated during these years, and the 1950 World Cup was exploited by statesmen, nation builders and politicians alike to showcase Brazil to the world – and to itself. The construction of the immense, modern Maracanã stadium in Rio was designed to shout out Brazilian modernity, prosperity and pride to the world. It was constructed using locally produced concrete, and its architecture was bold, innovative and futuristic. It was bigger than any of the Italian, French or Uruguayan stadiums that had hosted World Cups before. The 200,000 Brazilians who crowded in to watch Brazil play Uruguay in the final match, which would decide the winners of the tournament, believed that they would witness the coronation of their virtuous, multi-ethnic, flamboyant team over the hardworking but uninspirational Uruguayans. Famously, Brazilian administrators and politicians had already declared Brazil the winners before the match began. But Uruguay got two goals and Brazil only one, and two national legends were born – one for the winners and one for the losers.

For Brazilians, the Maracanãzo (the event at the Maracaña) created an anxiety about national failure and about hubris in sport. It also triggered the collapse of racial democracy and belief in the shared values of ethnic diversity. Black players – particularly Barbosa, the goalkeeper – were scapegoated for the defeat, creating a lasting legacy of racism towards defensive players, especially in the selection of the national team. The hardening of ethnic suspicions was also felt beyond sport, in wider society, such as in the styles of music being chosen to represent Brazil abroad.

For Uruguay, however, 1950 was the unexpected high point of international sporting achievement. The country had already won the championship on home turf in 1930, but this overturning of the odds by defeating the overwhelming favourites in Rio created a team of stars and legends. For the writer Eduardo Galeano, who listened to the match at home in Montevideo as a child, this was an event which defined a nation's identity, its history and its future:

> I was a young boy and football-crazy, and like every Uruguayan I was glued to the radio, listening to the World Cup Final. When the voice of the commentator Carlos Soyé transmitted to me the sad news of the Brazilian goal, my soul fell to the floor. That was when I turned to my most powerful friend. I promised God a number of sacrifices that I would make if he could only appear at the Maracanã and turn the game around.
>
> I was never able to remember the things that I had promised, and for this reason I was never able to fulfil my pledge. Also, Uruguay's victory in front of the biggest football crowd ever, had certainly been a miracle, but it had been a miracle of flesh and blood, the work of one man called Obdulio Vargas, our captain. Obdulio had brought cold blood to the game when the Brazilian avalanche endangered us, and then he had picked the whole thing up, lifted it by his shoulders and with guts and pure bravery he had pushed against the elements.[25]

Uruguay's victory, for Galeano, was born of hard work, skill, belief and not a little luck. For Brazil the defeat triggered a crisis of confidence; for Uruguayans it remained a beautiful moment when the odds were overturned and the nation's skill and perseverance were rewarded.

The 1950 World Cup was the fourth such tournament. In 1930 it had been held and won in Uruguay. In 1934 it was held and won in Italy. In 1938 it was held in France and won by Italy. By 1950 therefore, the honours were symbolically even between Europe and Latin America. Both had hosted the tournament twice and both had won it twice. During the first half of the twentieth century foreign influences were strong in Latin America – especially in terms of commerce, migration and culture – but they were as often welcomed and emulated as they were decried. Correspondingly, Latin American economies and societies presented telling innovations that were adopted by other regions. A good example is the development of the first combine harvester in Argentina, or the experimentation that led to the manufacture of the first plastics in Peru.[26] Yet international historians were often dismissive of these Latin American contributions to the state of the world, and some Latin Americans increasingly resented the way in which foreigners used them for their knowledge, products or enthusiasm when they didn't seem to get anything useful in return.

The Heir to Casement and Bingham? Che Guevara and Machu Picchu

Two years after the Maracanãzo, a young medical student set out on a continental journey. He started on a motorbike with a companion, Alberto Granados, later hitch-hiking on buses and by boat. It was a crucial turning point in his life, and that of Latin American history. The boy who hugged his mum and left home seeking girls, adventure and an education was Ernesto Guevara from Rosario, Argentina. The man he became was 'Che' Guevara, the icon of the Cuban Revolution and, in life and even more so in death, a global symbol of internationalism, solidarity and socialism.

In early 1953 the two men reached the Peruvian highlands and began the ascent up to Machu Picchu, the Inca citadel that had only recently been publicized by the u.s. archaeologist Hiram Bingham. Guevara, according to his travel diary, had begun a slow process of politicization during his travels through Chile's northern copper mining district. Here Guevara first began to have more profound thoughts about the people and places he encountered on his travels. At the open-cast copper mine of Chiquicamata he was shocked by the poverty and everyday dangers faced by the workers, 'these poor heroes who die in the war against nature [to mine the copper] ... when their only thought is putting food on the table at the end of every day'.[27]

Around Cuzco, in Peru, Guevara and Granados saw for the first time a largely indigenous population, triggering them to think seriously about the long continuities in Latin America's history. On observing the marvellous feats of stone engineering in Cuzco (where the Spanish conquistadores had built their houses and churches on top of the ruined but still sturdy walls of the Inca buildings), and at fortresses like Ollantaytambo, Guevara was cast into a spiritual state. He came to imagine himself as sharing the history and culture of the indigenous people who had built these edifices. He felt that the ignominy of the colonized peoples was his own. But, resentfully, he wrote that 'the grey stones have grown tired of imploring their gods to destroy the hated conquering race, and now they show only the tiredness of inanimate things which is only able to provoke the admiring exclamation of some tourist.'[28] At Machu Picchu, Guevara sought to distinguish himself from the North American tourists he saw wandering around the ruins. It was at Machu Picchu where Guevara found the inspiration to fuse his tourist's admiration for the relics of an indigenous civilization with his slow-burning political awakening. Leaving aside a discussion of the origins of the once 'lost' city, Guevara remarks:

> The undeniable thing, the most important thing, is that we have before us a pure expression of the most powerful indigenous race in the Americas, untouched by contact with the conquering civilization, and full of immensely evocative treasures in its walls, walls which have died from the boredom of no longer being. The magnificent scenery around it provides the ideal backdrop to inspire the dreams of anyone strolling through its ruins; North American tourists, hidebound by their practical view of the world, can place those representatives of the fallen people they have seen on their journey in among these once living walls, unaware of the moral distance separating them, since only the semi-indigenous spirit of the South American can grasp the subtle differences.[29]

Like the Chilean poet Pablo Neruda on Machu Picchu just a decade earlier, the soaring heights of the Andes, and the marks of indigenous native civilizations upon them, thrust Guevara into

Ernesto 'Che' Guevara (1928–1967) was born in Rosario, Argentina, and trained as a doctor. His politicized mother shaped his thinking about economics and society, and his intellectual formation was catalysed by a long trip around South America he took in 1952–3, later immortalized in a book and on film as the *The Motorcycle Diaries*. It was at Machu Picchu in Peru, when contemplating the Inca ruins, that Guevara proclaimed himself to be a Latin American internationalist rather than solely Argentinian. He later travelled to Guatemala and Mexico, where he met Fidel Castro and joined the project to liberate Cuba from the rule of Fulgencio Batista. Though initially charged with coordinating the medical part of the expedition, Guevara's loyalty and attention to detail quickly earned him the command of guerrilla units whose victory in the Sierra Maestra became the stuff of legend. His capacity for big-picture military strategy was combined with absolute ruthlessness in combat with the enemy, and indeed indiscipline within his own ranks. After the success of the revolution Guevara was put in charge of the ministry of industries, and later finance and the National Bank. He wrote obsessively, creating the influential

Che Guevara on a mule in Las Villas, Cuba, 1958.

theory of the guerrilla *foco* or focus which would lead social revolutions across the world, and defining the New Man who would give himself up for revolution. Both these ideas, as well as Guevara's own romantic image as the bearded, visionary revolutionary, were of immense significance as the Cuban Revolution spawned potential imitators across the world.

Guevara played his own part in the internationalization of his work and his image, leading Cuban efforts to globalize the revolution in Africa (especially in Angola and Ethiopia) and elsewhere in Latin America. Leading a *foco* group in Bolivia in 1967, he was finally tracked down by u.s. intelligence operatives in league with the Bolivian army, and extrajudicially executed and buried in an anonymous grave. His remains were returned to Santa Clara in Cuba in 1997. In death Che Guevara has become a global icon representing subversion and revolution which has been appropriated in the marketing of fashion, alcohol and many other products as well as in the promotion of the Cuban Revolution itself, to the extent that most people worldwide who hear his name or see Alberto Korda's famous image think he was born and bred in Cuba, rather than rural Argentina.[30]

Guevara's world view was defiantly global. Just before his death he wrote: 'We must definitely keep in mind that imperialism is a world-system, the final stage of capitalism, and that it must be beaten in a great worldwide confrontation. The strategic objective of that struggle must be the destruction of imperialism.'[31]

spiritual contemplation and political compromise. His own soul, he decided, must be 'semi-indigenous' as well as European. He could now write and act on behalf of the voiceless and marginalized *americanos*. Later, in a famous segment of his diaries, Guevara reports how he launched into an improvised speech in an Amazonian leper colony, exhorting his small audience to share his 'Latin American' identity and declaring that

> the division of America into uncertain and illusory nationalities is completely fictitious. We are one single mixed race which, from Mexico down to the Magellan Straits, presents notable ethnographic similarities. For this reason, trying to liberate myself from any leftover provincialism, I would like to raise a toast to Peru, and to United America.[32]

From this realization, Guevara began to elaborate a Latin American identity based on solidarity, community and humanitarian ideals. Only later, when in Central America and increasingly antagonized by Cold War interventions in the continent, did he turn away from medicine and towards politically motivated violence.[33]

Between the States and América: Knowing Culture

By 1950 popular culture had so expanded its reach across Latin American countries through new media – principally the radio – that it is fair to talk of the existence of (albeit often incomplete, fractured or fragmented) national identities based around traditions, cultures and a sense of shared political community. This was the hallowed goal which nation builders had been striving for since independence from colonial rule. National revolutions, as in Mexico, had in some places created the institutional framework for a national culture based on equality and respect rather than hierarchy and conservatism. Elsewhere educational projects in national history and national geography had slowly created a sense of shared belonging among different communities across national territories. In many areas continuing imperialism on the part of foreign powers served to catalyse people to think of themselves as different from, and threatened by, people who came from overseas. But it was popular culture, as expressed in music, stories and first and foremost sport, which created positive identities based on neither violence nor victimization but instead on play and pride, which would be the basis for national identities from then on.

One wonderful example of the intermingling of transatlantic peoples and cultures is tango. Think first of Carlos Gardel, the French-born Argentinian tango great, who died in a plane crash near Medellín, Colombia, in 1935. His body was taken on a hemispheric aero-cortège from Medellín to New York to Rio de Janeiro before being buried in Buenos Aires.[34] Another tango legend, Astor Piazzolla, used the texture of music to 'tanguificar el mundo' (remake the world in tango style), to fuse global influences and subvert them into something original. Tango has since been sold to the world as something instrumentally and authentically Argentinian, and a whole industry of teachers and tourism has sprung up around it in Buenos Aires and throughout the Argentinian diaspora worldwide.[35]

Economic historians are not afraid to talk of this period as one of early globalization.[36] Latin American economies felt the pressures of being locked into external relationships that shaped their trade and investments. Latin American people were under the same pressures, and as Borges and Guevara show us in their different ways, those external pressures became internalized at the very same time that national projects and nationalism were being asserted. This heady mixture created some tumultuous times in the middle of the twentieth century. Latin America has never developed in isolation from the interventions and intentions of other powers. There could be no vacuum in which new nations could grow unmolested. The Cold War was beginning.

This chapter has shown how Latin America's external economic relationships were based around particular products, which created long-lasting legacies for the ways Latin Americans thought about the world and the way the world thought about Latin America's place in it. Latin America evolved from somewhere to be conquered or learned about by outsiders (as in the nineteenth century) into a place whose people needed saving from the excesses of capitalism, or a place that had neglected its own history and needed help and education in order to come to understand its own past. In many ways both Roger Casement and Hiram Bingham were producing what Aníbal Quijano calls a 'geopolitical economy of knowledge', which again posited Latin Americans as the consumers of knowledge produced or invented by outsiders.[37]

Jorge Luis Borges's very short story 'El Etnografo' ('The Ethnographer') reflected on the ironies of all this.[38] He skewered u.s. imperial culture, and its use of social science research to further imperial aims, at the same time as he acknowledged the extent to which Latin American culture relied upon supposed u.s. cultural ascendency and was defined (as a relative failure) against it. The protagonist of the story 'which I heard about in Texas, but which occurred in another state' is Fred Murdock, a stereotypical young North American, neither blond nor brown, with 'nothing unique about him, not even the feigned individuality of the young'. Fred studies indigenous languages at university and is sent by his supervisor to live among an indigenous community in the West (which might as well be Latin America) and observe their rites and customs, to ingratiate himself until they tell him their secrets. Fred does as he is told, learning the language and assimilating himself, eventually tearing up his ethnographic notes, dreaming in the new language and coming to 'think in a manner which his own sense of logic rejected'. Eventually he is trusted enough for the elders to pass on the 'secret doctrine', and soon afterwards Fred leaves the community and returns to his university, informing his supervisor that 'he knew the secret and he had resolved not to publish it.' Fred concludes: 'The secret is not worth as much as the roads that led me to it. These roads, one has to wander along them.' For Borges, then, we might conclude, it is not in the indigenous cultures or in the intellectual universities where the truth of Latin America's history and identity lie: rather it is in the quest to discover oneself where meaning and significance can be found. The last line, as ever with Borges, brings such speculations back down to earth: 'Fred got married, got divorced, and is now one of the librarians at Yale.' Daily disappointments, in love as in work, were the inescapable backdrop to intellectual endeavour.

Two Argentinians, Ernesto Guevara and Jorge Luis Borges, came to represent for many outsiders the divergent natures of Latin America. The first was a charismatic revolutionary committed to social and economic equality and prepared to use violence to achieve his goals. The second was an eccentric, bookish intellectual whose astonishing literary feats inspired generations of writers across the world to find solace and creativity in libraries, encouraging multilingual and multicultural reading and contemplation. In the 1950s Latin America entered the Cold War period of global history. Then, again, two divergent paths were set out before it: communism and capitalism, the Soviet Union and the United States. Latin American peoples were caught between two superpowers, two dreams, two pathways to what they saw as progress and modernity. There were many Latin American victims of these clashes between projects, ideologies and visions of the future, and many Latin American perpetrators of the worst abuses.

SIX

Latin America in the Cold War

Not far from my home in Bristol there used to be a piece of anarchist graffiti on the side of a squat which featured an evil, snarling Uncle Sam character throwing fire bombs at innocent civilians. Alongside the picture was a roll-call of countries that had been victims of u.s. imperialism, with attempts to quantify the number of dead caused by u.s. interventions. Alongside Vietnam, Iraq and Afghanistan, Guatemala, Nicaragua, Chile and Colombia were featured. Although the image was not drawn by Bristol's most famous street artist, Banksy, it aspired to similar levels of universal recognition and broad-brush interpretation. It presented Latin America as one victim among many. Yet any understanding of the abuses committed by the u.s. in Latin America during the 1950s, '60s, '70s and '80s can only be attained by situating them in their historical contexts. In order to do this it is crucial to understand Latin American efforts to improve their security and protect their sovereignty in this period, and to assess the interventions of the Soviet Union alongside them. Neither must we forget that the guerrillas, torturers, terrorists and prison guards were overwhelmingly Latin Americans themselves.

Many Latin Americans were victims of the Cold War. 'Cold War terror – either executed, patronized, or excused by the United States – fortified illiberal forces, militarized societies, and broke the link between freedom and equality' in Latin America.[1]

Many Latin Americans railed against the United States' role in supporting tyrannical and abusive regimes. Perhaps the coarsest example of antiimperialist anti-Americanism of the mid-twentieth century was the Chilean poet Pablo Neruda's *Canto general*, whose final sections drew together a litany of U.S. abuses in Latin America, from the interventions in Cuba and Puerto Rico through exploitation of banana workers and copper miners. Neruda (1904–1973) had also visited Machu Picchu, a decade before Che Guevara, and in his famous *The Heights of Macchu Picchu* (Canto II of *Canto general*) he used the ruins to symbolize the continued presence, significance and value of indigenous culture in Latin America, suggesting that it was only here that white creoles such as himself (and later Guevara) could come to think of themselves as fully 'American', and therefore able to act for and speak for the downtrodden masses. Neruda was careful to situate his anti-Americanism as part of a broader historical invective against all forms of imperialism in the continent, from the Spanish, through the French and British, until it converged on U.S. barbarities in the twentieth century. Neruda's anti-Americanism was shaped by growing U.S. influence in Chile, which escalated during and after Salvador Allende's Unidad Popular presidency (with which Neruda was closely associated). The direct involvement of Richard Nixon's presidency in undermining Latin American democracy led Neruda to write his 'Call for the Destruction of Nixon', which contrasted the U.S.'s imperialism in the world – and beyond – with his own values of communism, peace and happiness. Neruda called Nixon a villain and a criminal and mocked his promotion of space exploration. He accused Nixon of genocide and wrote of an urge to use his poetry to kill the U.S. president, metaphorically, because he 'has killed so many here on earth'.[2]

For Neruda the role of the poet and artist in Latin America had moved from the romantic muse of his early career (the classic 'Twenty Love Poems and a Song of Despair' acting as a channel for the voices and aspirations of the people, to now serving as a witness to historical crimes and inequalities. Neruda died not long after the military coup of 11 September 1973 that overthrew Allende. For many authors the coincidence was too much, with some suggesting that Neruda died of a broken heart, his dreams for his country shattered by violence (unlike Allende, who shot himself in the presidential palace rather than be captured by the military coup leaders). In 2013 Neruda's corpse was disinterred, with debate continuing over whether he might have been, as his driver claimed, poisoned by the new military regime while in hospital.[3] Neruda's anger was latched onto by a generation of outsiders who assumed that Latin America had become irremediably anti-American during the Cold War.

This chapter demonstrates that this was certainly not the case. Foreign powers chiefly sought to support or exacerbate existing national or regional conflicts for their own benefits – they did not create these conflicts alone. Through a careful progression through major episodes in Latin American history of the 1960s and '70s, this chapter shows how the Cold War was but one of multiple relationships – economic, political and cultural – tying Latin America to the outside world in this period. Direct intervention by the u.s. in Latin American politics predated the Cold War by several decades, and by taking the long view of how the Cold War was 'Latin Americanized' we get a better sense of the many strange turns history took during these years.[4]

Latin America and the Second World War

During the Second World War the Allies looked to Latin American airspace as they sought to secure their access to natural resources (especially Venezuelan oil and Brazilian rubber) and continued control of the Panama Canal and Caribbean shipping routes.[5] Latin American states became pulled into the air conflict even as they professed neutrality in the early years of the war. German influence in the continent meant that it was certainly not a given that Latin America would support the Allies. The fact that Nazi activists and supporters later found asylum in Latin America, especially in the Southern Cone, after the war's end, serves to demonstrate a residual loyalty to ideologies linked to the Axis powers, though it can also be better explained by the existence of the millions of German and Italian migrants who arrived in Latin America in the three decades before the War. This created a considerable backflow of sympathy and kinship links for many of the defeated Germans. Juan Gabriel Vásquez's novel *The Informers* (2004) is a wonderful recreation of the tensions and anxieties that these long histories caused after 1945.

Histories of the global reach of the Second World War in Latin America generally only mention the role of the German ship the *Admiral Graf Spee* in the Battle of the River Plate in 1939, which was attacked by British ships and scuttled outside Montevideo. But Latin America was much more than a fearful observer hanging on to its neutrality and its silverware as war was waged in the oceans surrounding it. The political divisions that shaped discussion of the war in Europe were shared and mirrored in Latin America, with memories of the Spanish Civil War – and the thousands of exiles who arrived on Latin American shores in the late 1930s and early '40s bringing their stories with them – provoking debate over the rights and wrongs of the war. But Latin Americans also joined up in their thousands, including many Argentinians who volunteered to fight in the British Army. When Brazil entered the Second World War in 1942 on the side of the Allies, it did so with gusto. Brazilian air crews were trained in the u.s., and they attacked German submarines operating in the Atlantic with great success throughout 1943. Mexican attack planes also bombed German submarines in the Pacific and the Caribbean. Brazilians fought with some success in the Italian campaigns of 1943 and 1944.

The aviation industry in Latin America, described in an earlier chapter, became a field of intense competition during the Cold War years. u.s. airlines, planes and often pilots came to dominate as a direct result of a deliberate u.s. policy to promote its own aviation interests and to undermine other powers' companies as well as their national strategies. During the 1940s the u.s. used threats and the financial muscle of Pan Am as a means of squeezing out German or Axis-linked firms from aviation, which had had a strong presence in Brazil in particular. After the end of the Second World War this process continued with both commercial and geopolitical imperatives. One exception was Transportes Aereos Centroamericanos (taca), the Central American air network founded by the New Zealander Lowell Yerex. taca became a success by keeping its costs down and successfully buying and maintaining second- and third-hand aircraft, especially from Britain.[6]

Internationalism

The United Nations was founded in 1948, and Latin American states were among its strongest supporters. The UN offers a space where Latin Americans can be treated as equals within the international community – and as the foreign interventions on Latin American soil related in this book suggest, it should come as no surprise that this was perceived as valuable. Throughout the UN's history, Latin American states have taken a full part in its various bodies, missions and commissions. Colombians and Cubans were in Korea from 1950–63; Brazilians and Colombians were in Egypt in 1956; Argentinians and Brazilians were in Katanga from 1961–4; Peru sent men to the Golan Heights in the early 1970s; Argentinians have long been in Cyprus, and were enthusiastic participants in the lead-up to the first Gulf War in 1991.[7] In the twenty-first century Latin American participation in UN peacekeeping missions has become the norm. When the UN mission was attacked in Iraq in 2003, the UN's special representative to the country was killed, alongside over twenty others. He was a Brazilian, Sergio Vieira de Mello.

The peacekeeping mandates of the UN, however, often buckled beneath the geopolitics, subterfuge and proxy wars of the Cold War. Latin America suffered the ravages of the Cold War as much as any other area of the world, caused as much by covert guerrilla warfare as by the maintenance, over several decades, of unpalatable military regimes.

Populism in the Cold War

One of the first victims of the flexing of U.S. muscles in Central America in this period was the Nicaraguan leader Augusto Sandino. Sandino was a populist and nationalist who rose above traditional Liberal–Conservative divides in order to speak of class divisions and foreign enemies in the same voice. In 1927 he wrote a manifesto that attempted to combine his own sense of national belonging with a declaration of resentment and conflict against U.S. interventions in Latin America:

I am Nicaraguan and I am proud that in my veins flows, more than any other, the blood of the American Indian, whose regeneration contains the secret of being a loyal and sincere patriot. The bonds of nationality give me the right to assume responsibility for my actions on matters of Nicaragua and, therefore, of Central America and the entire continent that speaks our language . . .

I accept the invitation to the struggle and I myself will provoke it, and to the challenge of the cowardly invader and the traitors to my country I answer with my battle cry. My chest and that of my soldiers will form walls that the legions of Nicaragua's enemies will crash upon. The last of my soldiers who are soldiers for Nicaragua's freedom, might die, but first, more than a battalion of you, blond invader, will have bitten the dust of my rustic mountains . . .

Come, you gang of morphine addicts; come murder us in our own land, I am awaiting you, standing upright before my patriotic soldiers, not caring how many you may be. But bear in mind that when this occurs, the destruction of your grandeur will shake the Capitol in Washington, reddening with your blood the white sphere that crowns your famous White House, the den where you concoct your crimes.[8]

Sandino was assassinated in 1934 by opponents who proved much more friendly to the u.s. and to the large fruit company owners who had much influence over Central America in this period. A year before Sandino's murder, u.s. president Franklin D. Roosevelt inaugurated his 'Good Neighbor' policy, which aimed at pursuing peaceful cooperation with Latin America. The intention, part of Roosevelt's New Deal, was to create a stable hemisphere within which to relaunch the u.s. economy. It might be fair to summarize the Latin American reaction with the proverb 'once bitten, twice shy'. The debts owed by Latin American states to u.s. institutions were already reaching into the billions of dollars, according to u.s. estimates, and fear about non-repayment was the catalyst for attempts at rapprochement on the part of the u.s.[9]

At times the U.S. let loose a 'savage crusade, justified under the guise of the Cold War, against Latin American democratic movements'. The creation of national security states, particularly in Chile, Brazil and Uruguay, institutionalized torture and disappearances in directed, official campaigns of political persecution. In countries like Argentina, El Salvador and Guatemala the combination of influences from abroad with escalating domestic political conflict created a 'scattershot horror' in which the most frequent victims were civilians rather than political activists.[10] The physical presence of U.S. Marines in Nicaragua itself during the 1910s and '20s had already been a catalyst to forms of resistance against foreign interventions.[11]

The long-term pressures of urbanization, limited industralization and foreign investment combined after the Second World War in Latin America with ongoing political and ideological movements. Marxism and communism, already strong in many urban areas, retained substantial bedrocks of support into the 1940s and '50s and were sometimes encouraged or resourced by the USSR. Many communists pursued electoral success, an avenue that eventually produced the presidential election victory of Salvador Allende in 1970. Elsewhere charismatic individuals were able to consolidate themselves in power through populist actions, taking advantage of the opening up of the democratic franchise by appealing to the aspirational, the poor and, increasingly, women. Sometimes the Cold War opened space for these unconventional operators. The best example was Juan Perón, who was president of Argentina three times between 1946 and his death in 1974. His style and political legacy – Peronism – continue to be hugely significant half a century on. Perón's principal political strategy was to get newly urbanized labourers on his side by expanding social benefits while being aggressive towards 'national' and/or 'class enemies'. Massive public works programmes were introduced alongside the attempt at import-substitution-industralization, which was adopted in much of the continent to break the chains of 'economic dependency' and reduce the need to export raw materials which could create profit elsewhere rather than at home.[12] Crucial to Perón's support among Argentina's working poor was his first wife, Eva.

Eva Perón (1919–1952), or **Evita**, was born María Eva Duarte in rural Argentina in the midst of great waves of immigration, urbanization and industrialization that were transforming the country. In Buenos Aires she worked as an actress and won the hearts of many audiences as well as an ambitious military colonel, Juan Perón. When he became a president renowned for his populism, his young wife was an important factor in attracting poor provincial migrants to his cause. Her affinity with the *descamisados*, the shirtless ones, was a crucial support for Perón's regime. In particular she argued and fought for increased workers' rights and in favour of female suffrage. In a speech, Evita said: 'I have travelled the old countries of Europe, some of them devastated by war. There, in direct contact with the people, I have learned another lesson about life. That is the lesson of the humble, hard-working woman, who struggles together with man for recuperation and peace.' Widely hailed as a popular icon, her early death from cancer converted her into a national martyr whose name was constantly evoked in support of the causes she supported. She was immortalized in the musical *Evita* as well as through many charitable foundations and political activist groups.[13]

Poster with the portrait of
Eva Perón, 1948.

Latin American Culture in the United States

Before the Cold War U.S. power in Latin America had a long history dating back to the expression of interest enunciated in the Monroe Doctrine of 1823. Key processes included the acquisition of Mexican territory through offensive warfare in the 1830s and '40s, the construction of the Panama Railroad across Colombian territory in the Gold Rush of 1850s and '60s and the filibustering of U.S. citizens such as William Walker who acquired land and political authority in Central America. The Spanish–American War of 1898, leading to the independence of Cuba under American tutelage, and then the liberation of Panama from Colombian rule in 1903 and the construction of the Canal until its completion in 1914, opened a new phase for more aggressive, more overt intervention.

Unexpected avenues had been opened for Latin Americans, and Latin American culture, within the U.S. Fortino Mario Alfonso Moreno Reyes (1911–1993) for example was, as his comic creation Cantinflas, the first Latin American made into a global star through the medium of cinema. Born in a poor barrio of Mexico City, as a quick-witted young man he entered the growing entertainment industry as the capital rapidly urbanized. His comic turns were perfect for the silent films of the 1940s, yet the art and ambiguity of his performance meant that he was hard to pigeonhole. Sometimes his turns as Mexican peasants or the urban poor seemed to be ridiculing them, whereas at other times he seemed to be subversively mocking stuck-up elites. He represented for his audiences the comedy and chaos involved in Mexico's embrace of modernity and global culture in the mid-twentieth century. Cantinflas himself embodied many of these contradictions: at once in love with celebrity and anxious for Hollywood approval and, at home, a trade union organizer. Distinctly local in his roots, language and traditions, as a global media icon he came to represent Mexico for many Europeans and Asians whose only contact with the continent in the 1950s and '60s was through film. As an employee of Columbia Pictures he employed visual humour as well as Spanish-language jokes and irony in order to break into the U.S. market. Yet his appeal to Mexicans and Latin

Americans as an everyman was never able to supplant Charlie Chaplin or Groucho Marx, Cantiflas's contemporaries, in this lucrative area. In many ways Cantinflas's films, with their joyful wordplay and freedom of expression, continue to stereotype Latin American humour as somehow unintelligible to non-Spanish speakers. He was in this sense a particularly Latin American type of global superstar.[14] Stereotypes certainly abounded in Walt Disney's films aimed at the region, such as *The Three Caballeros* (1944).

Another perhaps more surprising star of the period was the Chilean Mapuche soprano Rayén Quitral (1916–1979). She became an unlikely opera superstar at mid-century, overcoming the obstacles to social mobility presented by her gender and ethnicity (female Mapuche Indians in this period tended to be seen as rural and excluded from national – yet alone international – culture, as Joanna Crow has shown[15]). She performed many of the classics of European opera at the great houses of New York, Mexico City, London and Buenos Aires. Cantinflas and Quitral, however, were the exceptions that proved the rule. Their long lives were the mirror image of the abbreviated lifespans of those politicians and activists who explicitly opposed u.s. power, like Augusto Sandino, Jacobo Arbenz or Salvador Allende.

Guatemala in the Cold War

For many historians, the experience of Guatemala in the 1950s was archetypal of u.s. actions in the continent. As told by Eduardo Galeano, this was the story of a liberal experiment gratuitously destroyed by u.s. imperialism, economic pressure and covert operations. Workers' rights and transport infrastructure were both expanded in an attempt to limit the power of United Fruit, 'the virtually untaxed and uncontrolled owner of vast lands and of the railroad and port'. The liberal president Juan José Arevalo, on leaving office in 1951, claimed that he had dealt with 32 conspiracies financed by United Fruit during his administration. His replacement, Jacobo Arbenz, embarked on agrarian reform, which caused alarm among foreign investors. In the u.s. there were fears that 'a Communist government had taken over'.[16] The U.S. ambassadors to the Central American republics worked out a plan for invasion, led by Guatemalan troops trained and equiped by the U.S., and escorted by U.S.-piloted F-47 bombers. Allen Dulles, head of the CIA but previously a director of United Fruit, cabled his congratulations.[17] Arbenz was forcibly removed from power and replaced by a friendlier regime – but political violence rumbled on, and on, and on, for four decades.

The violence in Guatemala between the 1970s and the '90s featured a 'scorched earth campaign that murdered over one hundred thousand Mayans and completely razed more than four hundred indigenous communities . . . By the time the war ended in 1996, the state had killed two hundred thousand people, disappeared forty thousand, and tortured unknown thousands more.'[18] The violence of the Cold War period was aided and abetted by imperial powers in terms of both arms sales and technical support, and how it fitted coherently with a century-long process of land colonization, racial inequality and political violence in Guatemala.

The Cuban Revolution

The most well-known episodes of Cold War history in Latin America involved violence or the threat of violence. The Cuban Revolution and its consequences are the events that cast a shadow over much of the period. Fidel Castro chose to use violence for his attempts to wrest power from the U.S.-backed mestizo leader Fulgencio Batista, seeing no prospect for democratic success. In 1952 Castro led an abortive attack on the La Moncada barracks and was arrested. In his trial he famously declared to the nation that 'History will absolve me' and that his rebellion would eventually be successful.[19] In 1957 Castro returned from his Mexican exile (where the Argentinian doctor Ernesto 'Che' Guevara had joined the group) and his boatload of guerrillas fought their way across the Sierra Maestra mountains. This was a slow process, with the guerrillas reliant on persuading local people to support them and feed them, and it was only in late 1958 that Batista's regime recognized that its time was up and fled the country for the U.S. On 1 January 1959 Castro, Cienfuegos and

Rigoberta Menchú (born 1959) won the Nobel Peace Prize in 1992 in recognition of her work in promoting and defending human rights in her native Guatemala. A member of the K'iche ethnic group, Menchú recorded her life story in a famous testimonial, *I Rigoberta Menchú*. In it she detailed her horrendously difficult life, the poverty, violence and hunger exacerbated by the Guatemalan civil war, which decimated the country and put indigenous communities directly in the line of fire of leftist revolutionaries, the state's armed forces and illegal paramilitary death squads. Menchú was dedicated to carving out space for peace and respect for indigenous rights. Although her narrative created controversy over the extent to which she had co-authored the book with a Venezuelan academic, Elizabeth Burgos, it was a global bestseller which put Menchú and her life story at the centre of much debate about Latin American armed conflicts and their effect on indigenous communities across the continent. In the early twenty-first century she entered democratic politics, standing for election as president and working with peace foundations and other NGOs. In her Nobel Prize speech, she said: 'I consider this prize, not as a reward to me personally, but rather as one of the greatest conquests in the struggle for peace, for human rights and for the rights of the indigenous people, who, for five hundred years have been split, fragmented, victim to genocide, repression and discrimination.'[20]

Rigoberta Menchú.

Guevara piled into Havana to inaugurate their new, revolutionary government.

At first there was a chance that a nationalist Cuban government led by Castro could have come to terms with the u.s. After all, the sugar and tourism industries had been fairly profitable, and u.s. investors and visitors had been key to both. Castro and Guevara were even photographed playing golf, which had become the ultimate symbol of an elitest, imperialist sport.[21] The question of who or what was foreign and who or what was Cuban became political. As Guevara himself commented: 'No country until now has denounced the American interference in Cuban affairs, nor has a single daily newspaper accused the Yankees of helping Batista massacre his people. But many are concerned about me [being] the meddling foreigner.'[22]

After the revolution, two of Havana's three golf clubs were requisitioned for other, more practical uses, while elsewhere in Latin America, such as the Country Club in Caracas, Venezuela, and at San Isidro, Lima, Peru, golf clubs spread over prime real estate territory to give the business elites space to relax and conduct deals away from the prying eyes of the public. But once in office Castro and Guevara were keen to embark on social and economic reform, and opposition to their takeover coalesced among Cuban exiles in the u.s. In 1961, 1,500 u.s.-backed mercenaries attempted to invade Cuba in the notorious failure known in English as the Bay of Pigs and in Spanish as Playa Girón. Cuban resistance combined with inept u.s. preparation and confused leadership to produce a damning and embarrassing defeat for the invaders. The Cuban singer-songwriter Silvio Rodríguez later immortalized the events as a victory for Cuban unity and togetherness over u.s. greed and imperialism, praising the 'black men and red men and blue men, the men of Playa Girón'.[23]

Castro himself was much more explicit and combative in his interpretation. Indeed many historians think that it was the attempted u.s. invasion of 1961 that turned Castro and his colleagues into the arms of the ussr. Whereas previously they had been pragmatists aiming only to secure the best deal for their island nation, after the Bay of Pigs they became more strident in their ideological assertions.[24]

A fortnight after the defeat of the invasion, and the capture of over 1,000 prisoners, Castro gave a speech to mark the 1 May celebrations. He concluded:

> The recent invasion shows how right we were to arm. At Playa Girón, they came to kill peasants and workers. Imperialism forced us to arm for defence. We have been forced to put energy and material and resources into that, although we would prefer to put them into more schools, so that in future parades there can be more athletes and school children. If our people were not armed, they could not crush mercenaries coming with modern equipment. The imperialists would have hurled themselves on us long ago if we had not been armed. But we prefer to die rather than surrender the country we have now. They know that. They know that they will meet resistance, and so the aggressive circles of imperialism have to stop and think.[25]

In March 1961 John F. Kennedy, president of the u.s., launched the programme of peaceful economic and political cooperation that would become known as the Alliance for Progress. (It is a source of irony that the attempted invasion of the Bay of Pigs in Cuba took place just one month later.) This programme succeeded in convincing some Latin American leaders, such as President Rómulo Betancourt in Venezuela, of the benefits of closer ties with the u.s. But many Latin Americans were suspicious of these supposedly friendly gestures. After Kennedy's assassination the plan lapsed into abeyance. Nelson Rockefeller visited the region at the end of the 1960s, charged by the new President Nixon with assessing the success or otherwise of the Alliance for Progress. Rockefeller concluded:

> There is general frustration over the failure to achieve a more rapid improvement in standards of living. The United States, because of its identification with the failure of the Alliance for Progress to live up to expectations, is blamed. People in the countries concerned also used our visit as an opportunity to demonstrate their frustrations with the failure of their own

governments to meet their needs ... demonstrations that began over grievances were taken over and exacerbated by anti-u.s. and subversive elements which sought to weaken the United States, and their own governments in the process.[26]

1962 World Cup in Chile

Elsewhere Latin America was taking a more assertive role in global cultural events as an acceptable intermediary between the two super-power blocs. Chile hosted the FIFA World Cup in 1962. Chilean elites intended their hosting of the prestigious tournament to embed a sense of national homogeneity, further economic progress and enhance the country's image on the world stage. They fell short of all three of their goals. Carlos Dittborn, a Santiago football club chairman, pleaded with FIFA that 'Because we have nothing, we want to do it all.' In modern parlance the World Cup was to regenerate Santiago and leave a legacy in economic as well as cultural terms. Nevertheless the boom in local, amateur, barrio clubs in the 1940s and '50s, emerging out of widespread dissatisfaction with the professional model and the disenfranchisement of working people, was not fully incorporated into the planning and organization of the World Cup. In part this was because of the devastation and chaos of an earthquake in 1960, which left tens of thousands dead and the authorities playing catch-up to put the tournament on at all. Relatively few foreigners came to watch, and if at all, Chile in 1962 was remembered elsewhere for the 'Battle of Santiago' where Chilean and Italian players brawled on the pitch. The British commentator David Coleman described it as 'the most stupid, appalling, disgusting and disgraceful exhibition of football possibly in the history of the game', and urged the authorities to expel both teams from the competition.[27] This was not how the Chilean authorities had wanted its World Cup to be represented on televisions around the world.

The Cuban Missile Crisis

The Cuban Missile Crisis of 1962 is one of the most famous episodes in Latin American history, at least for the generation of outsiders who feared that this conflict between the two superpowers of the Cold War would trigger the Third World War and a nuclear conflict that would destroy the world. Although television documentaries and movies have sensationalized and dramatized the events around the personalities of the three charismatic leaders involved – Kennedy, Castro and Khrushchev – it is more useful to understand the crisis in its long-term perspective. As the historian Richard Gott has noted, in the wake of the Spanish retreat from Cuba in 1898, and the departure of the U.S. in 1959, 'now it was the time of the Russian empire to assume the historic role of Cuba's defender.' Cuba was 'the epicentre of the crisis although not the place where decisions were made'.[28] Raúl Castro led the Cuban negotiations with the Russians, resolving such practical problems as how to keep Russian missiles below 20°C in Cuba's tropical climate, and how to keep them hidden during the long Atlantic sea crossing. In the midst of the crisis Kennedy declared a naval blockade and made a speech on television on 22 October 1962 in which he appealed 'to the captive people of Cuba':

I have . . . watched with deep sorrow how your nationalist revolution was betrayed and how your fatherland fell under foreign domination. Now your leaders are no longer Cuban leaders inspired by Cuban ideals; they are puppets and agents of an international conspiracy.[29]

Castro responded in turn the next night, placing U.S. actions within a long-term historical perspective and calling Kennedy a 'pirate':

He asked why the Americans had proclaimed a blockade when they own the seas already. [Henry] Morgan is the owner of the seas. I don't say [Francis] Drake, because Drake was a person of some renown . . . They can search through the archives . . . but in the history of piracy they will not find a precedent for any kind of this sort of action. It is an act of war in time of peace![30]

When Kennedy and Khrushchev ended the crisis, with the USSR removing the problematic missiles and the U.S. pledging not to invade Cuba and to remove its own missiles from Turkey, there was another telling omission. The Cubans did not have a say in the final negotiations, not even Castro (in Gott's words, he was 'entirely adjacent to these events'). Cuba had been the site of this standoff, but its national sovereignty was the last thing on the minds of the global imperial leaders who held its fate in their hands.[31]

Vatican II: Latin America at the Cutting Edge of Theology

At the same time as the world's material superpowers were going head to head over Cuba, the world's self-proclaimed spiritual superpower was considering how best to apply itself to the space left to it. The Catholic Church was at a crossroads. Because of its rapid population growth Latin America was home to a substantial minority of the world's Catholics, soon to be a majority. Pope John XXIII organized the Second Vatican Council (Vatican II) between 1962 and 1965. The global gathering of bishops and advisers saw Latin America's demographic weight bear fruit as never before. The resolutions adopted by the Council were heavily influenced by the left-leaning clergy living and working in the cities and shanty towns of rapidly urbanizing Latin America, particularly the Latin American Episcopal Conference (CELAM). Vatican II allowed Catholics much greater freedom than had previously been allowed in how they would express their faith. The Medellín conference organized by CELAM in 1968 to debate the application of Vatican II to Latin America brought together the strands of the radical theology that later became known as 'liberation theology', a belief and practice that encouraged bringing social as well as spiritual succour to the poor. Liberation theology and its most celebrated exponents, particularly the Peruvian Gustavo Gutiérrez and the Nicaraguan Ernesto Cardenal, attracted much attention and admiration across the world.[32]

Guerrilla Movements

Social activism was not confined to the Church, but was a consequence of the pronounced and increasingly visible social inequalities that had resulted from urbanization and limited industrialization. For many it was but a short step from political activism to the use of political violence, and the Cuban Revolution acted in some quarters as an inspiration. During the 1960s, as the long-term durability of the Cuban Revolution became more assured, Cuba began to invest resources in attempts to export its revolution internationally. Cuban troops were sent to Angola, the Congo and North Africa, with Che Guevara a driving force behind the strategy. (Cuba was not the only Latin American country doing this: the military regime in Brazil sent its own troops to Africa as part of its alliance with the U.S., and was ready for a proxy confrontation with Cuba.[33]) When governments turned to the right, the guerrillas opposing them were naturally left-wing: the Cold War context remained important, though practical support from the USSR was largely lacking.

In Latin America Cuban-style guerrilla *focos* (small groups who would act as a revolutionary vanguard, the idea being that they would eventually be welcomed with open arms by local populations, as in Cuba) sprang up across the continent, though the resources they received from Havana were rather limited and fitful. The Peruvian poet Javier Heraud joined one such group, the National Liberation Army, in 1963 after a short visit to Cuba. He was gunned down in Madre de Dios in the Peruvian Amazon in May that same year, becoming a romantic hero to some Peruvian intellectuals, as well as to the later leftist military regime of General Juan Velasco Alvarado (1910–1977, in power 1968–74).[34] The National Liberation Army (ELN) was also founded in Colombia in the mid-1960s, inspired by the Cuban example and attracting members from both communist-leaning peasants and urban intellectuals. The most celebrated of these was the Catholic priest Camilo Torres, who saw the guerrilla struggle as an extension of liberation theology, which urged Catholics to take the 'option for the poor' and struggle alongside ordinary people rather than enjoy the luxuries of office.

Torres died in 1966, immersed in the violent struggle against the Colombian state.[35]

One Hundred Years of Solitude

While Torres was in the mountains, immersed in his revolutionary struggle, the aspiring Colombian author Gabriel García Márquez was in Mexico City writing the novel that gave him international fame and which came to represent Latin American culture and literature for millions of people for the next two decades. *One Hundred Years of Solitude*, first published in 1967, is a sprawling family saga and an allegory of the nation and continent, providing a history of the fictional town of Macondo in order to critique Latin American history from the conquest to the present day. As part of the 'Latin American boom' of literature, *One Hundred Years of Solitude* was marketed to the world as the high point of magical realism, a literary style that rendered Latin America's marvellous, unbelievable realities in exotic, overblown and fantastic prose. International readers across the continent and the world lapped up García Márquez's vivid, colourful descriptions, sardonic and humorous mocking of human vanity and frailty, and ambitious chronicling of a world in turmoil. The book made its author a worthy winner of the Nobel Prize in Literature in 1982, by which time he had become tied to the genre of magical realism, which had spawned a thousand inferior imitators. In all the fuss over the originality of its literary style, many readers rather missed one of the central theses of the book: the role of foreigners in upsetting the social order and causing conflict and despair. The Cold War context of the time it was written helps us to see this very clearly.

'The birth and destruction of the fictional town of Macondo [in *One Hundred Years of Solitude*], along with the fortunes of the Buendía clan, are an allegory for economic imperialism', as Greg Grandin has observed.[36] The coming of a North American banana company, obviously symbolizing the United Fruit Co., transforms the town, bringing a railway and electric lights but also the state and its institutions – the police and army – into the lives of citizens who had previously been peripheral and even ignored. Their independence was transformed. Banana workers attempt to protect what they see as their rights to decent pay and working conditions, and in response the army orders a massacre of 3,000 of the protesters. One of the characters, José Arcadio Segundo, struggles to put into words the violence that he witnessed during the massacre, and the cataclysmic events produced by it culminate in wiping the plantation from the face of the earth.

García Márquez became friends with Fidel Castro, but he was no Cold War extremist. Nor was he a head-in-the-sand nationalist. He, like the other 'boom' writers – the Mexican Carlos Fuentes, the Argentinian Julio Cortázar, the Peruvian Mario Vargas Llosa and the Chilean Isabel Allende – was happy to acknowledge the European and U.S. influences upon his work (particularly James Joyce, William Faulkner and Cervantes). *One Hundred Years of Solitude* links foreign arrivals with happiness, ingenuity and joy as well as economic imperialism and unwelcome overtures. But the powerful central episodes of the novel, revolving around the banana company, sprang out of García Márquez's profound rage against U.S. imperialism in the continent in the 1960s, and signalled his growing sympathy for and solidarity with the Cuban revolutionaries.

Mexico at the Centre of the Sporting World: 1968–70

In Europe the year 1968 – and especially the month of May – is often remembered in global history for its outburst of youth and cultural rebellion. Student protests gave birth, its veterans remember, to a newly energized counterculture, out of which egalitarian political and social movements emerged. Paris was the symbolic centre of the protests and young people across Europe felt that they had become part of something new and exciting and that they were going to change the world. This movement catalysed a new wave of youth travel across Europe and Asia and eventually towards Latin America.[37]

But 1968 had a very different aura in Latin America. Indeed the fallout from the death of Che Guevara – the ultimate icon of the Cuban Revolution – cast a long shadow over youth and leftist protest movements. In 1967 Guevara was hunted down and shot by the

Bolivian armed forces in collaboration with CIA agents while he was trying to lead a rebellion of the Bolivian peasantry against their national elites.[38] The widely disseminated image of his naked corpse, Christ-like with bedraggled beard and hair, served to cement his image as revolutionary martyr, which was taken up globally during the 1970s.

Rather than liberation, therefore, this was a time of increasing military involvement in Latin American politics and cultural life. In Mexico, where the Institutional Revolutionary Party (PRI) had been in power for several decades since the Revolution, its political opponents attempted to use the country's hosting of the Olympic Games in 1968 to focus international attention on the lack of respect for democracy and human rights in Mexico. The massacre of student protesters, women and children in Tlatelolco in the build-up to the 1968 Olympic Games sent a fierce message from the state that it would use all possible avenues to present a stable and secure face to the world as global media attention centred on the country.[39] The government's subsequent cover-up of the extent to which its agents had caused the violence themselves served to show how important international opinion, and the role of sporting events in directing that attention, had become. Two years later the FIFA World Cup also came to Mexico, hot on the heels of the Olympics. This was the first tournament broadcast internationally on colour televisions, and those lucky enough to see the tournament on their screens witnessed the flowering of perhaps the greatest team ever – with Jairzinho, Carlos Alberto and others. But in most minds outside of Latin America, the 1970 Brazilian team is identified solely with one man: Pelé.

In 1970 Pelé's fame was

going into orbit. Almost alone among his generation of Brazilian players he had an agent and a manager . . . he was making enough to move in an entirely different social stratum from any Brazilian player hitherto. He had been declared a national treasure, trademarked his own nickname, signed up with Pepsi Cola, been incorporated into a popular telenovela and acquired his own radio shows.

The day after Pelé scored his 1,000th goal, 'the following day's newspapers, which in every other country on the planet covered nothing but the second Apollo moon landing, were split down the middle in Brazil. Apollo 12 on one side, Pelé on the other'.[40]

Brazil's victory in 1970 was praised internationally as a triumph of style, rhythm and natural talent – all characteristics that Brazilians had been happy to claim as their own since the days of Gilberto Freyre. But the reality was that the Brazilian team was the best prepared, having been the recipient of vast attention and resources from the military regime looking to harness the popular support of the *seleção* (team) for its own purposes. The squad had its own handmade, individually tailored boots, a special kit to cope with Mexico's humidity and a NASA-inspired fitness regime. It was careful preparation and attention to detail, combined with skill, that created a memorable victory over Italy in the final. 'The euphoria that surrounded Brazil's victory in the 1970 World Cup crystallized the already intimate relationship between football and the military-political complex in the country'.[41] But in the outside world, the colourful, smiling, celebratory image of Brazil at the 1970 World Cup in Mexico – epitomized by Pelé – was established in the mindset of the footballing world as firmly as if it were carved in stone.

Military Dictatorships: Bulwarks of the Cold War

It might seem odd to see the smiling, ebullient Pelé as a product of the Cold War. But Brazil's military dictatorship was not the only one that used culture, as well as politics and violence, to preserve the regime and win friends abroad. Other Latin American countries were soon also in serious need of an image overhaul. The 1970s became, especially in the Southern Cone, a decade of right-wing, military governments that used all means at their disposal to control their populations. The longest-serving military dictator was General Alfredo Stroessner, who ruled Paraguay for 35 years until 1989. All of them were supported by the United States as bulwarks against communism.

Upon first taking power at the beginning of the Cold War, Stroessner sought to demonstrate his anti-communist credentials to the outside world. In March 1955 a colony of Ukranian settlers in Paraguay were deliberately and falsely accused of harbouring pro-Soviet tendencies (the reality was that many had migrated from the communist USSR for political reasons), and most of the male population, several hundred people, were imprisoned and tortured. "'They didn't die of old age", one of their widows remembered, "they died young, like my husband, because of what they did to them in jail". The Stroessner regime began its political clampdown on these innocent foreigners, and then applied its methods of fighting communism to the population at large.[42]

Chilean military leaders acted as though they had the full support of the Nixon administration in the U.S. to do whatever they thought necessary in order to get rid of Allende's Unidad Popular government in 1973. President Nixon met with the CIA director Richard Helms along with the directors of multinational firms worried about their business interests in Chile. According to Christopher Hitchens's account, 'a series of Washington meetings, held within eleven days of Allende's electoral victory [in 1970], essentially settled the fate of Chilean democracy.'[43] Helms's notes of his meeting with Nixon reveal a desire to prevent Allende from even assuming the presidency:

> Not concerned risks involved. No involvement of the embassy. $10,000,000 available, more if necessary. Full-time job – best men we have . . . Make the economy scream, 48 hours for plan of action.[44]

Allende's government, however, survived three years of attempts to make its economy scream. Henry Kissinger, first as National Security Advisor and then as Secretary of State in 1973, gave his full support to covert attempts to undermine and overthrow Allende, including encouraging the murder of members of the military who would be hostile to coup attempts, such as General René Schneider, Commander-in-Chief of the Chilean army, who was murdered on 25 October 1970. Kissinger famously remarked that he had no intention of allowing a country to become Marxist 'just because its people are irresponsible'.

Pelé, captured during the session 'Can a Ball Change the World: The Role of Sports in Development' at the 2006 Annual Meeting of the World Economic Forum in Davos, Switzerland.

Pelé (born Edson Arantes do Nascimiento, in 1940 in Minas Gerais) became the first global football icon in the 1950s, '60s and '70s. Playing for Santos in Brazil and later the New York Cosmos in the U.S., he scored over 1,000 goals in a career that created long-lasting images of Brazil and Afro-Brazilians across the world. It was primarily Pelé's performances in the iconic gold and green jersey of the Brazilian national team in their World Cup teams of 1958, 1962 and 1970 that made him into a global celebrity. His assurance, playfulness, grace, power and rhythm captured the minds of football fans worldwide, particularly in 1970, the first World Cup tournament to be televised in colour. After retirement from playing, Pelé successfully exploited his position and fame for financial gain, taking roles in many major advertising campaigns. He also worked within Brazil to institutionalize sport, and as a United Nations ambassador. He was a key figure in Brazil's bid to host the 2014 World Cup.[45]

In 1973 Salvador Allende's left-wing elected government was over-thrown by a military coup, the culmination of several months of street protests, strikes, economic sabotage and political unrest. Chilean Air Force planes bombed the presidential palace, La Moneda, where Allende remained with his closest aides until he committed suicide. The military leaders behind the coup asserted that they were acting solely in the national interest, and that they wanted to rescue the country from unpatriotic leftists. General Augusto Pinochet soon emerged as the most ruthless and powerful of the military junta who had taken over. Photographs of the military leaders posing in uni-forms and sunglasses were broadcast and printed around the world, presenting them as hard-hearted, stern and dogmatic individuals like movie bad guys. Indeed, like the military regimes across the Southern Cone in this period, they were much worse than that. People linked to Allende's regime, people suspected of being political opponents and people who participated in activities that the junta deemed politically suspect (like amateur football, folk music or trade union-ism) were rounded up and detained in concentration camps. The most famous of these was the singer Víctor Jara, who was tortured and murdered in the Estadio Chile football stadium after having been ridiculed by his guards and asked to sing them a song.[46] Tens of thousands of Chileans were killed or disappeared.[47]

Human rights organizations, still in their infancy in this period, were catalysed to act to support the victims of the military regime and thousands of Chileans sought refuge and asylum elsewhere in Latin America, across Europe and in the UK. Solidarity groups were formed to support the exiles and fundraising concerts made the events in Chile central to many Europeans' notions of what Latin America was about. The spectacle of Andean pan-pipe bands touring city centres across the globe also dates from this period.

Having reached power on the back of strong international (though often covert) support, once in government Pinochet was able to return the favour. His administration sought to overturn the social-ization of the economy at which Allende had aimed, and wanted to tone down the power of the state ministries and bodies that the socialists had used to foment nation building and redistribution of wealth. Pinochet's economic advisers, Chileans who had trained in the theories of Milton Friedman at the University of Chicago, decided to use the Chilean economy to test what at the time were radical economic theories in terms of deregulation and privatization. The so-called 'Chicago Boys', while Chilean, came to be associated with the interests of U.S. investors and a small Chilean economic elite – who all benefited from these policies – as opposed to the majority of the Chilean people, who saw a great division between rich and poor being created in their country, which had previously been one of the most equal in Latin America.[48] Naomi Klein elaborated her theory of the 'shock doctrine', combining economic warfare and military intervention in a society, based on events in Chile in this period: she called this combination 'the Pinochet option'.[49]

Being an ideological ally of Ronald Reagan and Margaret Thatcher in the 1980s certainly helped Chile in economic terms, and within the Cold War context Pinochet was seen as a bastion against communism in a country where Marxists had been peacefully and democratically voted into office as recently as 1970. The Chilean armed forces were rewarded (and kept loyal) by a guaranteed slice of the national budget drawn from profits from the copper industry; much of this budget was spent on the latest gadgets and hardware from the U.S. and British arms industries. In 1989 Pinochet suffered a surprise (to him and his supporters, at least) loss in a referendum on whether he should continue in power, and he was eventually replaced as head of state by a succession of centre-left politicians from the Concertación alliance, culminating in Michelle Bachelet (2006–10), who had herself been tortured by Pinochet's administration in the 1970s. Bachelet was also Chile's first female head of state, and her continuing popularity secured her return to the presidency in 2014.

In 1993, when I was working as an English teacher in the centre of Santiago, Margaret Thatcher – herself recently booted out of office, though by a nervous Conservative Party rather than the electorate – came to Chile as she was promoting her memoirs. She visited Augusto Pinochet – though no longer president, he was still head of the armed forces and a senator – to thank him for his support and friendship over the years and, perhaps, to talk about the next batch

Augusto Pinochet (1915–2006) was the leader of South America's most notorious and repressive Cold War military dictatorship. He ruled Chile from the 1973 coup that ousted President Salvador Allende (who committed suicide in its midst) until a 1989 referendum on his continuing rule saw Chileans choose to begin the transition to democracy. Born in the Chilean port of Valparaíso, Pinochet entered the army at an early age and by the early 1970s was a senior and active opponent of Salvador Allende's leftist Unidad Popular coalition government. On 11 September 1973 he was one of the group of military officials who orchestrated the rebellion against Allende's rule, capitalizing on a drawn-out campaign to erode the economic basis of the government's legitimacy, fully supported by U.S. covert operations. The coup was violent and repressive, with suspected political opponents being locked up, tortured and/or murdered. Pinochet and the junta justified the coup by saying: 'the internal and external security of the country is in danger. The survival of our Independent State is at risk. If the government remains in power, it will prejudice the interests of the Republic and the Sovereignty of the People.'[50]

Pinochet quickly became the figurehead of the military junta and in the mid-1970s embarked upon a series of economic

The Chilean military junta and its head, Augusto Pinochet (centre front), in the Diego Portales building to celebrate the new constitution, 1973.

reforms masterminded by the Chicago Boys, a group of Chilean economists who had been trained in neo-liberalism in the U.S. The break-up of state monopolies and the privatization of strategic industries and education created an economic bonanza for the rich and those linked to the government while increasing inequality and pulling away safety nets from the poorest in society. Chile came to be seen as a success story of the International Monetary Fund and for free marketeers such as Margaret Thatcher, and during this period Chile imported great numbers of British weapons to support the dictatorship. While the referendum removed him as head of state, Pinochet remained as Commander-in-Chief of the armed forces until 1998, during which time he continued to cast a dark shadow over attempts to modernize and demilitarize Chilean society. In 1999 Pinochet was arrested in London and threatened with extradition to Spain to face charges of engineering the disappearance of thousands of Chilean citizens during his time in power. After lengthy legal and political manoeuvring he was released to return to Chile on medical grounds, where he survived another six years. In death he continues to symbolize the deep fractures and wounds in Chilean society which he had done so much to create.

of British aircraft to be ordered by the Chilean armed forces. I remember quite strikingly the respect in which Thatcher was held by the mainstream Chilean press, especially when she showed unexpected weakness by fainting in public the day after her interview with Pinochet.

The story of Pinochet's relationship with Great Britain had a tragicomic end. Flush with the proceeds of his sixteen-year term of office, Pinochet had taken to visiting doctors in London's renowned Harley Street to deal with his various medical problems. In 1998, to international amazement, Pinochet was arrested by the Metropolitan Police as part of an investigation into whether he should be extradited to Spain, where the authorities wished to try him for human rights abuses committed during his time in office, ostensibly against Spanish citizens in Chile. Pinochet and his supporters were incredulous; the Labour administration – many of whose supporters had campaigned against Pinochet in the 1980s – found itself stuck between its own declared 'ethical foreign policy' and the fear of legal precedent and the calls of treachery from Pinochet's supporters, both in London and back in Chile. Eventually, as is the way in these cases, a fudge was found. Pinochet was declared physically unfit to be prosecuted and was allowed to return to Chile, where he died surrounded by friends and family in 2006.[51] Like Stroessner, who died in exile in Brazil, and sundry other deposed military leaders, Pinochet was allowed the peaceful death that he denied to so many of his compatriots.

Chilean society remained fractured by the actions of the military government in the Cold War. Political activism and egalitarianism, once open and freely debated, became closed and hidden as people feared those who might betray them. Hesitant moves towards truth and reconciliation happened in Chile, as in Argentina and Peru, only a decade or more after most of the perpetrators had retired or died. In the search for justice, reparations and the acknowledgement of past crimes, the long support offered by international allies and NGOs played a major role.[52]

One of the most notorious transnational collaborations during the period of right-wing dictatorships in the Southern Cone was Operation Condor, in which 'disappeared' people, generally political prisoners or so-called social undesirables, were flown in aeroplanes over the Atlantic and dumped, often still alive, into the ocean. This probably represented the most extreme – though there is a lot of competition – and desperate abuse of human rights during this most terrible of periods. The use of the aeroplane as a method of murder is perhaps horribly reflective of the large numbers of human victims of air travel in Latin America. Beginning with Jorge Chávez, the Peruvian who died in the first air crossing of the Alps, there have been a run of mysterious and not-so-mysterious deaths linked to aeroplanes in the region. The direct opposite of Operation Condor is the celebrated 'miracle of the Andes' in 1972, when a Fairchild plane carrying the Old Christians Rugby Club from Montevideo to Santiago de Chile, via Mendoza in Argentina, crashed on top of the mountain. The perils and tribulations suffered by the survivors, who resorted to cannibalism while they awaited rescue, were immortalized in the film *Alive* (1993) and numerous television documentaries.[53] There were no survivors of Operation Condor.

1978 World Cup in Argentina

The 1978 World Cup held in Argentina is often held up as the prime example of a dictatorial, repressive regime manipulating sporting events in order to massage their own international profile and to win internal popularity by harnessing the emotive power of international sport. As historians and eyewitnesses have gradually revealed what happened in 1978, it has come to surpass anything that fictional writers could have invented.[54]

It is not that nothing was known in the outside world about human rights abuses in Argentina in the 1970s. News of the regime's use of forced 'disappearances' and the torture or murder of political opponents had reached international governments through the new human rights organizations that spread in the 1970s. The thousands of exiles who left Argentina in these years also took news with them, and sometimes founded solidarity groups in their new countries to raise awareness of the ongoing struggles back home. Amnesty International launched a targeted information campaign but, as Ezequiel

Fernández Moores has revealed, European companies turned a blind eye so as not to lose investments in sponsorship. Mercedes-Benz, Siemens and Telefunken all chose to continue their involvement with the competition.[55] Some European football players, most notably the German Paul Breitner, made political gestures, but most decided that Argentinian politics was none of their business. Within the Argentinian squad, players including Alberto Tarrantini had lost friends to political witchhunts even during the build-up to the tournament. Even they had mixed feelings about the event. Leopoldo Luque remembered:

> The fans seemed to forget the poverty and the deprivation in the big cities. . . . You could see in their eyes just how much it meant to them. We laboured under a huge responsibility to win the tournament for our people and help them to forget their suffering. How could we not win the World Cup for these people?[56]

Perhaps the least of the accusations against Jorge Videla's military regime was that they bribed or bullied the Peruvian national team to lose a key qualifying match so that Argentina could progress. Allegations that each Peruvian player received cash, or that Argentina loaned the Peruvian state many millions of dollars in free credit, or that 35,000 tonnes of grain were shipped to the Andean nation, all have some supporting evidence. One of the Peruvian players, Raúl Gorriti, told Jon Spurling that Videla and his security guards entered the Peruvian dressing room just fifteen minutes before kick-off, intimidating them so that they lost their nerve. Peru lost 6–0, and a wave of conspiracy theories were launched.[57]

During the 'dirty war' employed by the state against people it believed to be its opponents, there were many improvised torture chambers set up across the country. One of these was at the Argentine Navy Mechanical School, located within earshot of the stadium. Prisoners and their guards could hear the cries of joy each time a goal was scored. The players and the fans, however, could not hear the cries of pain from the torture camp. In 2009 the Argentinian footballing hero Ricky Villa (who later scored perhaps the most iconic goal at Wembley Stadium, for Tottenham Hotspur in their FA Cup Final victory over Manchester City) went to meet several of the Mothers of the Plaza de Mayo. This group has spent decades campaigning – most visibly by marching around the Plaza de Mayo in the centre of Buenos Aires – and demanding justice for their disappeared loved ones. 'But why didn't you speak out at the time, Ricky?' they asked him. Perhaps the career Villa enjoyed in the UK, alongside his compatriot Osvaldo Ardilles, provides part of the uncomfortable answer.[58] But they were not alone in preferring to remain silent about the sufferings of 1978.

The Cold War in Latin America was distinguished only by the often inexplicable horror of the atrocities launched against its own people. With hindsight, and as official documents have become available, some sense has been made of this period. No doubt historians will in the future be able to tie some of the threads together better than we have been able to do until now. Some good did come out of these years. In combating abusive regimes the seeds of a human rights movement in Latin America came into being, a movement that has been progressively strengthened through the 1990s and 2000s. We have seen that Latin America was far from a passive victim of the Cold War and that local leaders and peoples appropriated geopolitical moments for their own interests. Latin Americans also engaged in external Cold War interventions of their own, such as the Argentinian veterans of the Dirty War who gave counter-insurgency and military assistance in Central America; the Colombians who fought in the Korean War; and the Cubans who fought in Angola.[59]

Latin America became a defiantly and proudly nuclear-weapon-free continent during the Cold War, the final confirmation of a long trajectory towards disavowal of these weapons which had begun with the support given to the UN Committee on Disarmament in its various forms in the 1960s. In 1968 the Non-Proliferation Treaty was signed by countries worldwide, and Argentina, Brazil and Cuba were the only late signatories. In this Latin American states act as a beacon of the possible to the rest of the world, showing how through patience and negotiation the most destructive weapons can be laid aside.[60] The experience of negotiating transitions out of military regimes has enforced Latin America's 'multilateral orientation', meaning that the region is much better disposed towards working collaboratively than other countries with recent imperial pasts that have accustomed them to working on their own by necessity.[61] The development of the North American Free Trade Association (NAFTA), Mercosur (Southern Market) and the Free Bolivarian Association of the Americas (ALBA) in the post-Cold War years are testimony to this, though at the time of writing each is undergoing its own stresses and faces an uncertain future. Certainly there has been no lack of initiative in developing new forums and alliances within Latin America and its surrounding regions since 1990. The number of conferences organized by the Organization of American States involving heads of states, of specific ministries, is testament to the power of multilateral initiative.

Finally the Cold War saw Latin American states stake their claims to Antarctica. Argentina and Chile both asserted territorial sovereignty to parts of the southern landmass, and both these claims overlap with the British claim. It is to be hoped that the Antarctic does not become the focus of an oil- or other resource-driven desire for exploitation. If European powers were to come into conflict with aggressive Latin American states with a closer geographical claim, this would be another type of war altogether. As other imperial powers – the U.S. and the USSR – retreat from the region, older territorial colonial legacies could once more return to the fore.[62]

SEVEN

Violence and Exoticism

The 1980s witnessed many Latin American governments that were in thrall to the economic power and military might of the United States. Only Cuba was really able to avoid this trap, aided by stubbornness, support from the USSR and belief in the destiny of its national revolution, despite the fact that it suffered in economic and political terms from the trade embargo enforced by the U.S. until the present day. U.S. power was generally exerted through economic strength, close relations with collaborative Latin American elites and occasional use of force. The rise of the international trade in illegal narcotics in this period was closely linked to U.S. hegemony in Latin America, as the U.S. market was the major destination of all the narcotics produced in Latin America. The illegality of one of Latin America's major export products created enormous scope for sub-terfuge and extraordinary episodes in its history in these years. Drugs money and covert U.S. operations often appear as likely factors in unexplained events. On 24 May 1981, for example, Jaime Roldós, the president of Ecuador, died in a plane crash, the causes of which were never established because of the lack of a black box recorder onboard, and on 31 July 1981 Omar Torrijos, the leader of Panama since 1966, died in another plane crash whose causes have never been satisfactorily explained. Both leaders had followed policies that were not in line with those of the U.S., and it has been suggested that both deaths were murders carried out by U.S. covert operatives.[1]

Neo-liberalism, the IMF and the World Bank

The political scientist Javier Santiso has described this period as one when 'the entire continent danced an endless waltz of paradigms, changing step in time to the topics, lessons and consensus from the north'. The early 1990s Washington Consensus was perhaps the most widely adopted of these paradigms, urging as it did fiscal discipline, low inflation and structural economic reform. It resulted in large-scale privatizations, withdrawal of the state from certain areas including welfare and the promotion of free trade, all of which often ended up benefiting foreign investors and multinationals rather than the governments who introduced the policies.[2]

Scholars such as Francisco Panizza argue that during this period, governments and economic administrators across the region came to implement broadly similar economic policies for the first time since the general move to import–substitution–industralization of the 1960s. Commentators have, with hindsight, branded the economic policies of the late 1980s and early '90s 'neo-liberal', though this term was not used by anyone at the time. The neo-liberalism running through the 1980s and '90s made the continent resoundingly less equal since the gap between rich and poor – measured in terms of living standards, income and access to services – grew ever wider. Of course, this was not the World Bank's, or indeed anyone's, intention. In the 1980s especially the World Bank 'considered structural adjustment and market-led economic growth to be the primary means for reducing poverty'. Only in the mid-1990s was there recognition that market-led development might not bring the poor out of poverty on its own; hence the increasing fondness of Latin American countries for targeted monetary transfers like the Bolsa Familia (family allowance) in Brazil, a government welfare programme which directed cash into the accounts of poor families with minimal mediation.[3]

Reliable statistical evidence seems to support the link between neo-liberal economic policies and increasing inequality. The best way of measuring inequality is via the Gini coefficient, which measures the distribution of households according to total household income. It runs from 0 to 1, and the lower the Gini coefficient, the more equal the society. Uruguay has long been held to be one of the most equal societies in Latin America. In 1967 the Gini coefficient for households in the capital, Montevideo, was 0.33. It rose substantially during the 1980s, hovering between 0.41 and 0.44, before dipping back to 0.38 in 1993.

In Chile the Gini coefficient for households in Santiago was 0.5 in 1968, and had dropped to 0.47 by 1971, possibly as a result of Allende's government's attempts at wealth redistribution. From 1978 through to the mid-1990s the Gini coefficient rose above its previous level, remaining between 0.52 and 0.54 during the 1980s and '90s and suggesting a considerable rise in inequality during the Pinochet years.

As a final example, Brazil showed a clear trend towards accentuated inequality from the 1960s through to the '90s, ranging between 0.57 and 0.65, during which time it was the most unequal country in the continent. The peak of inequality occurred during the 1980s when structural economic reform, urged under the Washington Consensus, was having considerable social consequences across the country. One of the major achievements of the Cardoso and Lula presidencies since 1995 has been to focus on this and reduce inequality. In 2011 the Gini coefficient had been reduced to 0.52, its lowest recorded level in Brazil.[4]

The Peruvian novelist and 2011 Nobel Prize-winner Mario Vargas Llosa dryly appreciates the ironies here. In 1990 he ran in the Peruvian national presidential elections as an avowedly neo-liberal candidate against a dry but populist independent candidate, Alberto Fujimori. Vargas Llosa proclaimed that what Peru needed was an economic shock and readjustment to global circumstances. He acknowledged that this would have unfortunate but necessary negative short-term consequences. Fujimori and his supporters portrayed Vargas Llosa as an unpatriotic, callous outsider who had spent too long living outside the country (in Spain, France and the UK) and who must therefore be bereft of feelings for the economic well-being of ordinary Peruvians. Fujimori won the popular vote and duly followed an economic policy almost identical to that on which Vargas Llosa had campaigned. Fujimori also made a stark change in policy with regard to the ongoing guerrilla violence of the Shining Path, paying little heed to human rights legislation in a militarization of the conflict which resulted in an escalation of rural violence and, eventually, the capture of the Shining Path's leader and principal ideologue Abimael Guzmán. Fujimori's links to Japan (from where his family originated) won Peru some important trading concessions and investment opportunities: the number of Japanese cars on Peruvian roads increased dramatically in these years but power brought corruption and numerous abuses. Fujimori's government took the neoliberal ideology to new lows in the late 1990s, instituting a National Population Programme which aimed to limit population growth through mass sterilizations. Over 300,000 people were sterilized, most of them poor women from rural areas. Neoliberal doctrines dictated that health workers were given challengingly high targets for the number of operations to perform per month, regardless of the consent of those being sterilized. The country's first president of Asian origin was removed from power in 2000 (resigning via fax while on a visit to Japan) and remains in prison in Lima at the time of writing, having been given a long jail sentence for specific human rights abuses, and pleaded guilty to corruption and abuse of power.[5]

From the Falklands/Malvinas War to Diego Maradona

By 1981 the increasingly divided and incompetent military regime in Argentina led by General Jorge Videla had exhausted most of the short-term popularity it had won through organizing the World Cup triumph of 1978. Human rights abuses were brought to international attention ever more often by groups such as the Mothers of the Plaza de Mayo and increasing inequality was creating discomfort and anger on the streets. The junta decided to invade the Falkland Islands/Islas Malvinas, expecting that Great Britain would not have the resources, interest or political will to fight for them and that the military regime would thereby win some easy nationalist political kudos. An expedition formed of hundreds of young recruits was sent across the South Atlantic to occupy these last colonial outposts, which had long lost their significance to Britain as refuelling stations where ships had been loaded up with coal in the old days of steamship travel.

Neither side had a particularly convincing claim to sovereignty over the islands. Argentina had only briefly registered an interest between securing its own independence from Spain in the 1810s and the British occupation that began in 1833. Britain had used the islands principally as a coaling station through the late nineteenth century to supply its ships before or after they rounded the southern point of South America. The opening of the Panama Canal in 1914 drastically reduced the importance of that transoceanic shipping route, and the British presence in the Falklands for the subsequent years is best symbolized by the image of Isambard Kingdom Brunel's famous ship the ss *Great Britain* – the world's largest and fastest iron-hulled ship when it was launched in Bristol in the 1860s – which lay beached near Port Stanley in the Malvinas through the 1930s, '40s, '50s and '60s after it had finally ceased to be used as as a floating warehouse and coal barge. In 1970 a group of Bristol-based enthusiasts floated the wreck back across the Atlantic, apparently symbolizing, for the Argentinians who followed the news, the end of the British Empire's presence in the Falklands/Malvinas.

At least, that is what General Videla and his junta thought. British attempts at diplomatic negotiation were half-hearted, as the foreign secretary, Lord Carrington, and his friends could scarcely believe that the Argentinians would do something so rash as invading. Each side misunderstood the other. When news of the Argentinian invasion reached London Margaret Thatcher recognized the opportunity to win some political prestige for herself on the back of a potential military victory over Argentina. A Falklands task force was sent across the Atlantic. The actual war itself was relatively short, far more Argentinian than British troops were killed and the British flag was raised again in Port Stanley. The failure to regain the islands created a festering sore in Argentinian political discourse to the present day; in Britain refusal to negotiate over the sovereignty of the islands is one of few absolute foreign policy prerogatives that transcend political allegiance. The British colonial presence in the islands was actually increased as a result of the war: military defences were reinforced, a cricket club was formed and generous subsidies were awarded to British agriculturalists there.

In Argentina from 1982 the Malvinas became one major foreign policy objective that could unite much of the nation. In the 1982 World Cup, held just weeks after the end of the war, Argentina was not drawn against any of the teams from the UK, and a petulant young Diego Maradona was sent off against Brazil as his team failed to fulfil their potential as defending champions. In 1986, however, at the World Cup held in Mexico, things were different.

In 1986 Diego Maradona was at the peak of his footballing powers. In the quarter-finals of the World Cup in Mexico he led his Argentinian team out to play England. His first goal he scored with his hand, punching the ball into the net over the head of the English goalkeeper Peter Shilton, who had his eyes closed (as, apparently, did the referee). Maradona's second goal redeemed him in the eyes of everyone who saw it, either in the stadium or the millions watching on television. He dribbled round almost every English player with great intricacy and at incredible speed. He later described the goal, and its meaning, in his autobiography:

> When I was growing up in Fiorito I used to dream of one day scoring a goal like that on the pitch, and I did it in a World Cup, for my country and in a final. Yes, a final, because, for us, that is what it was, we were playing a final against England. Because it was about beating a country, not a football team. Even though we said, before the match, that football didn't have anything to do with the Malvinas, we all knew that a lot of Argentinian kids had died out there, that they had killed them as if they were little birds . . . And this was revenge, it was about getting back at them for the Malvinas. We all said, before the match, that we shouldn't mix things up, but this was a lie, a lie! We thought of nothing else – of course it wouldn't be just another game!
>
> It was about more than just winning a match, about dumping the English out of the World Cup. Somehow we blamed the English players for everything that had happened, for everything that the Argentinian people had suffered. I know that

Diego Armando Maradona (born Buenos Aires, 1960) was the greatest footballer to emerge from Argentina. The child prodigy from Fiorito epitomized the *pibe*, the kid with the flair, technique, skill and cunning to outwit his supposed elders and betters. From Boca Juniors to Barcelona, Maradona was hailed for his skills and the victories he gifted to his teams, and he went from there to Napoli. The new wealth he created with his feet he spent on socializing and presents for his family and hangers-on; he was also expert at using the new commercial opportunities of a globalizing world to maximize the financial benefit of his skills. In Italy his links with the criminal underworld became celebrated and scorned in equal measure, yet this was the scene of his greatest national footballing achievements. Representing his country with enormous pride, he led Argentina to victory as captain and star player in Mexico in 1986. In 1994 Maradona was thrown out of the World Cup in the u.s. after testing positive for cocaine use; from there his rancour and disillusion with sport sprang into fervour and engagement with left-wing politics, spells in Cuba and then a return as coach to the Argentina *selección* at the 2010 World Cup in South Africa. His team dazzled and then crashed to earth.[6] At the time of writing he is a tv celebrity.

Diego Maradona at the 2012 GCC Champions League Final.

it sounds crazy but that's the way we felt. The feeling was stronger than us: we were defending our flag, the dead kids, the survivors . . . [7]

Sport, in Maradona's hyper-emotional terms, had become a surrogate for warfare, an opportunity for the militarily defeated to inflict pain on the victors through whatever means. In addition to the Falklands/Malvinas conflict, the strong British influence on Argentinian economic and cultural life over two centuries may have created this subconscious desire for revenge. It is of course possible that Maradona was not aware of the luxury department store Harrods in Buenos Aires, the polo club and the substantial British community in the city and the pampas, or of the British construction of the railways, or the Barings Bank crisis that nearly bankrupted Argentina and left Britain relatively unscathed in the 1890s. But from a global perspective we can see the British unwillingness to relinquish the Falklands in 1981 and subsequently as part of a reluctance to step back from 200 years of close engagement with Latin America, an engagement which left significant economic, social and cultural legacies – of which this late imperial conflict over sovereignty is but one manifestation. (Each individual brings their own upbringing and ideology to the historical circumstances that shape their lives, of course. Leo Messi, the most talented footballer in the world since Maradona, and another Argentinian, plays in Europe for Barcelona. I have been unable to locate his opinion on the Falklands/Malvinas debate: Messi is a very different sporting and political animal from Maradona.)

Sport and Globalization

It is not difficult to identify other examples of ways in which increasing globalization, after the spread of cheaper air travel in the 1970s, brought Latin American sportspeople into career moves that transcended their origins in the developing world. The wave of baseball players entering the u.s. from the Dominican Republic, Cuba and Venezuela is a good example, with only a small minority reaping, like

Pedro Martínez, the dreamed-of rewards. The rest return home to watch the glamour on television. The LA Dodgers built a training camp in Santo Domingo in 1976 in order to stand the best chance of spotting, cropping and harvesting the best young Dominican players: this strategy has since been replicated by many other teams. In Santo Domingo the Campo Las Palmas director Rafael Avila told the young hopefuls: 'This is a test. If you fail here, you will return to your villages broken. Your family's future is in your hands.'[8] Of course, the hoovering up of young, impoverished talent into transnational scouting networks for the benefit of multinational, corporate sporting teams has become as common in baseball in the Dominican Republic as it is in football in West Africa or Brazil. Latin American footballers have become firmly established as part of the Turkish, English, Italian, Spanish, French and Russian leagues. Many have been extremely successful, such as Faustino Asprilla at Parma and Newcastle; Leo Messi, Ronaldo and Romário at Barcelona; Ivan Márquez at Inter Milan; or Hugo Sánchez and Ivan Zamarano at Real Madrid.[9] But other Latin American footballers have struggled to make the cultural transition from their own countries, suffering homesickness, adaptation problems or simply loss of form. The examples of Robinho at Manchester City and Juan Sebastián Verón at Manchester United are well known because the hugely inflated size of their transfer fees provoked great media attention and scurrilous reporting that brought them down to earth.[10] The challenge in the twenty-first century is to avoid the perils that befell the first generation of globalized sportspeople from emerging countries. Luis Suárez, the Uruguayan footballer who played for Ajax in the Netherlands and then Liverpool in England, might appear to be a case in point. Suárez had been widely criticized for his apparently cavalier attitude towards sportsmanship and foul play and was accused of racism, a case that was brought to a tribunal in 2011. Suárez was found to have used racist language against the black French defender Patrice Evra during a match between Liverpool and Manchester United. Suárez's defence was that the language he used was not supposed to be offensive, and that skin colour is routinely used in verbal speech and banter in his country of origin. He was banned for eight matches by the Football Association, and given lots of rather stern lectures by the media on the place of race-related language in the UK. But of course the bottom line in the globalized sports industry is money, related to performance, and during his time at Liverpool Luis Suárez was far and away the team's most effective player and its highest scorer, despite his various suspensions, including one for biting an opponent.

Suárez was the object of much criticism in the British media. His actions were deemed by commentators as un-British and as representative of the negative consequences brought about by the introduction of Latin American players. Liverpool FC staunchly defended Suárez from the racism charge and the FA tribunal revolved around the linguistic semantics of the context and tone in which words were used.[11] In the medium term Suárez's unique skills and talents on the pitch probably protected him from what might otherwise have been career-ending mistakes.[12] In other areas Latin Americans in European-dominated sports have often been the victims, rather than the perpetrators, of unsportsmanlike behaviour.

The best example here is cycling, specifically Colombian cycling. Because of a peculiar combination of French cultural influence with British expatriate mechanics in late nineteenth-century Bogotá, mixed with easy access to the nascent rubber industry and a challenging, mountainous topography, road cycling became a popular national sport in Colombia in the 1920s and '30s in a way that was unique outside Europe at the time. Colombia produced cyclists who were hardy, born at high altitudes and used to training there, and who therefore had the high number of red blood cells required by endurance athletes. The Vuelta a Colombia, or Tour of Colombia, was promoted enthusiastically by the new national radio stations whose poetic commentaries on the cycle race and the national territory it passed through united the nation in mid-century. This happened just as the country was turning in on itself and beginning half a century of civil warfare after the nationwide riots and looting that followed the assassination of the populist lawyer and liberal politician Jorge Eliécer Gaitán in April 1948.

Lucho Herrera and Fabio Parra were the two Colombian cyclists who spent years on European television screens in the 1980s, winning

Luis 'Lucho' Herrera (born 1961) was the Colombian cyclist who burst on to the European sporting consciousness with a series of devastating attacks in the Alps and Pyrenees during the Tour de France and Vuelta a España in the 1980s. His tiny frame, focused black eyes and unalterable resilience made viewers on television aware that this most Eurocentric of sports could be mastered by men from the ignored peripheries of the Andes.

Herrera came from Fusagasugá in Cundinamarca, and as a child rode bicycles in the thin mountain air as a way of getting around. He was soon spotted for his speed and endurance and enjoyed a spectacular amateur career in the 1970s. But it was his role in the Café de Colombia teams in the major European tours, alongside other Colombian climbers such as Fabio Parra, which immortalized him and gave his country a lasting sporting reputation worldwide that rivals that of Brazil and Argentina in football. Clad in the polka-dot jersey of the best climber in the tour, images of Herrera scaling mountain peaks with breathless Europeans trailing behind him were as vibrant a way of asserting Colombia's presence on the world stage as any other individual or group had achieved.

stages of the Tour de France and demonstrating impenetrable race faces with an apparently natural and symbiotic relationship with the mountains that they climbed. Behind Herrera and Parra, however, other, less gifted Colombian cyclists were used by the big European teams to trial training techniques, diets and performance-enhancing drugs before they were handed to the major French, Italian or Spanish leaders of the big teams. As Matt Rendell has shown in *Kings of the Mountains*, his splendid book on the history of Colombian cycling, these Colombian cyclists were the guinea pigs of professional cycling because of their lowly national origins and their relative lack (compared to the Europeans) of big financial clout or sponsorship. Many of these Colombians paid for their lack of status with their lives.[13] Some Colombian cyclists who continued living in the country in the off-season, such as Lucho Herrera, were kidnapped by guerrillas seeking financial ransoms. Since 2010 a major investment in young Colombian cyclists has begun to yield fruit. In 2013 Nairo Quintana finished second in the Tour de France, and Rigoberto Urán came second in the Giro d'Italia. Greater international success seems just around the corner.

The International Drugs Trade

Rumours linking cyclists with drug abuse were routine in the 1980s, of course, and methods were much more improvised and risky than Lance Armstrong's now notoriously well-planned and strategized doping scheme of the 2000s. But it was in the 1980s that Colombia itself became intimately linked in international public opinion with drug cultivation, drug trafficking and the violence that was intrinsically tied to narcoculture. Admittedly, some retired cyclists got mixed up in drug trafficking, just as Colombians from all sections of society did, as the so-called black economy came to dwarf legal economic transactions in the country in the early 1990s.

Drugs, especially cocaine, became in the 1980s the principal stereotype with which the world pigeonholed Latin America. The Andean countries where the coca leaf was traditionally grown were the first to be linked to cocaine, as quickly an economic system was set up in which coca leaves were grown in Bolivia or Peru, then transported to Colombia, where they were treated and manufactured into cocaine.

Colombia became the manufacturing centre and transhipment locus from which illegal narcotics were distributed to lucrative markets, first in the U.S., then Europe and eventually the rest of the world. Key to the evolution of this profitable enterprise were first, the decision of consuming regions such as North America and Europe to keep cocaine use illegal; and second, the risk-taking and gall of early entrepreneurs in and around Medellín, Colombia, who took on all rivals, used violence to protect their interests and maximized profit at every turn. The representative individual and chief villain in many accounts of this behaviour was Pablo Escobar.

On 27 November 1989 an assassin hired by Escobar planted a bomb on an Avianca plane from Bogotá heading for Cali. It exploded over Soacha in central Colombia, killing 110 people. The intention was to kill the presidential candidate César Gaviria, who was not in fact on the plane. Victims that Escobar did reach included Luis Carlos Galán, at the time the Liberal candidate for the presidency of Colombia, and the minister of justice, Rodrigo Lara Bonilla. In 1993 the number of homicides in Colombia reached 95 per 100,000 people, compared to the rates of 20–39 deaths per 100,000 that had been customary even during the period of intense political violence between 1960 and 1980.[14] The U.S. declared a War on Drugs against Colombian traffickers, though the amount of cocaine entering the U.S. declined only slowly.[15] In 1993, with Escobar's death, the illegal cartels learned that smaller operations and lower profiles would be their best chance of evading capture. They also learned from Escobar's mistakes, seeing that corrupting the Colombian state and its institutions (the judiciary, the police, the military and border officials) would be much more successful and lucrative than taking it on in an all-out war. Escobar's death in 1993 certainly ended his reign of terror against moralistic Colombian officials. But the amount of narcotics smuggled to the U.S. and the rest of the world did not decline – indeed it has consistently gone up ever since, following demand. The rise of paramilitary groups in Colombia in the 1990s

Pablo Escobar (1949–1993) was the drug trafficker who unleashed a private army of thousands of young assassins (*sicarios*) against his rivals and against the Colombian state in the 1980s and '90s. For many people outside of the country, Escobar came to epitomize the callous disregard for human life that seemed to consume Colombian society during this civil war. His outrageously extravagant materialist excesses – the parties, the prostitutes, the private zoo, all of which he enjoyed even when he was theoretically a prisoner of the Colombian authorities in the prison they allowed him to build, La Catedral – grabbed sensationalist media attention worldwide. The drugs trade from Colombia to the United States – first marijuana, then, with unprecedented financial benefit, cocaine – gave the ruthless young Escobar the route to move upwards through Colombia's famously stratified and hierarchical society.

But no matter how wealthy Escobar got, he always craved the social acceptance which could never completely be his because of his lowly origins in a Medellín barrio, the incredible, savage and relentless violence he employed and, least importantly, the illegal nature of his earnings. He tried his hardest through populist gestures such as providing social housing for the poor, building sports fields for the deprived and, later, by becoming a Liberal politician and senator. But eventually the U.S. was goaded into making him their Public Enemy Number One, and rival cartels allied themselves with paramilitaries and the Colombian military and intelligence services in order to kill him. He was shot fleeing across Medellín's rooftops. His death put only a temporary dent in Colombia's cocaine exports to the United States, though it did mark a serious reduction in the country's homicide rates, which were the highest in the world during Escobar's reign of terror.[16]

was originally catalysed by desires to combat Escobar and his narco-traffickers outside the reach of the law. But these groups quickly morphed into drug-trafficking entities themselves, and the long-standing Colombian leftist armed groups the FARC and the ELN were also drawn into the narcotics industry by virtue of the profits to be gained from channelling drugs and funds through the substantial sections of the Colombian territory that they controlled. By the mid-1990s it was no mistake to say that each gram of cocaine purchased in New York or London was helping to pay for ammunition or weapons that would kill Colombians, and Colombian agencies repeatedly made this argument, to little avail. By 2012 the UN estimated that 3.6 million Colombians had been displaced by the violence since 1997, much of this either directly related to or fuelled by the illegal narcotics industry.[17]

By 2000 some international observers had come to think that it was time to talk about the legalization of the drug trade in order to diminish the potential profits offered to those unscrupulous enough to use violence to protect their interests. The stories of displaced peoples repeat and emphasize the pain caused by the conflict.[18] Partially in response to the increased militarization of the Colombian anti-narcotics policy, much of the drug-related profits and violence have in recent years migrated to Mexico. Mexican citizens have begun to feel the brunt of the clash between regular and private armies and the damage to their institutions caused by a rampant illegal economy, contraband and corruption.[19] There are two constants in the history of drug trafficking in Latin America in the last quarter-century: the victims are primarily Latin American and the consumers are primarily not.

Political Violence and its International Context: Peru

One side effect of the increasing Colombian monopoly on the cocaine industry during the 1980s and '90s was that it gradually filtered proceeds away from armed groups elsewhere in the Andes. Peru's armed conflict was at its most intense in the late 1980s and early '90s. The Shining Path group were inspired by Mao Zedong and the Peruvian intellectual José Carlos Mariátegui, and they took their brand of revolutionary politics to the Peruvian highlands, achieving remarkable popularity in the lands around Ayacucho where their founder, Abimael Guzmán, had been a lecturer in philosophy. Shining Path extended a reign of terror across the Peruvian country-side and into the cities in the late 1980s, but theirs was primarily a national strategy, and their victims were often indigenous or poor mestizo Peruvians who happened to find themselves on the wrong side of the conflict. The Truth and Reconciliation Commission, held at the end of the violence, eventually concluded that the Peruvian armed forces' attempts to fight back against the Shining Path and other groups had caused more deaths than the rebels themselves. All sides waged wars using fear and extortion as their weapons, and of the estimated 70,000 deaths, the vast majority were innocent civilians rather than rebels or soldiers.[20]

Peru's other major armed rebel group in this period was the Movimiento Revolucionario Túpac Amaru (MRTA), named after the Inca hero who had fought against Spanish colonialism, but actually a Marxist revolutionary group much more closely linked to, and inspired by, the Cuban experience. The MRTA was hit hard by the militarization of the conflict under President Fujimori in the early 1990s, as the Shining Path had been, but in 1996 it launched its most famous and audacious attack. In order to garner maximum publicity for their cause, and to maximize their possibilities of success, the MRTA elaborated a plan that would guarantee it attention from the international community.

On 17 December 1996 MRTA members disguised as waiters took over the residence of the Japanese ambassador in Lima, where he was hosting a diplomatic reception to which all the great and good of Peruvian society had been invited. President Fujimori had not been able to attend, but the Foreign Minister was there, alongside many ambassadors, cultural figures, business leaders and other politicians. The stunt attracted media attention from across the globe, since many countries had citizens among the hundreds of hostages. At the time I was working for Amnesty International at their Lima office, a dozen blocks from the compound, and we were deluged with requests for background information on the MRTA and what they might want or do.

The MRTA's public pronouncements requested the release of their colleagues being held as political prisoners in Peruvian jails, calls for greater social equality in Peru, attacks on the neo-liberal economic policies being carried out by Fujimori's administration and demands for the lessening of the Japanese influence in Peruvian development organizations. As time went on the International Red Cross, the Archbishop of Lima, Juan Luís Cipriani, and a team of international ambassadors negotiated the liberty of all of the foreign hostages, leaving 72 male Peruvians inside. As the siege continued international public attention waned, only to be startlingly re-awakened on 22 April 1997 when Peruvian commandos stormed the building from tunnels excavated beneath the residence and from neighbouring properties. Rumours of the impending attack, and the involvement of U.S., Israeli and/or British special forces, had long been circulating in Lima. (The noise of the tunnels being dug had been hard to conceal, even by playing loud rock music.) Most of the MRTA members were playing their daily game of indoor football when the armed forces entered, and therefore were unarmed. All of the MRTA members were killed in the episode, in which all the hostages were freed. This provided a substantial boost to Fujimori's flagging popularity, both nationally and internationally, and he ruled for another three years. The combination of violence, utopian visions and melodrama made this a popular episode of Latin American history for the outside world's news agencies, and Ann Patchett's novel *Bel Canto* (2001) captured some of it in fiction.

The kidnapping of foreigners briefly became a standard and lucrative business rather than a one-off experiment for the FARC guerrilla organization in Colombia. Although accurate comparative statistics are not available, before drug trafficking infiltrated the organization around the mid-1990s, kidnapping and other forms of extortion provided the group's principal revenue streams. Foreigners, either those working for international firms or naive tourists, were regularly captured and held in isolated regions until friends, family or insurers paid out ransoms of thousands or millions of dollars.

Explicit admissions as to the extent of ransoms paid were seldom made, but the memoirs written by released hostages make it plain that this is what happened.[21] The payment of international ransoms was another way in which non-Colombians contributed to financing the violence in the country.

Traffickers used drug mules as a means of transporting hidden parcels of cocaine directly to their markets. Mules were often low-status individuals who hoped that they could make enough profit from one journey to set themselves up for life. Initially they came solely from the country of origin of the drug to be transported; then, as customs officers became smarter at selecting individuals to be stopped and searched – and travelling on Colombian or Peruvian passports became an easy way to guarantee being stopped in airports – the mule industry also became globalized and more cosmopolitan. In 2008, for example, 8,500 people were arrested in Spain for trafficking cocaine into or within the country. Of these 61 per cent were Spanish (and most likely responsible for much of the internal trafficking). The picture is likely to be similar elsewhere. Although the actual 'bulk of the trafficking towards Europe still seems to be in the hand of Colombian organized crime groups', individuals of diverse nationalities were being arrested in Spain with drugs in their possession: 970 Colombians, 288 Moroccans, 249 Dominicans, 151 Nigerians, 113 Ecuadorians, 110 Romanians, 72 Portuguese, 26 French and 37 Britons.[22]

Music and the Cultural Representation of Latin America on the World Stage

Horrific though the examples above are, the 1990s also saw global-ization create avenues though which a more positive image of Latin America could emerge out of the shadow of decades of news reports and fictional recreations of economic failure, dictatorships, guerrillas and violence. The increase in the number of television and radio channels through the 1980s made space available for non-standard musical genres, and foreign language films, to reach much wider audiences across the world. At first exiled left-leaning bands such as Inti-Illimani and Illapu from Chile dominated the Latin American sections of world music stores, and with their carefully chosen exotic instruments – most famously the pan-pipes and the charango – they gained wide followings. Inti-Illimani, who spent long years in Italy, came to combine the folkloric instruments that had made their names before the 1973 coup with classical motifs and full orchestral arrangements. Their 1999 album *Sinfónico*, recorded after Inti-Illimani returned to Chile during the transition to democracy, is a marvellous melding of the two influences on their career and representative of the historical forces that created them in the 1970s shaped them during exile.

Folk groups like Inti-Illimani and political vocalists like Mercedes Sosa were never likely to reach the kind of stardom that was offered by the commencement of dedicated music television channels such as MTV, which launched in 1981. One Latin American who did reach a broader audience was Juan Luis Guerra, the Dominican merengue artist. The cool rhythms and sensuous dancing were combined, in Guerra's performances, with lyrics evoking a sense of common endeavour with the people. His most famous song, '*Ojalá que llueva café*' (1989), reflected on the plight of farmers during economic hardship, and its refrain – 'I hope it rains coffee' – was one of hope in the future and the improvement of opportunity and equality. Merengue had been popularized by the dictatorship of Rafael Trujillo in the 1950s and '60s as a central part of the Dominican national identity he wanted to forge. Juan Luis Guerra and many other bands took it out of the Dominican Republic and spread its style across the Spanish-speaking world, to the extent to that today scholars talk of 'diasporic merengue'.[23]

As pop culture became increasingly globalized, Latin American musicians who dropped their politics – or who didn't have any to speak of – were able to develop a global reach. In this they built on the pioneering success of artists like Pérez Prado and Celia Cruz, and others who made their names in salsa and merengue clubs in the U.S., particularly New York.[24] Crucial to any crossover success was singing in English, however. The principal precondition of Gloria Estefan's success, for example, was that her Latin American roots were originally pushed to the background, and that she sang in English.

Estefan (born 1952) was the most successful 'Latin' pop star in the U.S. to emerge during the MTV period of the 1980s and '90s. Her route to fame, as well as her musical trajectory, is very revealing of many of the processes traced in this book. Like many Cubans born in the mid-twentieth century, Estefan's grandparents had migrated from Asturias, northern Spain. Her father worked as a bodyguard for the wife of President Fulgencio Batista, so upon the triumph of the Cuban Revolution the Estefan family went immediately into exile in the U.S., settling in Miami when Gloria was seven. After taking a university degree in Psychology and French, Estefan worked as a translator and interpreter at Miami International Airport, where she was once approached by the CIA to infiltrate Cuba as a U.S. spy.[25] Estefan's singing career began in English but this changed with the 1993 album *Mi tierra*, which featured the longing title track about Cuba, calling the island 'The land that aches, the land that gives', and lamenting that 'your land sighs if you are not there, you cannot forget the land where you were born, because it has your roots and what you left behind'.[26] From then until the present she has continued to be a vocal supporter of Cuban opposition movements based in the U.S.[27] Gloria Estefan made her name as a pop star in the U.S., and then worldwide, singing in English with her band The Miami Sound Machine. In her later career she has sung as often in Spanish as in English, balancing the tightrope of remaining 'mainstream' while reaching out for authenticity by singing in her mother tongue and touching on subjects with supposed 'Latin' rather than 'Anglo' appeal.

One artist who took the opposite direction, and with it achieved even greater success, is Shakira. In the autumn of 2012, when revising an early draft of this book, I asked some of my first-year undergraduate students at the University of Bristol to name the most influential Latin American alive. (My final-year and second-year students had named Lula da Silva, Hugo Chávez and Gabriel García Márquez.) My first-year class, who were all born in or around 1994, were unanimous that Shakira was the most significant living Latin American. Their explanations were revelatory. Although the majority of the class were female, all the students agreed that she was a role model for women in terms of achieving success in a male-dominated environment while remaining authentic and true to her own identity, her roots and her social conscience. In this Shakira's charitable work through her Pies Descalzos foundation, which provides educational opportunities to underprivileged Colombian children, has been as important as her music.

Shakira's success in the global marketplace might be explained by the way that she has marketed her sexuality, specifically her exotic, sensuous, somehow Colombian sexuality, to the voracious male voyeurs who watch her music videos. But probably even more important is the fact that she appeals to females as much as males, with an identity that encourages and revels in male attraction but clearly sets out her own control of the encounter. Her 2005 duet with Wyclef Jean, 'Hips Don't Lie', is a classic lesson in the exoticization of Shakira's Colombian origins and sexuality, drawing attention to the language barrier and using it as a signal to further interest and attraction, but given greater power by her singing partner being a black Haitian rapper, as both acknowledge in the salsa- and Cumbia-style song's lyrics.[28]

For her millions of fans, Shakira evoked a sense of authenticity and pride in her own identity that inspires people across the world to be happier in their own skins and sexualities. This was a major achievement. Latin American pop stars who have achieved success in the u.s. have not all been able to bask so easily in the acclaim. Perhaps they were only too aware of themselves as artificial constructs of the media and music industries, forced to flaunt exoticism and sexuality that they did not feel at home with. The example of Ricky Martin, the Puerto Rican pop sensation of the late 1990s, is a case in point. Born in 1971 as Enrique Martín Morales, he was a child star with a boy band and then went on to solo success. His 'Livin' La Vida Loca' combined Spanish with English phrases in order to target the crossover markets and remind viewers and listeners in the Anglophone world of his difference and sensuous nature. It was over a decade after this major success that Martin felt able to come out as homosexual, despite and perhaps because of the constant rumours and scaremongering about him in the press and online. Martin's difficulty to come out as a homosexual, despite his large gay following

Shakira Isabel Mebarak Ripoll (born 1977) was born in Barranquilla on Colombia's Caribbean coast into a family of Middle
Eastern heritage. A child prodigy, her singing and dancing brought
her national attention as a teenager; she achieved her international breakthrough with her third album, *Pies Descalzos (Bare
Feet)* aged just eighteen. Shakira was recognized for her tuneful
songs and was equally adept at rock 'n' roll and dreamy ballads.
Her own brand of belly dancing was crucial in launching her as
a global megastar and made her a fixture on music television
channels in the late 1990s. Exploiting her visual image as the
personification of Latin American exotica, Shakira embarked upon
a deliberate strategy of anglification, learning English and producing both English and Spanish versions of her next albums. In
this way she was able to remain a classic star in Latin American
music as well as transcending her sex symbol status in English-
language music. Buoyed by her stratospheric commercial success,
Shakira launched her Pies Descalzos Foundation, which promotes
early years education in poor areas of Colombia. In 2010 her song
'Waka Waka (This Time for Africa)' was the theme of the FIFA
World Cup in South Africa; the video for it was downloaded half a
billion times on YouTube. At the time of writing Shakira is by far
the world's most famous Colombian, and dedicates herself as
much to motherhood, her charitable projects and mixing with the
global philanthropic elite as to her music.

Shakira on the red carpet event for *The Voice* season 4, House of Blues, West Hollywood.

in concert halls across the world, perhaps says something about the limits placed upon Latin American global superstars and the conditions within which they are able to access contracts, publishers and concert tours. With his own charity foundation now working against human trafficking, Martin is following Shakira's lead by using his wealth for philanthropic causes and on behalf of Latin Americans unable to access the opportunities that he has had.

Shakira and Ricky Martin may be the most celebrated of the many examples of Latin Americans who asserted themselves and promoting their cultures on the world stage at the end of the century, surfing the waves of globalization and leveraging maximum benefit from their skills, beauty and/or good fortune. They provide an interesting end point for this chapter. The 1980s and '90s were on one level a 'lost' period for social and economic progress in the continent, with economic crisis, defaults, hyperinflation and political turmoil the backdrop to gradual democratization. Francisco Panizza has argued that the returning democracy took a while to embed itself, strengthening as it did civil society and buttressing wider socioeconomic indicators of well-being. Although several major traditional Liberal and Conservative parties did virtually go to the wall, this did not bring the end of political organization. New political parties, such as the Partido Trabajador in Brazil, which eventually brought Lula da Silva to the presidency, stepped up to fill that vacuum. The ascent of the free market in the 1980s and '90s may have been a tough time for activists trying to organize from the bottom of society up, even with international support, but it did create a certain degree of strength and resilience in civil society, which began to flourish in the beginning of the twenty-first century as economic conditions changed. Latin American leaders were also a degree freer to control their own destinies in the new century, because the previous regional superpower, the u.s., had other things on its mind.

EIGHT

Unleashed from Empire?

D id Latin America's relationship with the rest of the world change on 11 September 2001? The critic John Beverley thinks so, suggesting that Latin American cultural politics have been qualitatively different since 11 September 2001. This, he argued, was because of the sharp opposition between the 'pink tide' of left and left-of-centre governments gaining power in Latin America and the increasingly aggressive neo-conservatism holding influence in Washington. It is certainly the case that something changed in u.s. policy towards Latin America on that date, though it was probably due to rising indifference rather than conscious political change.[1]

This chapter examines the years between 2000 and 2014, culminating with the awarding of the 2014 World Cup and 2016 Olympic Games to Brazil by the international football federation (FIFA) and the International Olympic Committee (IOC). Is there a new recognition that Latin America has shed its dependence on the rest of the world, that it has negotiated the globalized world with the new confidence of Venezuela's Hugo Chávez and Brazil's Lula da Silva? What about the rise in mass migration from Latin America to Europe and North America? Are we simply seeing renewed *interest* in Latin America rather than any qualititative change in relationship, because of the demographic movements and the so-called Latinization of the u.s.? How significant are these new Latin American diasporas?

I was in Bogotá on 11 September 2001, researching my doctoral thesis. Dedicated as I was to my studies, and anxious not to waste a minute of my precious time in the archives, I remained in the manuscripts room of the Biblioteca Luis Ángel Arango all day even when the news of events in the U.S. broke. I listened to radio coverage along with the archive supervisor, and only saw the images for the first time on the cover of the special issue of the newspaper *El Espectador* when I walked back to my room in the suburbs that evening. I had been planning to go along to see what reception Colin Powell, U.S. Secretary of State, would get on his visit to the city that evening. Press reports had suggested that students were preparing a protest against the U.S. presence in Colombia but, of course, Powell never came to Bogotá – he went straight back to the U.S. With hindsight Powell's decision to drop everything symbolizes the Bush administration's attitude to Latin America after 9/11. Plan Colombia, which had been President Clinton's expensive attempt to purchase an end to the drugs and guerrilla wars in Colombia, was now shifted primarily into Colombian hands to try to achieve the project's aims of ending the long civil war. U.S. Relations with Mexico and much of South America were reduced to endless statements that free trade agreements were the only game in town. Indifference and incompetence governed U.S.–Latin American relations. The attempted coup against Hugo Chávez in Venezuela in 2002 was a farce precisely because everyone involved seemed to be waiting for someone better organized or better briefed to come in and sort it out. No one did, and despite the U.S. funding and encouragement, Chávez returned to power, re-energized and more determined than ever to blame Bush – whom he mockingly called the 'devil' and 'Mr Danger' – for Venezuela's often considerable economic ills.

The preoccupation of the United States political and military elites with the Middle East, Iraq, Afghanistan and Pakistan benefited Latin America in many ways since 2001, enabling its leaders to have more confidence in their own paths towards the future, and to be less fearful about the consequences of not towing the continental line (though the president of Honduras, Manuel Zelaya, overthrown by a military coup in 2008, the legitimacy of which was allowed to go unquestioned by Hillary Clinton, might have a thing or two to say about that, as might Fernando Lugo, the leftist Paraguayan priest who was booted out from office by a recalcitrant congress in 2011 with only a very tenuous constitutional framework for their actions).

There have been many social, economic and cultural changes in Latin America in the last decade that suggest new roads and processes for the future, as well as many continuities with the past.

Projections of New Latin American Voices and Testimonies

One of these changes has been in Latin American writing. The blending of fantasy and reality that was magical realism – *lo real maravilloso*, in Alejo Carpentier's famous formulation – has now been succeeded by a literary voice more rooted in reportage, journalism and documentary film-making. The genre of *testimonio*, though critiqued by some scholars outside the region as essentially inauthentic, has given a voice – or rather, a channel through which to publicize that voice – to groups in Latin American societies that previously remained outside the mainstream.

The most famous work of *testimonio* in the late twentieth century was *I, Rigoberta Menchú*, written by a Guatemalan woman of indigenous heritage who told a vivid and often shocking tale of her involvement in the country's civil warfare. Menchú was later awarded the Nobel Peace Prize for her efforts to protect human rights in the midst of appalling conditions both for herself and for her people (discussed in the previous chapter). Academics in the discipline of Latin American Studies, both in the u.s. and in the uk, have emphasized the crucial role of Elizabeth Burgos, the France-based anthropologist who played a key role in transcribing and shaping Menchú's voice in the bestselling text. The debate over what is and what is not a *real* voice of indigenous Latin America deflected attention away from the social and political injustices in Central America that Menchú sought to highlight, and to which her Nobel Prize (for Peace, not Literature) was meant to draw attention.

The rise of *testimonio* as a literary genre was reflected by the use of first-person testimony for political motives as a way of healing wounds caused by past conflicts. Democratic successor or transitional administrations, such as those of Alywin and Lagos in Chile, Menem in Argentina or Paniagua and Toledo in Peru, felt or were unable to use the criminal courts to try military dictators or people

who had committed abuses of human rights under military dictatorships. Inspired by the South African Truth and Reconciliation
Commission, and with an equally strong religious backing, Latin
American democracies invested large amounts of resources, effort
and hope in storytelling. In the short term there were considerable
disappointments. In Guatemala in 1998 the publication of a report
by the Archdiocese of Guatemala into human rights abuses during
the military conflict, titled 'Never Again', led to the assassination of
the principal author, Bishop Juan José Gerardi, at his home.[2]

In Chile and Argentina the findings of Truth Commissions
enabled more accurate accounts of what had happened during the
military dictatorships to be written and publicized, focusing on the
extent of human rights abuses and disappearances that had not been
reported or documented during the dictatorships themselves.[3] In
Peru the publications of the Truth and Reconciliation Commission
exposed the involvement of state forces in the political violence of
the 1980s and '90s, which in numerical terms overshadowed the
number of murders committed by the Shining Path. Outside of Latin
America these commissions won media attention and much praise
from international human rights organizations. It was hoped that
this bout of truth-telling would prove cathartic and that these societies would never again descend into the downward spiral of political
violence, secrecy and partisanship. With the world watching and
attentive, it was hoped, human rights in Latin America would be
better protected. Within these societies now declared 'post-conflict',
however, the commissions and their detailed, documented reports
were not able to fully close circles of violence, betrayal and revenge.
Legal cases against Pinochet and Fujimori, and against the many
surviving Argentinian officers who had been complicit in torture,
rumbled on outside of the international media spotlight.

The most obvious example of a writer who employed a kind of
testimonio to step out of the shadow cast by magical realism is
Colombia's Héctor Abad Faciolince. Reacting against his compatriot
García Márquez at the same time as being inspired by him, Abad's
biggest selling book so far, *El olvido que seremos* (*Oblivion, A Memoir*,
2006), combines the whimsical and romantic autobiography of the

author's early years with a gritty, document-based history of Medellín in the late 1980s. At the centre of both strands is the author's father, Héctor Abad Gomez, whose affectionate, indulgent and endearing bond with his only son accentuates the heartbreak of the final chapters as Abad Faciolince details the minute-by-minute chain of events that led to his father's murder by paramilitaries in broad daylight in the centre of Medellín in 1987. For the reader the book is tear-inducing and life-affirming. For the author literature comes to give testimony to the terrible experiences of Colombian society during the apogee of paramilitary power in the late twentieth century. Abad Faciolince tells how

> For many years, I secretly kept this bloodstained shirt, with lumps that turned brown and black with time. I don't know why I kept it. It was as if I wanted to have it there to goad me, to keep me from forgetting whenever my conscience grew numb, like a spur to memory, like a promise to avenge his death. When I wrote this book I burned [the shirt] too, since I understood that the only revenge, the only memento, and also the only possibility to forget and to forgive, consisted in telling what happened, and nothing more.[4]

Remembering the past with honesty and without embellishment has become the ambition of these authors, essential to providing the region with the possibility of a future with sovereignty and social justice. Crucial to this endeavour is the translation of their literature into French, English, German, Chinese and other languages, so that Latin American realities can be known as widely as possible and lessons learned from the past.

The Pink Tide

The three most pressing issues affecting Latin America in the twenty-first century are nations, regionalism and globalization, according to the international relations expert Gian Luca Gardini.[5] In terms of nations Gardini sees the rhetoric about a so-called pink tide of

Luiz Inácio Lula da Silva, or **Lula** (born 1945), became president of Brazil in 2003 and quickly came to represent a modernized Brazil that was open to foreign investment, self-confident and financially stable, all in marked contrast to the corrupt, bankrupt and unstable regimes that in the eyes of the world had preceded him. Lula was a trade union organizer who became the central figure in Brazilian left-wing politics in the 1980s, standing unsuccessfully several times until finally being elected as the first new president of the twenty-first century. With his trademark beard and charismatic smile he seemed to represent the occupation of power by the leftists who had long been frustrated in opposition. Yet Lula could only stay in power by manipulating the existing political structures, maximizing political relationships of clientism and sensibly redistributing the proceeds of the raw materials bonanza linked to Chinese investment. He became personally associated with the Bolsa Familia and Forme Zero programmes, with their stated aims of remedying inequality through raising living standards at the bottom end of society. On a continental scale he forged good working relationships across Latin America, and not only with the pink tide of leftist governments.

Lula was a pragmatic leader who recognized that Brazil's growing economy could be employed to make it a regional powerhouse, rather than looking exclusively to Europe, Asia or North America for its allies. To Lula can be attributed much of the success of Mercosur as a trading bloc and the increasingly fraught efforts of the richer global north to reach trade agreements with the poorer global south. The culmination of Lula's strategy to make Brazil a true global power will be the designation of a permanent seat on the UN Security Council, long a goal of Brazilian foreign policy. The staging of the World Cup and the Olympics is aimed at demonstrating Brazil's centrality to the world of culture. Lula thought that Brazil was improving its position in the world, telling a journalist in 2006 that 'in the past, if the United States sneezed, we caught pneumonia. Today, if the United States sneezes, we sneeze too.'

Lula da Silva, 35th President of Brazil, 2007.

left-leaning governments (initially Bachelet's Chile, Lula's Brazil, Chávez's Venezuela and Kirchner's Argentina) as masking a wider and more significant pragmatism that has influenced most Latin American states as they deal with the effects of post-Cold War globalization. One good example of a state that has projected a leftist image since 2002 is Argentina, initially under the leadership of Néstor Kirchner. Kirchner (like his successor, his wife Cristina Fernández) maintained the support of social movements by approaching elections on a largely populist and nationalist ticket. He was able to present his government as resisting imperialism and the global forces that had undermined Argentina during the financial crises of previous years, while continuing to do business with the world, particularly through expanding exports.[6]

Commentators across the world remarked on how Lula and Bachelet embraced economic pragmatism and managed to use commodity export wealth to maintain popularity through wealth redistribution. There were other attempts to manipulate free markets in favour of equality. 'Fair trade' became a brand that consumers of coffee and bananas in the u.s. and Europe looked for to legitimize their purchase. The Fairtrade Foundation label and the marks of other fair trade organizations aimed to guarantee to consumers that profits would be directly relayed back to the producers rather than being siphoned off by multinational conglomerates. For coffee this has been a relatively successful endeavour during the past decade – many of the major brands now market themselves as 'fair trade' companies, though specialists continue to dispute the details.[7] The production and sale of bananas is much more problematic. Foreign banana producers in Colombia were found to have paid paramilitary fighters to protect their plantations in the 1990s. European Union quotas heavily distorted the banana market in order to protect former colonies of the UK and to disadvantage Latin American producers. Nevertheless Ecuadorian and Costa Rican bananas have managed to infiltrate major overseas markets in the last decade. 'Ecuador has fought tenaciously for unrestricted access to the EU banana market . . . how far that could have benefited growers is uncertain. In the increasingly cut-throat competition for market share, the prize tends to go to those whose workers accept the lowest pay', as Gordon Myers argues.[8]

Perhaps the most delightful example of this ability to combine political principle and economic reality was Hugo Chávez's anti-imperialist speeches, which caused great offence in the u.s., while maintaining and indeed cementing close trade links, especially in petroleum, with that very same country.

Marketing Indigeneity

The test for this new pragmatism comes not from suit-wearing states-men but from areas of the continent where the indigenous popula-tion remains in the majority. The concept of 'indigeneity' has been used to strike up comparisons, parallels and collaborations with indigenous groups across the continent and the world. There have been some considerable successes in getting the concerns of indigenous peoples in the Andes, Central America and Mexico onto global agendas. The Zapatista movement in Chiapas, Mexico, was one attempt in the 1990s, using the imagery of the leftist guerrilla groups but with a new language focusing on negotiation, acceptance, tolerance and transformation. Subsequent movements in Ecuador and Bolivia in particular have focused the minds of their govern-ments on how to protect the interests of the indigenous peoples who make up the majority of their countries' populations. The politics of these governments have sometimes been labelled 'ethnonationalism'.[9] One good example of ethnonationalist policy is how these govern-ments have sought to persuade the UN or the broader international civil society to 'buy' reserves of gas and oil that lie beneath indigen-ous lands and/or sites of particularly environmental importance (such as the rainforests that provide homes for most of the planet's biodiversity), revealing where the fault lines of potential conflicts may lie in the future.[10] The natural environment has long been a marker of the success or failure of economic progress, and a symbol of nations' abilities to live in harmony with forces larger than human-kind, as Rupert Medd has recently shown for Peru.[11] President Morales of Bolivia has emerged as one of the key figures here.

Juan Evo Morales Ayma, known as **Evo** (born 1959), has put Latin America's indigenous communities firmly at the centre of global discussions of rights, environment and commerce at the beginning of the twenty-first century. Born into an Aymara family in the Bolivian provinces, Morales worked with his parents as a subsistence farmer before moving into organized politics. First coming to national attention as a labour organizer in the 1980s and '90s among producers of the coca leaf, Morales owed his political rise to his ability to straddle traditional left-wing, class-based activism and those indigenous groups long excluded or marginalized from Bolivian politics.

In the wake of several national political crises, triggered by neo-liberal economic policies enacted by traditional leaders taking instructions from the World Bank and free-market economists, Morales was elected president of Bolivia in 2006 as the candidate of the Movement for Socialism (MAS). Despite strident opposition from landowners, some businessmen and separatists in the Santa Cruz region, Morales's government successfully pursued its agenda of 're-founding' the Bolivian nation-state. Bolivia has been declared 'plurinational' in its new constitution, representing the equality of all of the many indigenous communities and language groups who are Bolivian citizens. New agreements have been sought with foreign hydrocarbon firms with the aim of ensuring a fairer distribution of the profits from the exploitation of oil and gas deposits.

Crucial to Morales's ideology is the affirmation of diversity within Bolivia, and this carried him into regional alliances with Hugo Chávez in Venezuela and their Bolivarian project of closer Latin American integration. Although not the first indigenous president in Latin American history (that was Benito Juárez, in Mexico in 1858), Evo Morales has become a constant reference point for people across the world who now know that America's indigenous peoples are not the docile, excluded communities they were once thought to be.

Evo Morales, 80th President of Bolivia, 2006.

Morales speaks of Bolivia's problems within a global context:

> Unless we put an end to the capitalist system, it is impossible to imagine that there will be equality and justice on this planet earth. This is why I believe that it is important to put an end to the exploitation of human beings and to the pillage of natural resources, to put an end to destructive wars for markets and raw materials, to the plundering of energy, particularly fossil fuels, to the excessive consumption of goods and to the accumulation of waste.[12]

Increased communication between indigenous groups across the continent, especially via the Internet, means that they are able to co-ordinate their claims and elaborate strategies to push forward claims to citizenship and agrarian reform, for example; this continental scope makes them more effective. In this their actions mirror those taken at state institutional level. Gardini puts much faith in the ability of transcontinental economic and political organizations to act as bulwarks in support of democracy, economic progress and environ-mental security in twenty-first-century Latin America. Analysing the growth of Mercosur, the Andean community, the Organization of American States and the Inter-American Court of Human Rights, Gardini asserts that the 'quest for regional unity remains strong'. But at the same time he acknowledges that the pull of indigeneity and growing localism as a response to globalization means that unity, nationalism, regionalism and diversity continue to pull in opposing directions on most occasions. As Peter Wade has shown, concepts of race and ethnicity in Latin America are rooted in everyday cultural practices: that means they continue to trigger political actions and loyalties. In Brazil, this has meant the increasing pride displayed as a 'black nation', as part of the expansion of commercial and cultural links with Africa under presidents Cardoso, Lula and Rousseff.[13]

On the local level the effects of globalization have transformed environments, cities and individual lives. Wendy Call studied the effects of globalization on the Mexican isthmus of Tehuantepec over several decades. She describes, in her book *No Word for Welcome* (2011), a longstanding defender of village life who had resisted urbanization and the construction of a highway. Eventually a branch of the u.s. supermarket chain Wal-Mart (Aurrera in Mexico) opens just down the way. The man eventually takes his five-year-old son to the shop. Call reminds us that 'the four-lane highway and the Wal-Mart are highly visible signposts of globalization, while the istmeños' victories are invisible, nonevents'. The man and his son don't buy anything: they play and enjoy the free air conditioning.[14]

A final example of the unexpected consequences of globalization for local and indigenous cultures in Latin America is the mountain-ous peak of Aconcagua, the highest summit in the Americas. With the arrival of air travel and the professionalization of mountaineering equipment, the Plaza de Mulas – the base camp for those hundreds of people annually who scale the peak – has become an English-speaking, dollar-exchanging, cosmopolitan hangout. Plaza de Mulas demonstrates that 'if globalization is about the homogenizing tendencies of dominant particularities, then it is u.s. culture that tends to set the daily routine.'[15] Parts of Latin America have become adjuncts of the global adventure tourism industry. In Plaza de Mulas, as in Aguas Calientes by Machu Picchu, local identities and politics can only now exist in relationship with or in opposition to these continuing foreign presences. The guides who take tourists up the mountains remain proud of their lands, and able to tell stories and negotiate encounters for their own benefit and for the benefit of their towns and peoples.

Chinese Commercial Expansion

One of the principal themes of media commentators on Latin American matters in the last few years has been the expansion of Chinese financial and commercial power into the region. It is very easy, but probably misguided, to foresee a waning of u.s. influence creating space for a growing Chinese hegemony. Yet this book has attempted to demonstrate the very different types of imperial opponents from which Latin Americans have defended themselves, or which they have welcomed with open arms, over the last two centuries. After the relative autonomy allowed by Spain and Portugal, upset only by attempts at reform and imperial crisis, followed the free-trading commercial power of Great Britain, the 'informal empire' and the cultural influence of France, Italy and Germany. Then, seeping westwards and then southwards from the mid-nineteenth century, came u.s. imperial expansion, with territorial acquisition at its heart and a sense of Manifest Destiny compelling its agents to overthrow rulers and assert its values. In the Cold War the u.s. came up against a similar foe in the Soviet Union, catalysing a new period of covert interventions and political violence alongside the struggle for commercial predominance.

Since 2004 China has invested its excess of capital in the parts of Latin America that contain the raw materials it needs to feed its growing manufacturing and industrial sectors: Chile, Brazil, Ecuador, Argentina and Peru. President Hu Jintao visited the region in 2004 and catalysed a huge boom in commerce from China. Initially China invested solely in raw materials but in recent years it has expanded into other sectors. Peruvian and Chilean exporters, for example, now provide over 80 per cent of China's fishmeal imports, which go to feed Chinese chickens, and therefore Chinese workers.[16] China has sought to divide and rule Latin America to some extent, preferring to develop bilateral relationships with favoured client states rather than working with regional bodies. This stymied the attempts of Hugo Chávez and others to build regional economic and political blocs that might in future resist the incursions of foreign powers. Although Chinese power has created new hopes of a South–South axis that thwarts the continued influence of the U.S. and Europe, it is also 'clear that Chinese companies are changing Latin America. But what is not clear is how Latin America is changing to deal with this.'[17] It is certainly apparent that renewed extraction of raw materials for export abroad is again having significant effects upon Latin America's natural environment. Ecuador, for example, has received major Chinese investment in its oil industry, and the government of Rafael Correa has received major criticisms from the environmental and indigenous groups that once supported him.[18]

High commodity prices have benefited Latin American producers this century, especially since early 2006. China, North America and the EU are all big purchasers of Latin America's raw materials. The profits that sales of oil, metals, gas and agricultural produce have accrued for private companies and nationalized state companies have been employed variously in state building, welfare and redistributive projects, the enrichment of elites and a more expansive foreign policy. The global financial crisis of 2008 had a limited effect in Latin America, compared to the U.S. and Europe, because the region's banks were not exposed to toxic assets to the same degree. However, between 2009 and 2013, the numbers of tourists visiting the region has not escalated to the number that had been hoped for, and inward investment from the U.S. and Europe has stalled. Tourist numbers do continue to rise, however, as travelling Greeks and Spaniards are replaced by travelling Chinese, for example. Remittances from Latin Americans living abroad have also continued to rise, bringing U.S.\$64 billion to the region in 2009.[19] It is also to be expected that Chinese communities that trace their history back to nineteenth-century migrations to Latin America will enjoy an increase in political power: for example, the estimated 4.2 million Peruvians who have some Chinese lineage and whose presence in Peruvian life is most obviously observed in the more than 4,500 popular *chifa* restaurants in Lima, which blend Chinese and Peruvian cuisines.[20] The quesion of whether this cultural position will translate into political power remains moot.

Hugo Chávez and the New Independence

Even as Latin American leaders look to the future, they ground their political discourse, and the way they look at the world, upon their countries' histories. One good example is the way the mortal remains of Simón Bolívar have been treated and debated in contemporary Venezuela. Bolívar's remains (excluding his heart, which stayed back in Santa Marta, Colombia, after his first exhumation in 1842) lie in what is now the National Pantheon in the centre of Caracas, which was consecrated as such in the 1870s under the watchful eye of the caudillo President Antonio Guzmán Blanco. Guzmán Blanco is famed for his attempts to modernize Venezuela, to overhaul its urban planning in the model of Haussmann's Paris, and for his populist authoritarianism. Guzmán Blanco gave the definitive shift to the Bolivarian cult, erecting statues, renaming avenues and orchestrating the publication of the 32 volumes of Bolivarian documentation assembled by Daniel O'Leary (who died in 1854 as British ambassador in Bogotá, Colombia).[21] Whereas in the 1870s the National Pantheon occupied a secluded, rural setting in between urban Caracas and the northern mountain range separating it from the Caribbean – and with an awe-inspiring view of the city, combining peace and tranquillity with scope and horizon – it has now been fully overtaken by

Hugo Chávez (1954–2013) was one of the dominant figures in Latin America's relationship with the rest of the world in the early twenty-first century. A mestizo with ancestral roots in Venezuela's indigenous and black populations, he was a populist president who came to define his politics as 'socialism for the twenty-first century'. Born in provincial Venezuela's interior plains, in 1992 he led a failed coup attempt against the democratic government of Carlos Andrés Pérez, which had implemented neo-liberal shock economic policies that triggered widespread anger and resentment. When released from prison, Chávez began his mainstream political career, winning the presidential election of 1998 on the back of generalized dissatisfaction with the political elite, and proclaiming that he would govern in the manner of Simón Bolívar.

Chávez presided over a new constitution that put participatory democracy at the heart of the state and pledged to redistribute the country's oil wealth away from the rich and towards the poor, especially the urban poor. A crucial part of his programme was his

Hugo Chávez speaking at the 2003 World Social Forum in Porto Alegre, Brazil.

internationalism, embracing Iran, China and Libya and trying to rebuild Bolívar's dreams for a united Latin America, most obviously with his Alianza Bolivariana para las Américas (ALBA). A master of the lengthy televised address, Chávez presented himself as everyone's favourite uncle, cracking jokes, singing songs and being rude about political enemies, both within the country and abroad. His bête noire was George W. Bush, whom Chávez labelled 'Mr Danger' during a speech at the UN in 2004, a nod to the novel Doña Bárbara (1929) by ex-Venezuelan president Rómulo Gallegos. Chávez survived a brief U.S.-backed coup in 2002 and a massive strike within the state-run oil company PDVSA in 2003, both of which hardened his political antipathy towards the old economic and political elite, who were very slow to organize politically against him. In 2012 he won a presidential election against the united opposition candidate Henrique Capriles, and despite treatment in Cuba for cancer he died in office.[22]

urban development, and looks on to a concrete plaza and a series of dual carriageway flyovers. Despite frequent architectural makeovers on both the inside and the outside, the Pantheon still feels like a hangover from another more patriotic era that had been left behind by urbanization and development. But inside, Bolívar's remains have not been left to rest in peace.

The memorial ceremony held in Caracas to commemorate the life of Hugo Chávez on Friday 8 March 2013, was an international event as well as a national moment of mourning and political transition. As I watched the live Venevisión webstreaming in the UK, I reflected on some of the historical parallels with the death and burials of Simón Bolívar, Chávez's historical lodestar. International attendance at the memorial service appeared to demonstrate a markedly ideological pattern. Bolivia, Iran, Brazil and Cuba were well represented. Argentina's president Cristina Fernández de Kirchner paid her respects but left before the ceremony on medical advice. The U.S. sent two minor but sympathetic politicians, and Britain was represented only by its ambassador to Venezuela. In the days leading up to the memorial service there was much media speculation as to where Chávez would be buried. Opposition figures suggested that the immense new mausoleum constructed to house the remains of Simón Bolívar in the centre of Caracas would now be adopted to shelter Chávez's mortal remains alongside those of his great hero. Others speculated that the convention establishing a minimum 25-year waiting list for burial to the National Pantheon might be waived in the case of President Chávez. The new mausoleum for Bolívar, which is an annex to the existing National Pantheon, has attracted much media interest on the basis of its size (it is huge), its shape (it looks like a skateboard ramp) and its considerable cost. Bolívar's remains have been in the National Pantheon since the 1880s, when a former church was converted into a space of memory dedicated to individuals who had given their lives in service to the Venezuelan Republic.

In the National Pantheon a statue to Bolívar occupies the space of the altar, leaving *El Libertador* to physically take over the space formerly occupied by religion. This is as good an example as any of the way in which nineteenth-century nation-states in Latin America tried, in the century after independence from Iberian colonial rule, to replace religious iconography of Church, monarch and Spain with patriotic martyrs and new national identities. In Venezuela, as the historian Germán Carrera Damas showed 50 years ago, the 'cult of Bolívar' fitted the bill and was taken up by politicians and generals of all political ideologies from the mid-nineteenth century onwards.[23] Dedicating this church to Bolívar, placing statues of him across the country and calling *'Viva Bolívar!'* at political rallies: it was easy to think between 1999 and 2013 that Hugo Chávez invented all of this, but nothing could be further from the truth.

The tomb of Bolívar enclosed within the National Pantheon was visited by luminaries including Vladimir Putin, Evo Morales and Lula da Silva, as Chávez made it into a unmissable stopping point on a Bolivarian tour of the capital. In 2010 much of Hispanic America marked the bicentenary of its separation from Spanish colonial rule. Although the first declarations of independence had been issued in 1809 (in Quito, Ecuador and Cartagena, Colombia) and other regions first declared their separation in 1811 – including Venezuela – 2010 was chosen as the year in which the continent as a whole would come together to celebrate the end of colonialism. Of course – and I write as someone who participated in many of the historical symposia, conferences and lectures that took place in Europe and the Americas to mark the date – the whole thing was a largely arbitrary excuse for regimes to spend money on celebrations and events that they hoped would shore up their own popularity and legitimacy. The bicentenary of 1810 was chosen because Mexico, the largest country with the most money to throw at the celebrations at the time, had a clear event and date to mark: the 1810 Grito de Dolores issued by the priest Miguel Hidalgo.

In 2011 Venezuela organized a wide array of projects to celebrate its own bicentenary – though, as in Mexico, independence had only been assured a decade later, in this case with the 1821 Battle of Carabobo, the bicentenary of which Chávez had pledged to attend, as president, in 2021. To commemorate 1811 historical research projects were funded, entire barrios repainted, health centres opened and political battles waged, all in the name of Bolívar and independence.

Political murals festooned urban walls and banners hung from the balconies of public buildings, all declaring the ongoing urgency of maintaining Venezuela's independence. In 2011 in Caracas I witnessed the major night-time parade organized by the government in which 200 years of history were synthesized into a three-hour rolling, acrobatic, choreographed and orchestrated tableau whose subject-matter ranged from the heroes of independence and their heroism to the discovery of oil and the subsequent struggles of unionized workers. I have never seen so many fireworks, or roller skates, in my life. This was a revolutionary history, publicly funded, massively televised and disseminated, in which Bolívar kicked open the door that became a national, proud and ongoing history. It was part of a project that had little time for the niceties of traditional historical interpretation and a great appreciation of the value of symbolic gestures in linking history to the daily revolutionary programme of overhauling Venezuelan society. In early 2010, for example, Chávez and President Rafael Correa of Ecuador presided over a ceremony in which the supposed remains of Manuela Sáenz, Bolívar's lover, were buried in the National Pantheon. Nobody at the time tried to hide the fact that Sáenz had been buried, in 1856, in a mass pauper's grave in Paita, northern Peru, and that it was probable that none of the earth being so honoured in Caracas in 2010 had any remaining physical link to her. However the symbolic gesture reached beyond the particles to display broad appreciation for the sacrifices of independence, which played very well in Chávez's constituency. The writer and historian Elías Pino Iturrieta reflected at the time that 'the intention (of the government) is to manipulate history but also to "revolutionise" the Bolivarian cult'. The BBC cited a Chávez supporter, a student called Silvester Montillo, who explained his reasons for supporting the reburial: 'Some people have criticised the government for spending money on this', he said. 'But they don't understand what it stands for. It doesn't matter to us whether there are traces of her DNA in the urn or not. What's important is that Manuela Sáenz represents the history of Venezuela and the history of all Latin America.'[24] It is this sense of the grand narrative of history and a revolutionary interpretation of it that Chávez and his administrations so successfully tapped into with their core supporters and which put them at the vanguard of change – change with a long historical backstory.

Ever since his election as president in 1998, and with increasing prominence in the wake of the 2002 attempted coup against him, Hugo Chávez liked to mention in his public addresses that Bolívar might not have died, in 1830, of the drawn-out battle against tuberculosis that he lost under the care of a French doctor, Alexandre Prospero Reverend, on the Caribbean coast of Colombia, in Santa Marta. Instead, Chávez speculated, Bolívar might have been the victim of poisoning; and that poisoning might have originated in Bolívar's political enemies; and those enemies might have been foreigners, like Dr Reverend; and might even have been from the u.s. After he was first diagnosed with cancer, Chávez mused on television that there might be a u.s. plot to infect Latin American leftist leaders with cancer in some new, secret way.

A team of u.s. scientists examined the case in 2010, and published their findings. They noted that arsenic poisoning was indeed a possibility, but that this may have come from the water system in Lima, Peru, where Bolívar had lived for a year in 1825–6. Like a posthumous game of Cluedo, it really might have been the lead piping. Alternative explanations include the suggestion that the arsenic was contained in a medical remedy.[25]

On 15 July 2010 Bolívar's coffin was opened up in a ceremony with Chávez in attendance but without fanfare. It was subsequently broadcast on national television in an interlude of the president's own show *Aló Presidente*. Presumably the low profile was adopted in order to avoid protesters disrupting the event. On the film Chávez is heard to say 'Viva Bolívar. It is not a skeleton. It's the Great Bolívar, who has returned.'[26] Debate over the act itself, and what meaning might be extracted from the remains, continued to colour political debate in Venezuela until Chávez's death. In the UK, thanks to the media coverage, more people know that Hugo Chávez disinterred Simón Bolívar than know about his economic redistribution plans or election victories. Latin American history shapes its present and acts as a lens through which the world views it.

Religion and the Churches

The devotion to patriotic martyrs, and the overwhelming passion for exhumations and pantheons, are evidence of the continuing legacy of Catholicism in Latin America at the beginning of the twenty-first century. Indeed, in terms of numbers of churchgoers, the Catholic Church has never been more influential in the region. Contraception remains difficult to get hold of in countries such as Chile and Colombia, where the Church's influence remains strong, and abortion laws have struggled to make it through houses of representatives where practising Catholics have followed the Vatican's teachings against abortion. Divorce has also remained hard to access for many women because of the Church's power. Many countries, such as Nicaragua, have even repealed some of their more progressive laws on women's rights and reproductive health in deference to Church campaigns. The role of Catholic NGOs – and, indeed, the NGOs of other denominations – in funding campaigns relating to reproductive health remains a controversial area in many countries.[27] Although HIV/AIDS has not reached the same epidemic proportions as in sub-Saharan Africa (the total number of people living with HIV in the region was estimated at 1.4 million in 2011) certain regions such as urban Mexico, Brazil, the Dominican Republic and Peru witness particular concentrations. Continued silence or stigma in the public sphere attached to homosexuality across most of Latin America means that it has been difficult to disseminate a consistent sexual health message in the last two decades, and the legacy of aggressive Church teaching against homosexuality is certainly an issue.[28]

Many observers from outside see the massive rise in the number of Protestants in Latin America as evidence of the cultural power of the U.S. and the influence of its evangelical efforts directed towards the south. There were 18.6 million devotees of Pentecostalism back in the 1980s, but by the 1990s even the Latin American Catholic Bishops Conference was reporting 8,000 converts to Protestantism from Catholicism every day. At the time of writing there are few reliable statistics but it is evident that Evangelicalism is booming in its traditional heartlands of Central America and Brazil as well as in urban centres across the continent. Some reports state that Guatemala now has more Protestants than Catholics, although many claims that 'Latin America is turning Protestant' rely as much on their televisual prominence as on objective data.

Nevertheless the form of Protestantism that has taken root in Latin America shows several continuities with the Catholicism that believers have left behind. Pentecostalism offers individual salvation, emotion and communion with the divine, providing a full feeling of community and solidarity in the face of social inequality, globalization and political disenfranchisement. The Catholic Church has struggled to convince younger, urban believers that its strict hierarchies and often intransigent views on modern life still belong to them.[29] Pentecostalism has started to make inroads into the international face of Latin America, first with the military dictator turned corrupt president Efraín Ríos Montt in Guatemala (on trial for genocidal crimes at the time of writing), and then with the footballers of Brazil's 2006 World Cup final, particularly Kaká and Lucio, who wore T-shirts emblazoned with 'Jesus Loves You' and made great play of dedicating their achievements on the pitch to their God.[30] The appointment of an Argentinian, Jorge Mario Bergoglio, as Pope Francis I in 2013 might be expected by some to shore up Catholicism in Latin America. It remains to be seen how effective his moderate conservatism will be in bolstering the Catholic Church during an era of rapid social change.

Connectivity

At the beginning of the twenty-first century, Latin America's communication links to the world are strong but significant gaps remain. Just as the railways of the nineteenth century and the roads and airports of the twentieth connected some groups but not all, similar omissions can be detected from the most recent data. In 2010 the Corporación Andina de Fomento published a hefty volume called *Latin America 2040: Breaking Away from Complacency, an Agenda for Resurgence*. The contributors argued that there remains much to be done to embed democratic governance, human rights and economic prosperity in the region, though their approach might be classified as broadly optimistic about the capacity of institutions, states and market forces to support these things.

In 2010 no single Latin American country had more than 9.8 fixed broadband connections per 100 inhabitants. That was Chile: but Nicaragua had 0.8 per 100, Paraguay 2.2 and Peru 2.8. That is a lot of people with scarce, limited or zero access to the Internet. Mobile phone technology – and its development to allow mobile users to access online services through their phones – may remedy this exclusion. In 2009 Argentina had 129 mobile phone subscriptions per 100 inhabitants, Uruguay 113, Brazil 98 and even Mexico, with one of the lowest figures, had 76.[31] Enduring digital exclusion shows that no technological innovation – from the railways to the telegraph, from the radio to television to the telephone – has yet managed to overcome the legacies and inequalities of Latin America's historical relationship with the world. Will online communication be any different?

Branding, public relations, marketing and communications are relatively new industries but follow historical patterns. Amaranta Wright's research into the consumer research carried out by the Levi's jeans company in Latin America showed how designs and brands are mapped onto the spatial, gendered, ethnic and class-based divisions that shape the continent's contemporary history. Selling and buying a particular type of trousers or mobile phone is understood – both by buyers and sellers and by those who cannot afford to buy, or those who choose not to – as a way of accessing a way of life that is imagined as being located elsewhere, often in North America. Can fashion – available to all, especially through extensive faking and bootlegging – overcome historical patterns of inequality? This also seems unlikely.[32]

Remembering the Falklands/Malvinas War

In September 2008, as the credit crunch and financial crisis broke, President Cristina Fernández de Kirchner of Argentina addressed the UN General Assembly. She warned that rather than a 'tequila effect' crisis, where problems in emerging economies infected richer countries, 2008 might be understood as a 'jazz effect', meaning that it 'emanated from the first economy of the world to the rest'. Brazil's Lula da Silva, speaking at the same event, 'blamed "speculators", "adventurers", and "opportunists" for an economic and financial crisis that, he claimed, had spawned "the anguish of entire peoples"'. More radically, President Morales of Bolivia claimed that the General Assembly was meeting at a time of rebellion against misery and poverty, and against the effects of climate change and privatization policies throughout the world'.[33]

Some leaders never tire of complaining how foreign countries and multinational companies are enacting a 'new imperialism' against them. Cristina Fernández de Kirchner's attitude to non-Latin American interests in Argentina since she came to power can be taken as a case in point. As I was writing the final draft of this chapter, her government took out a full-page advertisement in many British newspapers to reiterate her displeasure at the ongoing British presence in the Falkland Islands/Islas Malvinas. I quote extensively from it here because the text demonstrates the marked continuities and memories of the historical past I have been detailing in this book. She wrote:

One hundred and eighty years ago on the same date, January 3rd, in a blatant exercise of 19th-century colonialism, Argentina was forcibly stripped of the Malvinas Islands, which are situated 14,000 km (8,700 miles) away from London.

The Argentines on the Islands were expelled by the Royal Navy and the United Kingdom subsequently began a population implantation process similar to that applied to other territories under colonial rule.

Since then, Britain, the colonial power, has refused to return the territories to the Argentine Republic, thus preventing it from restoring its territorial integrity.

The Question of the Malvinas Islands is also a cause embraced by Latin America and by a vast majority of peoples and governments around the world that reject colonialism.

In 1960, the United Nations proclaimed the necessity of 'bringing to an end colonialism in all its forms and manifestations'. In 1965, the General Assembly adopted, with no votes against (not even by the United Kingdom), a resolution considering the Malvinas Islands a colonial case and inviting the two countries to negotiate a solution to the sovereignty dispute between them.

This was followed by many other resolutions to that effect.

In the name of the Argentine people, I reiterate our invitation for us to abide by the resolutions of the United Nations.[34]

The British Prime Minister disputed this interpretation of the original invasion and repeated British policy that the sovereignty of the islands resides in the people who live there. In 2013 the islanders voted in a referendum which, their leaders claim, demonstrates a clear lack of interest in devolving or sharing some sovereignty with Argentina. The oil companies currently exploring the ocean bed within British/Falkland territory will have taken note of this, especially in the light of the Argentinian decision in 2012 to nationalize the YBF part of the Spanish oil company exploring in the country, Repsol.[35] The lesson of this book regarding the transformations in Latin America's relationship with the rest of the world over the past two centuries suggests that there will be no quick resolution to this conflict, which will most likely continue to evolve as an intrinsic part of the historic relationship between Britain and Latin America – intertwined, not always as equals, with interlinked and unpredictable economic, political and cultural issues. Diego Maradona pointed this out, and made major political points, with his goals and behaviour in 1986. Sport again provided a way of highlighting and understanding the tensions in this relationship when, in 2012, in the build-up to the Olympic Games held in London, the Argentinian government produced a television advertisement which featured the hockey player Fernando Zylberberg. He was filmed exercising in front of some of the islands' major landmarks, including the Globe tavern and a quintessential red British telephone box; the strapline was: 'To compete on English soil, we train on Argentine soil.' While stylishly made and humorously disrespectful, the power of the advert was subsequently subverted by many factors outside of Fernández de Kirchner's control: Zylberberg was not selected to take part in the games; and Argentina went out of the hockey competition at the quarter-final stage (the unfancied Brits went one round better). Even better, however, it emerged that the advert itself was created by the Buenos Aires office of WPP, the British multinational advertising firm founded by Sir Martin Sorrell, a renowned British patriot.[36]

The Latinization of the United States

Since the very beginning of the independent history of the United States of America in the late eighteenth century there have been people living there who might nowadays be classified as Latino or Latin American immigrants. The earliest of these did not necessarily need to travel in order to pass through immigration, given that it was the United States itself that expanded in order to take over the areas it calls home: nowadays these regions are the U.S. states of New Mexico, California, Texas, Nevada and Arizona. During the late nineteenth and early twentieth century many Latin Americans worked in the U.S., chief among their number the famous Cuban patriot José Martí. At mid-century the trickle in northwards migration started to increase in volume, and the wave of political refugees of the 1960s and '70s reached the U.S. and Canada as much as Europe. Political exile, as well as economic migration or the personal quest for a better life, continued to be a reason to move – often but not necessarily permanently – to the U.S. throughout the rest of the century. This experience was positive for some, more difficult for others, and created new generations labelled as 'Hispanic' or 'Latino' even though the children born in the U.S. were often the ones who left behind their Spanish, Portuguese or indigenous languages and embraced English and the American dream.[37] The previous chapter looked at the rise to fame of Hispanic superstars such as Gloria Estefan and Shakira.

Since 2000 Latin America – and particularly the new group shorn of their status as Americans, known as 'Latinos' or 'Latinas' – have occupied a lot of attention in the U.S. media and academy due to the increasing coverage of illegal migration across the border from Mexico. This debate has been covered in popular argument in simple good/bad terms – that is, the good immigrant who 'makes it' and achieves the American Dream, versus the bad immigrant who allegedly brings criminality in his or her wake. In many universities scholars have shied away from this often ugly and unpleasant debate and focused on the people in between, the *chicano*, mixed-ethnicity residents of the borderlands between cultures. The 'frontiers' of this book's title did not disappear with Independence. Border-crossing remains politically significant – and often physically dangerous. The cultural background of this debate has become politicized in recent years, with some observers arguing that Barack Obama's electoral victories in 2008 and 2012 can be explained by his 'capturing' of a 'Hispanic' or 'Latino' vote.[38] The politics of migration are not so simple. Many Latin American immigrants have been recruited into the U.S. armed forces and have served in Afghanistan and Iraq since 2001. Their involvement in overseas warfare in U.S. uniform demonstrates once again the multifaceted nature of Latin America's engagement with the world, today as in the past two centuries. U.S. military bases, most controversially Guantánamo Bay on Cuba, are explicit reminders of these interlinked histories.

The delicate balances of identity tend to be steamrollered over and forgotten in the mainstream media. In its focus on positive stories, and in persuading North Americans to come to terms with the many millions of Latin Americans in their midsts, Hollywood has played a major role. As John Nieto-Phillips has observed, 'much of the foreign press's newfound fascination for Latinos [in the U.S.] can be attributed to Hollywood, which has disseminated considerable footage of steamy Latins (speaking English with muted accents) making their debut in America'. Salma Hayek (a Mexican actress of Lebanese and Spanish ancestry) and Antonio Banderas (a Spaniard) became representative of positive Latin American characters. Jennifer Lopez exploited the allure of her ethnicity and sexuality and turned it into a marketable commercial product. 'Hollywood has done little to complicate Latino images and, instead, has exploited stereotypes and "success stories" to meet popular tastes and expectations.'[39] In 2014 the Mexican Alfonso Cuarón became the first Latin American to win an Oscar for best director – for *Gravity*, a film made in the UK, about a space mission. Criticizing Hollywood for pandering to what its audience wants seems akin to booing a footballer for scoring goals, but the point stands: the versions of Latin American-ness that have been popularized worldwide by the early twenty-first century have, by necessity, been broad, sometimes inaccurate generalizations. As this book has shown by the diversity of its subject-matter and by its incompleteness, it is rarely possible to provide an 'authentic' representation of a continent that is so varied culturally, politically, ethnically and economically.

The Export of Sporting Cultures: Football Coming Home?

In 2012 there were 1,169 Brazilian footballers professionally contracted outside of their home country, 606 of them in Europe.[40] In Europe alone, therefore, there could be 55 entire teams made up solely of Brazilian footballers in action at any one time. Since 2000 Brazil has regularly been the most represented nation in the quarter-finals of the UEFA Champions League, easily surpassing Spain, Argentina and Italy, and well ahead of England, whose teams have won the tournament several times in that period.

Commentators have seemed to accept the fate of the country's globetrotting players. Jon Cotterill of TV Globo (Brazil's largest broadcaster) said in 2012:

> It's almost a given: it's accepted that there are so many players who start their careers here and then go off to Europe or wher-ever it may be. I've never really seen any complaints of: 'Oh, there's so many of our players leaving.' Maybe just now and then when there is a big star leaving.[41]

Indeed Brazilian-born players have now gone on to play for other national teams – such as Marcos Senna, who won the World Cup with Spain in 2010, and Eduardo with Croatia. In 2013 the biggest star of the moment, Santos's Neymar, signed a lucrative contract to ply his trade in Barcelona, following in the footsteps of Romário, Ronaldo and Ronaldinho. This pattern provides a neat feeling of the circularity of historical change at the end of our story, which complements the many British players who represented Brazil, Uruguay and Argentina in the very first international matches a century ago. What comes around goes around, though this time it looks and feels a world apart and acts, passes and scores in a very different way.

In 2014 the World Cup finals returned to Brazil after a 64-year absence. The government aimed to use the finals – and the Olympics, to be held in 2016 – to showcase a modernized country, a proud member of the BRIC group of nations, a new world leader with a young and vibrant culture. Part of this turning outwards towards the world is expressed in linguistic terms. While President Lula da Silva encouraged bilingualism (Portuguese and Spanish), the arrival of multinational corporate sponsors, as well as cosmopolitan footballers, triggered a rush to learn English in all sectors of Brazilian society, from small businesses and taxi drivers to prostitutes and beach vendors.[42] In June 2013 Brazil hosted the FIFA Confederations Cup, a warm-up for the World Cup involving the champions of each continental football confederation: Brazil beat Spain 3–0 in the final in the refurbished Maracanã stadium. But of much more interest than the football itself were the mass protests that swept across the country during the competition. Protesters, mobilized through social media, drew the world's attention to the massive investments in stadiums and football-related infrastructure, and how this contrasted with the social inequality and corruption that were popularly believed to be linked to the staging of the World Cup. Banners bearing legends such as '1st World FIFA, 3rd World Health and Education' were displayed to global audiences during marches that were initially triggered by rising public transport prices. The fact that FIFA will not pay any tax in Brazil during the World Cup was repeatedly returned to by commentators such as the footballer turned politician Romário, who argued that 'only FIFA is profiting, and this is one more good reason to go on the streets and protest.'[43]

As the eyes of the world's media turn back towards Latin America for the 2014 World Cup and the 2016 Olympic Games, it finds that Latin American culture has been part of this world all this time, only without attracting much consistent attention. Latin American migrants to the u.s., we know, have created a community of many millions linked by culture, language and increasingly political identity. Demographic change in the u.s. has prompted some, such as Samuel Huntingdon, to fear that the 'real' identity of the u.s. will be undermined by Latin American immigration.

But many of the same people who evoke a sense of fear at immigration take classes in salsa, zumba, tango or capoeira, the Latin American dance sensations which provide social interaction and an opportunity for dancing to North Americans and Europeans who have let dance and physicality fall out of their lives. The teachers of these classes are often Cubans, Colombians and Argentinians, and many of the students are British, German or North Americans. Salsa conventions have become a major industry, with dance schools evolving into corporations. But many of the classes are also filled with Latin American migrants, looking for a space in Chicago, Wolverhampton, Berlin or Oslo where they can assert their continued sense of Latin American identity despite their geographical dislocation from their original homelands.[44]

Carlos Alberto Torres, the Brazilian football legend whose strike ended an iconic Brazilian goal against Italy in the 1970 World Cup, which will be replayed a million times in the run-up to the 2014 World Cup, is on board for preparations for this tournament. A world-cup winner himself, he knows that nearly 200 million Brazilians will be desperate for their team to win the competition on home soil, partially to avenge the still-lingering pain of defeat in the Maracanãzo in 1950. Carlos Alberto reminds us, however, that despite the game's primordial importance in Latin American culture, and for Brazilian national pride, football is still only a game, and many factors will play a part in determining the outcome, including skill, luck, and the referees.[45] The weight of history will also play its part.

REFERENCES

Latin America and the World: An Introduction

1 Eduardo Galeano, *Open Veins of Latin America: Five Centuries of the Pillage of a Continent* (London, 1973); Oscar Guardiola-Rivera, *What if Latin America Ruled the World? How the South will take the North into the 22nd Century* (London, 2011).

2 Charles Jones, *American Civilization* (London, 2007), p. 52; C. A. Bayly, *The Birth of the Modern World, 1780–1914: Global Connections and Comparisons* (Oxford, 2004).

3 Niall Ferguson, *Empire: How Britain Made the Modern World* (London, 2004); Niall Ferguson, *Civilization: The Six Killer Apps of Western Power* (London, 2011).

4 José Moya, 'Introduction', in *Oxford Handbook of Latin American History*, ed. Moya (Oxford, 2011); Walter Mignolo, *The Idea of Latin America* (Oxford, 2004).

5 Leslie Bethell, 'Brazil and "Latin America"', *Journal of Latin American Studies*, XLII/3 (2010), pp. 457–85.

6 Online at www.latinobarometro.org.

7 Moya, 'Introduction', pp. 4–5, 7–8.

8 The following discussion of the three broad areas borrows heavily from Moya's explanation in his introduction to the *Oxford Handbook of Latin American History*. He extends the schema to cover the Americas as a whole.

9 Moya, 'Introduction', pp. 2–3.

10 For example Bayly, *The Birth of the Modern World*.

11 Moya, 'Introduction', p. 10.

12 Aníbal Quijano, 'Coloniality of Power and Eurocentrism in Latin America', *International Sociology*, XV/2 (2000), pp. 215–32.

13 Nestor García Canclini, *Hybrid Cultures: Strategies for Entering and Leaving Modernity* (Minneapolis, MN, 1995); Fernando Ortiz, *Contrapunteo cubano del tabaco y el azúcar* (Havana, 1940).

14 For a general overview with good coverage and detail see Teresa A. Meade, *A History of Modern Latin America, 1800 to the present* (Oxford, 2010), Edwin Williamson, *The Penguin History of Latin America* (London,

2008), or Will Fowler, *Latin America since 1780* (London, 2008). Leslie Bethell, ed., *The Cambridge History of Latin America* (Cambridge, 1986) remains a classic reference work.

15 Marcello Carmagnani, *The Other West: Latin America from Invasion to Globalization* [in Italian, 2003], trans. Rosanna M. Giammanco Frongia (Berkeley, CA, 2011).

16 Ibid., pp. 116–17.

17 Jones, *American Civilization*, p. 89. See also Felipe Fernández-Armesto, *The Americas: A Hemispheric History* (London, 2003).

18 See Richard J. Evans, 'Prologue: *What is History* – Now?', in *What is History Now?*, ed. David Cannadine (London, 2002), pp. 1–18.

ONE: Goodbye, Colonial Worlds: Independence

1 Rafe Blaufarb, 'The Western Question: The Geopolitics of Latin American Independence', *Hispanic American Historical Review*, CXII/3 (2007), pp. 742–63; Anthony McFarlane, *War and Independence in Spanish America* (London, 2014).

2 Martin Robson, *Britain, Portugal and South America in the Napoleonic Wars: Alliances and Diplomacy in Economic Maritime Conflict* (London, 2011).

3 Klaus Gallo, *Great Britain and Argentina* (Basingstoke, 2001).

4 Racine, '"This England, This Now": British Cultural and Intellectual Influence in Spanish America in the Independence-Era', *Hispanic American Historical Review*, XC/3 (2010), pp. 423–54.

5 Simón Bolívar, 'Letter Inviting Governments to a Congress in Panama, 7 December 1824', reproduced in *Simón Bolívar and the Bolivarian Revolution, Introduced by Hugo Chávez*, ed. and trans. Matthew Brown (New York, 2009), p. 166; for his 'final lament': John Lynch, *Simón Bolívar: A Life* (New Haven, CT, 2006).

6 Simón Bolívar, 'The Jamaica Letter' (1815), in *Simón Bolívar*, ed. Brown, pp. 40–64.

7 David Brading, *The First America: The Spanish Monarchy, Creole Patriots and the Liberal State, 1492–1867* (Cambridge, 1991); María Teresa Calderón and Clément Thibaud, *La majestad de los pueblos en la Nueva Granada y Venezuela (1780–1832)* (Bogotá, 2011).

8 Cecilia Méndez, *The Plebian Republic: The Huanta Rebellion and the Making of the Peruvian State, 1820–1850* (Durham, NC, 2005).

9 Peter Blanchard, *Under the Flags of Freedom: Slave Soldiers and the Wars of Independence in Spanish South America* (Pittsburgh, PA, 2008).

10 David Geggus, ed., *The Impact of the Haitian Revolution in the Atlantic World* (Columbia, SC, 2001).

11 Rebecca Cole Heinowitz, *Spanish America and British Romanticism, 1777–1826* (Edinburgh, 2010); Racine, '"This England, This Now"'; D.A.G. Waddell, 'British Neutrality and Spanish–American Independence: The Problem of Foreign Enlistment', *Journal of Latin American Studies*, XIX/1 (1987), pp. 1–18; John Lynch, 'British Policy and Spanish America,

1783–1808', *Journal of Latin American Studies*, I/1 (1969), pp. 1–30.

12 Gabriel B. Paquette, 'The Brazilian Origins of the Portuguese Constitution', in *Connections after Colonialism: Europe and Latin America in the 1820s*, ed. Matthew Brown and Paquette (Tuscaloosa, AL, 2013), pp. 108–38.

13 Matthew Brown, *Adventuring through Spanish Colonies: Simón Bolívar, Foreign Mercenaries and the Birth of New Nations* (Liverpool, 2006), pp. 13–30.

14 Charles Stephenson, *The Admiral's Secret Weapon: Lord Dundonald and the Origins of Chemical Warfare* (Woodbridge, 2006).

15 David Cordingly, *Cochrane the Dauntless: The Life and Adventures of Admiral Thomas Cochrane, 1775–1860* (London, 2007); Brian Vale, *A War Betwixt Englishmen: Brazil against Argentina on the River Plate, 1825–1830* (London, 2001).

16 Eric Van Young, *The Other Rebellion: Popular Violence, Ideology and the Mexican Struggle for Independence, 1810–1821* (Stanford, CA, 2001); Timothy Anna, *Forging Mexico, 1821–1835* (Lincoln, NE, 1998); Will Fowler, 'The *Pronunciamiento* in Mexico', in *Connections after Colonialism*, ed. Brown and Paquette, pp. 48–63.

17 Jordana Dym, *From Sovereign Villages to National States: City, State and Federation in Central America, 1759–1839* (Albuquerque, NM, 2006); Matthew Brown, 'Inca, Sailor, Soldier, King: Gregor MacGregor and the Revolutionary Caribbean', *Bulletin of Latin American Research*, XXIV/1 (2005), pp. 44–70.

18 See the discussion of this debate in Brown and Paquette, 'Introduction', in *Connections after Colonialism*.

19 Frank Griffith Dawson, *The First Latin American Debt Crisis: The City of London and the 1822–1825 Loan Bubble* (London, 1990); Leslie Bethell, ed., *Brazil: Empire and Republic, 1822–1930* (Cambridge, 1989); Kirsten Schultz, *Tropical Versailles: Empire, Monarchy and the Portuguese Royal Court in Rio de Janeiro* (New York, 2001).

20 Rebecca Earle, '*Padres de la patria* and the Ancestral Past: Celebrations of Independence in Nineteenth-century Spanish America', *Journal of Latin American Studies*, XXXIV/4 (2002), pp. 775–805; Hendrick Kraay, *Race, State and Armed Forces in Independence-Era Brazil, 1790s–1840s* (Stanford, CA, 2001).

21 On debates over the meaning of the nation, see José Carlos Chiaramonte, *Nation and State in Latin America: Political Language During Independence* (Buenos Aires, 2010).

22 This is nicely described in the Chilean author Isabel Allende's novel *Daughter of Fortune* (New York, 2000).

23 Simón Bolívar to Juan José Flores, in *El Libertador: Selected Writings of Simón Bolívar*, ed. David Bushnell (Oxford, 2004).

TWO: Building Nations, Looking for Models

1 For Colombia see Alfonso Múnera, *El fracaso de la nación: Región, clase y raza en el caribe colombiano, 1717–1821* (Bogotá, 1998).

2 Manuel Llorca-Jaña, 'Of Shipwrecks, "Savages" and Seamen: British Consular Contacts with the Native People of Southern South America during the 1820s and 1830s', *International Journal of Maritime History*, XXIV/2 (2012).

3 Joanna Crow, *The Mapuche and Modern Chile: A Cultural History* (Gainsville, FL, 2013).

4 John Lynch, *New Worlds: A Religious History of Latin America* (London, 2012).

5 Alistair Hennessey and John King, eds, *The Land that England Lost: Britain and Argentina, A Special Relationship* (London, 1992).

6 Matthew Brown, *The Struggle for Power in Post-Independence Colombia and Venezuela* (London, 2012), chapter 7.

7 Charles Darwin, *Journal of Researches into the Natural History and Geology of the Countries Visited during the Voyage of HMS 'Beagle', Round the World* (London, 1845).

8 Brown, *The Struggle for Power*, chapter 6.

9 David Rock, *Argentina, 1516–1982* (London, 1986).

10 Frank Griffith Dawson, *The First Latin American Debt Crisis: The City of London and the 1822–1825 Loan Bubble* (London, 1990), p. 249.

11 Michael P. Costeloe, *Bonds and Bondholders: British Investors and Mexico's Foreign Debt, 1824–1888* (Westport, CT, 2003).

12 See Bolívar's decree abolishing slavery, and explanatory note, in Matthew Brown, ed., *Simón Bolívar: The Bolivarian Revolution* (New York, 2009), pp. 65–6.

13 Andrew Pearson, Ben Jeffs, Annsofie Witkin and Helen MacQuarrie, *Infernal Traffic: Excavation of a Liberated African Graveyard in Rupert's Valley, St Helena* (London, 2012).

14 Leslie Bethell, *The Abolition of the Brazilian Slave Trade: Britain, Brazil and the Slave Trade Question, 1807–1869* (Cambridge, 1970); James Walvin, *Crossings: Africa, the Americas and the Atlantic Slave Trade* (London, 2013).

15 Domingo Sarmiento, *Facundo: Civilization and Barbarism* [1845], ed. and trans. Kathleen Ross (Berkeley, CA, 2003).

16 Joy Logan, *Aconcagua: The Invention of Mountaineering on America's Highest Peak* (Tucson, AZ, 2011), p. 27.

17 Doris Sommer, *Foundational Fictions: National Romances of Latin America* (Berkeley, CA, 1992); Joan Lee Skinner, 'Family Secrets: Incest in Jorge Isaacs' *Maria*', *Hispanic Review*, LXXVI/1 (2008), pp. 53–69.

18 Guy Thomson, ed., *The European Revolutions of 1848 and the Americas* (London, 2001).

19 Brown, *The Struggle for Power*.

20 Jay Sexton, *The Monroe Doctrine: Empire and Nation in Nineteenth-*

Century America (New York, 2011); Will Fowler, Santa Anna of Mexico (London, 2007).

21 Robert E. May, Manifest Destiny's Underworld: Filibustering in Antebellum America (Durham, NC, 2002).

22 Eduardo Galeano, Open Veins of Latin America: Five Centuries of the Pillage of a Continent (London, 1973), p. 210; mirrored in Oscar Guardiola-Rivera, What if Latin America Ruled the World? How the South will Take the North into the 22nd Century (London, 2011); for the contrasting view see Stephen Charge, 'Great Britain and the War of the Triple Alliance', unpublished MA dissertation, University of Bristol (2010).

23 Thomas Whigham, 'The Paraguayan War: A Catalyst for Nationalism in South America', in I Die With My Country, Perspectives on the Paraguayan War, 1864–1870, ed. Hendrick Kraay and Thomas Whigham (Lincoln, NE, 2004), p. 179.

THREE: Raw Materials, Raw Wounds

1 Bill Albert, South America and the World Economy from Independence to 1930 (London, 1982).

2 Cited in Peter Winn, 'British Informal Empire in Uruguay', Past and Present, LXXIII/1 (1976), p. 112.

3 Andre Gunder Frank, Capitalism and Underdevelopment in Latin America: Historical Studies of Chile and Brazil (New York, 1967).

4 This debate is neatly covered in the work of Florencia Mallon, reproduced and introduced in Orin Starn, Carlos Ivan Degregori and Robin Kirk, eds, The Peru Reader: History, Culture, Politics (Durham, NC, 2005), pp. 181–99. On the global history of guano, see Gregory Cushman, Guano and the Opening of the Pacific World (Cambridge, 2013).

5 Marcello Carmagnani, The Other West: Latin America from Invasion to Globalization [in Italian, 2003], trans. Rosanna M. Giammanco Frongia (Berkeley, CA, 2011), p. 144.

6 Peter Cain and Anthony Hopkins, British Imperialism, 1688–2000 (London, 2001), p. 248.

7 Alan Knight, 'Rethinking Informal Empire in Latin America (especially Argentina), in Informal Empire in Latin America: Culture, Commerce and Capital, ed. Matthew Brown (Oxford, 2008), pp. 23–48.

8 See for example Carmagnani, The Other West, pp. 157–8.

9 C. A. Bayly, The Birth of the Modern World, 1780–1914: Global Connections and Comparisons (Oxford, 2004), p. 403.

10 A good overview is Stefan Rinke, '¿La última pasión verdadera?: La historia del fútbol en América Latina en contexto global', Iberoamericana, VII/27 (2007), pp. 85–100.

11 Paul Garner, Porfirio Díaz (Harlow, 2001), quote on p. 163.

12 Rory Miller, 'Introduction', in Fútbol, Futebol, Soccer: Football in the Americas, ed. Miller and Liz Crolley (London, 2007), pp. 3–4.

13 Richard Giulianotti, 'Football, South America and Globalisation:

Conceptual Paths', in *Fútbol, Futebol, Soccer*, ed. Miller and Crolley, pp. 37–51, p. 38.

14 Richard Giulianotti, *Football: A Sociology of the Global Game* (London, 1999), pp. 6–7.

15 G. Mascarenhas, 'Várzeas, Operários e Futebol: uma outra Geografia', *GEOgraphia*, IV/8 (2002), pp. 84–92; Adrian Hamilton, *An Entirely Different Game: The British Influence in Brazilian Football* (Edinburgh, 1998).

16 Bonnie M. Miller, *From Liberation to Conquest: The Visual and Popular Cultures of the Spanish–American War of 1898* (Amherst, MA, 2011).

17 Peter Hulme and William Sherman, eds, *The Tempest and its Travels* (London, 2000).

18 Christopher Abel, *José Martí: Revolutionary Democrat* (London, 1986).

19 José Martí, 'La crisis y el Partido Revolucionario Cubano', 19 August 1893, in Martí, *Obras Completas*, ed. Jorge Quintana (Caracas, 1964), vol. I, p. 665, quoted in Louis A. Pérez Jr, *Cuba and the United States: Ties of Singular Intimacy* (Athens, GE, 1997), p. 79.

20 Drago, cited in Carmagnani, *The Other West*, p. 197.

21 Charles Jones, *American Civilization* (London, 2007), p. 69.

22 Gabriel García Márquez, *One Hundred Years of Solitude* [Mexico City, 1967], trans. Gregory Rabassa (London, 1978), p. 116.

23 Aims McGuinness, *Path of Empire: Panama and the California Gold Rush* (Ithaca, NY, 2009).

24 Alan Knight, 'The Mexican Revolution: Bourgeois? Nationalist? Or was it Just a Great Rebellion?', *Bulletin of Latin American Research*, IV/2 (1985), pp. 1–17. Carmagnani, *The Other West*, p. 197, sees Versailles as a 'humiliation' for Latin America.

25 Jones, *American Civilization*, p. 73.

FOUR: New Exchanges, New Markets

1 Colin Lewis, 'Britain, the Argentine and Informal Empire', in *Informal Empire in Latin America: Culture, Commerce and Capital*, ed. Matthew Brown (Oxford, 2008), pp. 99–123.

2 Juan Bautista Alberdi, 'Bases y puntos de partida', cited in Winthrop Wright, 'Foreign-owned Railways in Argentina: A Case Study of Economic Nationalism', *Business History Review*, XLI/1 (1967), pp. 62–93.

3 Adapted from Rosemary Thorp, *Progress, Poverty and Exclusion: An Economic History of Latin America* (Oxford, 2000), appendix table x.2, p. 363.

4 Lewis, 'Britain, the Argentine and Informal Empire'.

5 Dwayne R. Wisbeck and Robert M. Pike, *Communication and Empire: Media, Markets and Globalization, 1860–1930* (Durham, NC, 2007), p. 68.

6 Ibid., p. 90.

7 Hermes Tovar Pinzón, 'Tras las huellas del soldado Pinzón', in *Memorias de un País en Guerra: Los Mil Dias, 1899–1902*, ed. Gonzalo Sanchez and Mario Aguilera (Bogotá, 2001).

8   Matthew B. Karush, *Culture of Class: Radio and Cinema in the Making of a Divided Argentina, 1920–1946* (Durham, NC, 2012).

9   Willie Hiatt, 'Flying "Cholo": Incas, Airplanes and the Construction of Andean Modernity in 1920s Cuzco', *The Americas*, LXIII/3 (2007), pp. 327–58; David Goldblatt, *The Ball is Round: A Global History of Football* (London, 2006).

10 Miguel Tinker Salas, *The Enduring Legacy: Oil, Culture and Society in Venezuela* (Durham, NC, 2009).

11 C. A. Bayly, *The Birth of the Modern World, 1780–1914: Global Connections and Comparisons* (Oxford, 2004), p. 178, briefly uses the example of incomplete Mexican industrialization to differentiate the region from Europe and the U.S. in this period.

12 Adriana Bergero, *Intersecting Tango: Cultural Geographies of Buenos Aires, 1900–1930* (Pittsburgh, PA, 2008), p. 16.

13 Dan Hagedorn, *Conquistadors of the Sky: A History of Aviation in Latin America* (Miami, FL, 2010), p. 15.

14 Ibid., pp. 32–3, 87–8, 103, 128.

15 Ibid., pp. 124–6.

16 Ibid., p. 170.

17 Jordan Goodman, *The Devil and Mr Casement: One Man's Struggle for Human Rights in South America's Heart of Darkness* (London, 2009); Mario Vargas Llosa, *The Dream of the Celt* (London, 2012).

18 Nicholas Reeve and John R. Taylor, *Howard Carter and the Quest for Tutankhamen* (London, 1992).

19 Excerpts from the 1913 edition, including the original photos, can be viewed at http://ngm.nationalgeographic.com.

20 Hiram Bingham, *Inca Land: The Incredible Story of the Discovery of Machu Picchu* [1922] (Washington, DC, 2003), p. 196.

21 Ibid., pp. 199–206.

22 Amy Cox Hall, 'Collecting a "Lost City" for Science: Huaquero Vision and the Yale Peruvian Expeditions to Machu Picchu, 1911, 1912, and 1914–15', *Ethnohistory*, LIX/2 (2012), pp. 293–321.

23 Statistics taken from José C. Moya, *Cousins and Strangers: Spanish Immigrants in Buenos Aires, 1850–1930* (Berkeley, CA, 1998), p. 56.

24 Ibid., p. 149.

25 Bayly, *The Birth of the Modern World*, p. 440, sets this phenomenon against similar developments in Tasmania, the U.S. and southern Africa.

26 Michael Goebel, 'Gauchos, Gringos, Gallegos: The Assimilation of Italian and Spanish Immigrants in the Making of Modern Uruguay, 1880–1930', *Past & Present*, 208 (2010), pp. 191–229.

27 The literature on these subjects is large and growing: see for an introduction the work of Jeffrey Lesser, *Immigration, Ethnicity and National Identity in Brazil* (Cambridge, 2012), and *Re-thinking Jewish Latin Americans* (Arizona, NM, 2008).

28 For good introduction to Vasconcelos, Rivera and the cultural ferment that was Mexico in this period, see Gilbert M. Joseph and Timothy

J. Henderson, eds, *The Mexico Reader: History, Politics, Culture* (Durham, NC, 2003), pp. 15–20.

29 Bertrand M. Patenaude, *Trotsky: Downfall of a Revolutionary* (New York, 2010).

30 Ricardo Güiraldes, *Don Segundo Sombra* (Buenos Aires, 1926).

31 Jorge Icaza, *Huasipungo* (Quito, 1934). For a clear introduction to *indigenismo*, see Rebecca Earle, *The Return of the Native: Indians and Myth-making in Spanish America, 1810–1930* (Durham, NC, 2008).

32 Rómulo Gallegos, *Doña Bárbara* (Caracas, 1929).

33 As used in Hugo Chávez's TV show *Aló Presidente*, and also in his famous speech at the UN General Assembly in September 2006 when he referred to Bush as smelling of sulphur like the Devil.

34 Doris Sommer, *Foundational Fictions: National Romances of Latin America* (Berkeley, CA, 1992); Fernando Coronil, *The Magical State: Nature, Money and Modernity in Venezuela* (Chicago, IL, 1997).

35 Aníbal Quijano, 'Coloniality of Power and Eurocentrism in Latin America', *International Sociology*, XV/2 (2000), pp. 215–32.

36 See the holdings listed at the Khipu Database Project at Harvard University, http://khipukamayuq.fas.harvard.edu.

37 John Hemming, *The Search for El Dorado* (London, 2001).

FIVE: Beneath a New Empire

1 Charles Bergquist, *Coffee and Conflict in Colombia, 1886–1910* (Durham, NC, 1996).

2 Figures for each year represent three-year average values. Adapted from Rosemary Thorp, *Progress, Poverty and Exclusion: An Economic History of Latin America* (Oxford, 2000), appendix table vii.2, p. 346.

3 On income tax revenue see ibid., p. 346.

4 Victor Bulmer-Thomas, *The Economic History of Latin America since Independence* (Cambridge, 1995), p. 102.

5 Marcello Carmagnani, *The Other West: Latin America from Invasion to Globalization* [in Italian, 2003], trans. Rosanna M. Giammanco Frongia (Berkeley, CA, 2011), p. 203.

6 James Dunkerley, *Rebellion in the Veins: Political Struggle in Bolivia, 1952–1982* (London, 1984).

7 Adapted from Thorp, *Progress, Poverty and Exclusion*, appendix table vii.3, p. 347.

8 Greg Grandin, *Fordlandia: The Rise and Fall of Henry Ford's Forgotten Jungle City* (New York, 2009), p. 194.

9 Adapted from Thorp, *Progress, Poverty and Exclusion*, appendix table 1, p. 313.

10 Charles Jones, *American Civilization* (London, 2007), p. 53.

11 R. Bacelli, *Jardim America* (São Paulo, 1982).

12 These paragraphs on the origins of football in Brazil draw on Matthew Brown and Gloria Lanci, 'A Transnational Investigation of Football and Urban Heritage in São Paulo, 1890 to 1930', in *Global Play: Football*

Between Region, Nation and the World in Latin American, African and European History, ed. Stefan Rinke and Christina Peters (Stuttgart, 2014), pp. 17–40.

13 E. Blay, *Eu não tenho onde morar: vilas operarias na cidade de São Paulo* (São Paulo, 1985).

14 Eduardo P. Archetti, *Masculinities: Football, Polo and the Tango in Argentina* (Oxford, 1999), pp. 82–5.

15 Noel Maurer and Carlos Yu, *The Big Ditch: How America Took, Built, Ran and Ultimately Gave Away the Panama Canal* (Princeton, NJ, 2010).

16 Table from George Reid Andrews, *Afro-Latin America, 1800–2000* (Oxford, 2004), p. 155.

17 Table ibid., p. 155.

18 Kevin Foster, *Lost Worlds: Latin America and the Imagining of Empire* (London, 2009), pp. 66–72.

19 Alejo Carpentier, *The Kingdom of this World* (Havana, 1949). For an introduction to marvellous reality and 'magical realism', see Gerald Martin, *Journeys through the Labyrinth: Latin American Fiction in the Twentieth Century* (London, 1989).

20 Edwin Williamson, *Borges: A Life* (London, 2004).

21 Boris Fausto, *A Concise History of Brazil* (Cambridge, 1999).

22 Gilberto Freyre, *The Masters and the Slaves: A Study in the Development of Brazilian Civilization*, trans. Samuel Putnam (New York, 1964, first published in Portuguese in 1934).

23 John Charles Chasteen, 'The Pre-history of Samba: Carnival Dancing in Rio de Janeiro, 1840–1914', *Journal of Latin American Studies*, XXVIII/1 (1996), pp. 29–30. Micol Seigel, *Uneven Encounters: Making Race and Nation in Brazil and the United States* (Chapel Hill, NC, 2009).

24 Gilberto Freyre, in *Correio da Manhã*, 5 June 1938, cited in David Goldblatt, *The Ball is Round: A Global History of Football* (London, 2008), p. 282. For a good introduction to Brazilian football culture, see Alex Bellos, *Futebol: The Brazilian Way of Life* (London, 2002).

25 Eduardo Galeano, *El fútbol a sol y sombra* (Montevideo, 1998), p. 100, my translation.

26 Jones, *American Civilization*, p. 55.

27 Ernesto 'Che' Guevara, *The Motorcycle Diaries: A Journey Around South America*, trans. Ann Wright (London, 1995), p. 117.

28 Guevara, *Motorcycle Diaries*, p. 153.

29 Ibid., pp. 95–6.

30 Jon Lee Anderson, *Che Guevara: A Revolutionary Life* (New York, 1997).

31 Che Guevara, 'Message to the Tricontinental, the Executive Secretariat of the Organization of the Solidarity of the Peoples of Africa, Asia, and Latin America (OSPAAAL)', 19 April 1967, in *Che Guevara Reader: Writings on Politics and Revolution*, ed. David Deutschmann (Havana, 2003), p. 358.

32 Guevara, *Motorcycle Diaries*, p. 196.

33 For more on Guevara's travel writing see Rupert Medd, *Travel Writing and the Peruvian Environment: Testing Nature and Coloniality*, unpublished

PhD thesis, University of Bristol (2013).

34 Simón Collier, *The Life, Music and Times of Carlos Gardel* (Pittsburgh, PA, 1986).

35 Guillermo Anad, *Tango, transmodernidad y desencuentro* (New York, 2011), p. 10.

36 Victor Bulmer Thomas, Roberto Conde and John Coatsworth, *Cambridge Economic History of Latin America* (Cambridge, 2006).

37 Aníbal Quijano, 'Coloniality of Power and Eurocentrism in Latin America', *International Sociology*, XV/2 (2000), pp. 215–32.

38 Jorge Luis Borges, 'El etnógrafo' (1969). John Beverley drew my attention to Mabel Montaña's reading of this story, which I drew on, in his *Latinamericanism after 9/11* (Durham, NC, 2011), pp. 79–83.

SIX: Latin America in the Cold War

1 Greg Grandin, *The Last Colonial Massacre: Latin America in the Cold War* (Chicago, IL, 2004), p. xiv.

2 Pablo Neruda, *Canto general* (Santiago, 1950); Pablo Neruda, *A Call for the Destruction of Richard Nixon and Praise for the Chilean Revolution*, trans. Teresa Anderson (Cambridge, MA, 1980); Adam Feinstein, *Pablo Neruda: A Passion for Life* (London, 2004).

3 Jonathan Franklin, 'Chilean Poet Pablo Neruda's Body to be Exhumed over Murder Claims', *The Guardian*, 8 April 2013.

4 Gilbert Joseph and Daniella Spenser, eds, *In From the Cold: Latin America's New Encounter with the Cold War* (Durham, NC, 2008).

5 Dan Hagedorn, *Conquistadors of the Sky: A History of Aviation in Latin America* (Miami, FL, 2010), pp. 332–3.

6 Ibid., pp. 383–5, 400.

7 Charles Jones, *American Civilization* (London, 2007), p. 73.

8 Augusto Sandino, 'Political Manifesto', Nicaragua, July 1927, in *Nicaragua: Sandinista Peoples' Revolution Speeches by Sandinista Leaders*, ed. Marcus Bruce (London, 1985), reproduced in Alexander Dawson, *Latin America since Independence: A New Interpretation* (London, 2010), p. 154.

9 Marcello Carmagnani, *The Other West: Latin America from Invasion to Globalization* [in Italian, 2013], trans. Rosanna M. Giammanco Frongia (Berkeley, CA, 2011), pp. 200–201.

10 Grandin, *The Last Colonial Massacre*, p. xiv.

11 René de la Pedraja, *Wars of Latin America, 1899–1941* (Jefferson, NC, 2006), p. 435.

12 David Rock, *Argentina, 1516–1982* (London, 1986).

13 Mariano Ben Plotkin, *Mañana es San Perón: A Cultural History of Perón's Argentina* (London, 2002). Quote from Evita Perón, 'Speech on the Granting of Female Suffrage in Argentina, 23 September 1947' ('Anuncio de la Ley del Voto Femenino'), at El Historiador, www.elhistoriador.com.ar, my translation.

14 Jeffrey M. Pilcher, *Cantinflas and the Chaos of Mexican Modernity*

(London, 2001). Jean Franco, *The Decline and Fall of the Lettered City: Latin America in the Cold War* (Cambridge, MA, 2002), pp. 24–8.

15 Joanna Crow, *The Mapuche and Modern Chile* (Miami, FL, 2013), pp. 109–13.

16 Dwight D. Eisenhower, 1963, cited in Eduardo Galeano, *Open Veins of Latin America: Five Centuries of the Pillage of a Continent* (London, 1973), p. 127.

17 From Galeano, *Open Veins*, pp. 127–8.

18 Grandin, *The Last Colonial Massacre*, p. 3.

19 Nicola Miller, 'The Absolution of History: Uses of the Past in Castro's Cuba', *Journal of Contemporary History*, XXXVIII/1 (2003), pp. 147–62.

20 Rigoberta Menchú, with Elizabeth Burgos-Debray, *I, Rigoberta Menchú: An Indigenous Woman in Guatemala* (London, 1983). Quote from Rigorberta Menchú, 'Nobel Prize Speech, 1992', reproduced in *The Guatemala Reader: History, Culture, Politics*, ed. Greg Grandin, Deborah T. Levenson and Elizabeth Oglesby (Chapel Hill, NC, 2011), p. 590.

21 There is virtually no academic literature on the history of golf in Latin America, so you will have to take my own anecdotal experience of walking around the perimeter fences of the golf courses referred to here as evidence for the exclusivity of the sport, especially compared to the public, open links courses in Fife, Scotland. For a fascinating analysis of how golf is seen as a way of accessing business and career advancement in the U.S. for disadvantaged Latino/a migrants, see Jody Agius Vallejo, 'Latina Spaces: Middle-class Ethnic Capital and Professional Associations in the Latina Community', *City and Community*, VIII/2 (2009), pp. 129–54.

22 Cited in Amaranta Wright, *Ripped and Torn: Levi's, Latin America and The Blue Jean Dream* (London, 2006), p. 173.

23 Silvio Rodríguez, 'El Playa Girón' (1975). The song was ostensibly about a boat also called the Playa Girón, and the fishermen who worked on it, though the extra meaning of the final stanzas is clear.

24 For much of this section I draw on Richard Gott, *Cuba: A New History* (London, 2004).

25 Fidel Castro, 'Cuba is a Socialist Nation', address to the May Day celebrations, 1 May 1961, Havana, in Dawson, *Latin America since Independence*, p. 208.

26 Nelson Rockefeller, cited in Jeffrey Taffet, *Foreign Aid as Foreign Policy: The Alliance for Progress in Latin America* (London, 2007), pp. 185–8.

27 Brenda Elsey, *Citizens and Sportsmen: Fútbol & Politics in 20th-century Chile* (Austin, TX, 2012). Coleman's introduction and tirade, and clips from the match, can be viewed at www.youtube.com.

28 Gott, *Cuba: A New History*, pp. 197–200; also Nicola Miller, 'Reassessing The Cuban Missile Crisis: The Post-Cold War Historiography', in *War and Cold War in American Foreign Policy, 1942–1962*, ed. Dale Carter and Robin Clifton (London, 2001), pp. 211–39.

29 Kennedy, 22 October 1962, cited in Gott, *Cuba: A New History*, p. 205.

30 Castro, 23 October 1962, cited ibid., p. 205.

31 Ibid., p. 207.

32 Gustavo Gutiérrez, *A Theology of Liberation* (London, 1988, first published in Spanish 1973); for an introduction to Vatican II, see John Lynch, *New Worlds: A Religious History of Latin America* (London, 2012), pp. 355–6.

33 Charles Jones, *American Civilization* (London, 2007), p. 74.

34 Javier Heraud, *Poesias completas y cartas* (Lima, 1976). Brondy's homage to his friend is at pp. 9–10. The posthumous edition of Heraud's poems was supported by Velasco's government.

35 Camilo Torres, *Revolutionary Priest: His Complete Writings and Messages*, ed. J. Gerasi, trans. J. De C. Alcantara (London, 1973).

36 Gabriel García Márquez, *One Hundred Years of Solitude* [Mexico City, 1967], trans. Edith Grossman (London, 1968); Eduardo Posada-Carbó, 'Fiction as History: The Bananeras and Gabriel García Márquez's *One Hundred Years of Solitude*', *Journal of Latin American Studies*, xxx/2 (1998), pp. 395–414; Grandin, *The Last Colonial Massacre*, p. 170.

37 Richard Ivan Jobs, 'Youth Movements: Travel, Protest and Europe in 1968', *American Historical Review*, cxiv/2 (2009), pp. 376–404.

38 Jorge Castañeda, *The Life and Death of Che Guevara* (London, 1997).

39 Claire Brewster and Keith Brewster, *Representing the Nation: Sport and Spectacle in Post-Revolutionary Mexico* (London 2010).

40 David Goldblatt, *The Ball is Round: A Global History of Football* (London, 2008), pp. 380–81.

41 Ibid., p. 627.

42 Jorge Rubiani, 'The Tragedy of Fram', in *The Paraguay Reader*, ed. Peter Lambert and Andrew Nickson (Chapel Hill, nc, 2013), pp. 249–53.

43 Christopher Hitchens, *The Trial of Henry Kissinger* (London, 2001), p. 56.

44 Helms, notes on meeting with the President on Chile, 15 September 1970. The handwritten notes, alongside declassified records of the u.s. involvement in Chile in the period, can be viewed at www.gwu.edu/~nsarchiv.

45 Pelé, *The Autobiography* (New York, 2008).

46 Joan Jara, *Victor: An Unfinished Song* (London, 1998).

47 Marcus Taylor, *From Pinochet to the 'Third Way'* (London, 2006).

48 Steve J. Stern, *Remembering Pinochet's Chile* (Durham, nc, 2004).

49 Naomi Klein, *The Shock Doctrine* (London, 2007).

50 Augusto Pinochet, 'Proclamation of the Junta of the Armed Forces and the Police, 11 September 1973' ('1973 09 11 Junta Militar. Bando Nro. 5. Junta Militar'), at www.archivochile.com, Dictadura Militar: Documentos Junta Militar y Gobierno Dictatorial de Pinochet, my translation.

51 Andy Beckett, *Pinochet in Piccadilly: Britain and Chile's Hidden History* (London, 2002).

52 Steve Stern, *Reckoning with Pinochet: The Memory Question in Democratic Chile, 1989–2006* (Durham, nc, 2006).

53 *Alive: The Miracle of the Andes*, dir. Frank Marshall (1993).

54 On fictional renditions of this subject, see David Wood, 'Playing by the

Book: Football in Latin American Literature', *Sport and Society*, XII/1 (2011), pp. 27–41.

55 Ezequel Fernández Moores, 'The Many Faces of Argentina '78' (2003), available at www.playthegame.org.

56 Luque, cited in Jon Spurling, *Death or Glory: The Dark History of the World Cup* (London, 2010), p. 55.

57 Spurling, *Death or Glory*, pp. 58–60.

58 Ibid., p. 63. For the Mothers of the Plaza de Mayo, see www.madres.org.

59 Ariel C. Armony, 'Transnationalizing the Dirty War: Argentina in Central America', in *In From the Cold*, ed. Joseph and Spenser, pp. 134–6.

60 Jones, *American Civilization*, p. 77. Carmagnani has a less positive interpretation: see Carmagnani, *The Other West*, pp. 217–18.

61 The quote is from Carmagnani, *The Other West*, p. 219.

62 Klaus Dodds, *Pink Ice: Britain and the South Atlantic Empire* (London, 2002).

SEVEN: Violence and Exoticism

1 For the conspiracy theories see John Perkins, *Confessions of an Economic Hit Man* (San Francisco, CA, 2004).

2 Javier Santiso, *Latin America's Political Economy of the Possible: Beyond Good Revolutionaries and Free-marketeers* (Boston, MA, 2007), p. 3.

3 Francisco Panizza, *Contemporary Latin America: Development and Democracy Beyond the Washington Consensus* (London, 2009), p. 151.

4 Gini figures are from Thorp, *Progress, Poverty and Exclusion*, appendix table viii.i, 352, and more recent figures from BBC Online, 8 October 2012, www.bbc.co.uk.

5 Mario Vargas Llosa, *A Fish in the Water: A Memoir* (London, 1994), originally published as *El pez en el agua* (Lima, 1993); Catherine M. Conaghan, *Fujimori's Peru: Deception in the Public Sphere* (Pittsburgh, PA, 2006). To listen to stories of the sterilizations, see Quipu Project: A Living Documentary, at www.quipu-project.com (accessed 13 March 2014).

6 Jimmy Burns, *Hand of God: The Life of Diego Maradona*, revd edn (London, 2010).

7 Diego Maradona, *Yo Soy El Diego* (Buenos Aires, 2000), pp. 129–30, my translation. Watch the goals on YouTube. See Burns, *Hand of God*, for a good discussion of the match – which he calls 'Falklands Round 2' and the other goal, pp. 156–66.

8 PBS, 'The New Americans', www.pbs.org.

9 John Foot, *Calcio: A History of Italian Football* (London, 2006), pp. 470–72.

10 Grant Farred, 'Fiaca and Veron-ismo: Race and Silence in Argentine Football', *Leisure Studies*, XXIII/1 (2004), pp. 47–61.

11 'The Football Association and Luis Suarez: Reasons of the Regulatory Commission', 30 December 2011, available at www.thefa.com.

12 Ben Carrington, 'Introduction: Sport Matters', *Ethnic and Racial Studies*,

XXXV/6 (2012), pp. 961–70.

13 Matt Rendell, *Kings of the Mountains: How Colombia's Cycling Heroes Changed their Nation's History* (London, 2002), pp. 199–200.

14 Frank Safford and Marco Palacios, *Colombia: Fragmented Land, Divided Society* (Oxford, 2002), p. 360.

15 See statistics presented in the United Nations Office on Drugs and Crime's World Drug Report (2012) accessible at www.unodc.org. On this period of Colombian history see Forrest Hylton, *Evil Hour in Colombia* (London, 2008).

16 Mark Bowden, *Killing Pablo: The Hunt for the World's Greatest Outlaw* (New York, 2001).

17 UNHCR 2012 Colombia report, available at www.unhcr.org.

18 Max Schoening and Sibylla Brodzinsky, eds, *Throwing Stones at the Moon: Narratives of Colombians Displaced by Conflict* (New York, 2012).

19 The supposed 'Colombianization' of Mexico remains a moot point; see for example Fernando Escalante Gonzalbo, 'Puede México ser Colombia? Violencia, narcotráfico y Estado', *Nueva sociedad*, 220 (2009), pp. 84–96.

20 Report of the Truth and Reconciliation Commission (Lima, 2003), available in English at www.cverdad.org.

21 A readable example of the genre is Tom Hart-Dyke and Paul Winder, *The Cloud Garden: A True Story of Adventure, Survival and Extreme Horticulture* (London, 2005).

22 UNODC, World Drug Report (2012), p. 99.

23 Julie A. Sellers, *Merengue and Dominican Identity: Music as National Unifier* (New York, 2004), pp. 73, 150–52, 173–4.

24 See Walter Clark, 'What Makes Latin American Music "Latin"?: Some Personal Reflections', *Music Quarterly*, XCII/3–4 (2009), pp. 167–76.

25 She revealed this in media interviews in 2009, see for example *People*, 3 March 2009, www.peopleenespanol.com.

26 Gloria Estefan, 'Mi tierra' (1993), my translation.

27 In 2011 Gloria Estefan recorded seven hour-long shows on BBC Radio 2 about the history of Latin American music, which can be downloaded free from www.bbc.co.uk.

28 Shakira and Wyclef Jean, 'Hips Don't Lie', from Shakira, *Fijación Oral* (2005). The video of course can be viewed on YouTube. It visually reinforces all the points made here.

EIGHT: Unleashed from Empire?

1 John Beverley, *Latinamericanism after 9/11* (Durham, NC, 2011).

2 Archdiocese of Guatemala, *Guatemala, Never Again* (Guatemala City, 1998).

3 Greg Grandin, 'The Instruction of Great Catastrophe: Truth Commissions, National History, and State Formation in Argentina, Chile, and Guatemala', *American Historical Review*, CX/1 (2005), pp. 46–67.

4 Héctor Abad Faciolince, *Oblivion, A Memoir*, trans. Ann McLean and

Rosalind Harvey (Tiverton, 2010), p. 211.

5 Gian Luca Gardini, *Latin America in the 21st Century: Nations, Regionalism, Globalization* (London, 2011).

6 Daniel A. Cieza, 'From Menem to Kirchner: National Autonomy and Social Movements in Argentina', in *Empire and Dissent: The United States and Latin America*, ed. Fred Rosen (London, 2008), pp. 188–204.

7 Peter Luetchford, *Fair Trade and a Global Commodity: Coffee in Costa Rica* (London, 2011), pp. 179–85.

8 Gordon Myers, *Banana Wars: The Price of Free Trade, A Caribbean Perspective* (London, 2004), p. 135.

9 Martin Edwin Anderson, *People of the Earth: Ethnonationalism, Democracy and the Indigenous Challenge in Latin America* (New York, 2011).

10 Jonathan Watts, 'World's Conservation Hopes Rest on Ecuador's Revolutionary Yasuni Model', *The Guardian*, 3 September 2012.

11 Rupert Medd, 'Travel Writing and the Peruvian Environment', unpublished PhD thesis, University of Bristol, 2013.

12 James Dunkerley, 'Evo Morales, the "Two Bolivias", and the Third Bolivian Revolution', *Journal of Latin American Studies*, XXXIX (2007), pp. 133–66. Quote from Evo Morales, 'Speech to United Nations, 21 April 2008' ('Nueva York, 23 de Abril de 2008'), www.un.org/esa/socdev/unpfii/documents/statement_morales08_es.pdf, my translation.

13 Gardini, *Latin America*, p. 88; Peter Wade, *Race and Ethnicity in Latin America* (London, 2008); André Cicalo, 'From Racial Mixture to Black Nation: Racialising Discourses in Brazil's African Affairs', *Bulletin of Latin American Affairs*, XXXIII/1 (2004), pp. 21–7.

14 Wendy Call, *No Word for Welcome: The Mexican Village Faces the Global Economy* (Lincoln, NE, 2011), pp. 291–3.

15 Joy Logan, *Aconcagua: The Invention of Mountaineering in America's Highest Peak* (Tuscon, AZ, 2011), p. 217.

16 Robert Evan Ellis, *China in Latin America: The Whats and Wherefores* (Boulder, CO, 2009), p. 152.

17 Gastón Formés and Alan Butt Philip, *The China–Latin America Axis: Emerging Markets and the Future of Globalisation* (New York, 2011), pp. 95–6, pp. 133–5.

18 Ellis, *China in Latin America*, p. 122.

19 Claudio M. Loser, 'Successful Macroeconomic Performance: Launching Long-Term Reforms', in *Latin America 2040*, ed. Harinder S. Kohli, Claudio M. Loser and Anil Sood (New Delhi, 2010), pp. 113–15.

20 Ellis, *China in Latin America*, p. 149.

21 Gustavo Vaamonde, *Oscuridad y confusión: el pueblo y la política venezolana del siglo XIX en las ideas de Antonio Guzmán Blanco* (Caracas, 2004).

22 Bart Jones, *Hugo! The Hugo Chávez Story, from Mud Hut to Perpetual Revolution* (Hanover, 2007); Oscar Guardiola-Rivera, 'Hugo Chávez Kept his Promise to the People of Venezuela', www.guardian.co.uk, 5 March 2013; Hector Abad, 'After Chávez: There are Many Flavours to the Left

in Latin America', *The Observer*, 10 March 2013, www.guardian.co.uk.

23   Germán Carrera Damas, *El culto a Bolívar* (1969).

24   Will Grant, 'Manuela Saenz', BBC Online, 5 July 2010, www.bbc.co.uk.

25   Paul G. Auwaerter, John Dove, and Philip A. Mackowiak, 'Simón Bolívar's Medical Labyrinth: An Infectious Diseases Conundrum', *Clinical Infectious Diseases*, LII/1 (2011), pp. 78–85.

26   Quotes, and translations, from *The Scotsman*, 16 July 2010.

27   See for the case of Peru, Jelke Boesten, *Intersecting Inequalities: Women and Social Policy in Peru, 1990–2000* (University Park, PA, 2010), pp. 76–81.

28   UNAIDS, '2012 Fact Sheet', www.unaids.org.

29   Teresa A. Meade, *A History of Modern Latin America, 1800 to the Present* (Oxford, 2010), pp. 297–9.

30   See for example Anne Thomas, 'Brazilian Football Lucio Offers All Glory to God', *Christianity Today*, 13 June 2006.

31   Kohli, Loser and Sood, eds, *Latin America 2040*, p. 227.

32   Amaranta Wright, *Ripped and Torn: Levi's, Latin America and The Blue Jean Dream* (London, 2006), particularly pp. 203–23.

33   In this paragraph I draw the primary sources from Francisco Panizza, *Contemporary Latin America: Development and Democracy Beyond the Washington Consensus* (London, 2009), p. 251.

34   Cristina Fernández de Kirchner to David Cameron, www.guardian.co.uk, 3 January 2013.

35   Francisco Perejil, 'Argentina expropia a Repsol su filial YBF', *El País*, 17 April 2012.

36   For Sorrell's reaction, see www.guardian.co.uk, 4 May 2012.

37   A nice introduction to the detail here is Marita Eastmond, 'Reconstructing Life: Chilean Refugee Women and the Dilemmas of Exile', in *Migrant Women: Crossing Boundaries and Changing Identities*, ed. Gina Buijs (Oxford, 1993), pp. 35–54.

38   See the discussion in Lisa García Bedolla and Kerry L. Haynie, 'The Obama Coalition and the Future of American Politics', *Politics, Groups and Identities*, 1/1 (2013), pp. 128–33.

39   John Nieto-Phillips, 'Afterword: Echoes of Colonialism: Peninsulares, Wholesome Hispanics, Steamy Latins', in *Interpreting Spanish Colonialism: Empires, Nations and Legends*, ed. Nieto-Phillips and Christopher Schmidt-Nowara (Albuquerque, NM, 2005), p. 251.

40   Jamie Jackson, 'The Journey Boys from Brazil', *The Observer*, 14 October 2012, pp. 8–9.

41   Jon Cotterill, quoted ibid.

42   Reported by Maria Martin from São Paulo, in *El País*, 8 January 2013.

43   Romário de Souza Faria, 'I Supported Brazil's World Cup Bid, but the Expense is now Crippling Us', www.guardian.co.uk, 24 June 2013.

44   Matt Rendell, *Salsa for People Who Probably Shouldn't* (London, 2010).

45   Carlos Alberto Torres, FIFA ambassador, interview reported in *La Gazzetta DF*, 5 December 2013, www.lagazzettadf.com.

BIBLIOGRAPHY

Abad Faciolince, Hector, *Oblivion, A Memoir*, trans. Anne McLean and
 Rosalind Harvey (Tiverton, 2010)
Abel, Christopher, *José Martí: Revolutionary Democrat* (London, 1986)
Albert, Bill, *South America and the World Economy from Independence to 1930*
 (London, 1982)
Allende, Isabel, *Daughter of Fortune* (New York, 2000)
Anad, Guillermo, *Tango, transmodernidad y desencuentro* (New York, 2011)
Anderson, Jon Lee, *Che Guevara: A Revolutionary Life* (New York, 1997)
Anderson, Martin Edwin, *People of the Earth: Ethnonationalism, Democracy
 and the Indigenous Challenge in Latin America* (New York, 2011)
Anna, Timothy, *Forging Mexico, 1821–1835* (Lincoln, NE, 1998)
Archdiocese of Guatemala, *Guatemala, Never Again* (Guatemala City, 1998)
Archetti, Eduardo P., *Masculinities: Football, Polo and the Tango in Argentina*
 (Oxford, 1999)
Auwaerter, Paul G., John Dove, and Philip A. Mackowiak, 'Simón Bolívar's
 Medical Labyrinth: An Infectious Diseases Conundrum', *Clinical
 Infectious Diseases*, LII/1 (2011), pp. 78–85
Bacelli, R., *Jardim America* (São Paulo, 1982)
Bayly, C. A., *The Birth of the Modern World, 1780–1914: Global Connections
 and Comparisons* (Oxford, 2004)
Beckett, Andy, *Pinochet in Piccadilly: Britain and Chile's Hidden History*
 (London, 2002)
Bellos, Alex, *Futebol: The Brazilian Way of Life* (London, 2002)
Bergero, Adriana J., *Intersecting Tango: Cultural Geographies of Buenos Aires,
 1900–1930*, trans. Richard Young (Pittsburgh, PA, 2008)
Bergquist, Charles, *Coffee and Conflict in Colombia, 1886–1910* (Durham, NC, 1996)
Bethell, Leslie, 'Brazil and "Latin America"', *Journal of Latin American Studies*,
 XLII/3 (2010), pp. 457–85
——, ed., *The Cambridge History of Latin America* (Cambridge, 1986)
——, ed., *Brazil: Empire and Republic, 1822–1930* (Cambridge, 1989)
——, *The Abolition of the Brazilian Slave Trade: Britain, Brazil and the Slave
 Trade Question, 1807–1869* (Cambridge, 1970)
Beverley, John, *Latinamericanism after 9/11* (Durham, NC, 2011)

Bingham, Hiram, *Inca Land: The Incredible Story of the Discovery of Machu Picchu* [1922] (Washington, DC, 2003)

Blanchard, Peter, *Under the Flags of Freedom: Slave Soldiers and the Wars of Independence in Spanish South America* (Pittsburgh, PA, 2008)

Blaufarb, Rafe, 'The Western Question: The Geopolitics of Latin American Independence', *Hispanic American Historical Review*, CXII/3 (2007), pp. 742–63

Blay, E., *Eu não tenho onde morar: vilas operarias na cidade de São Paulo* (São Paulo, 1985)

Boesten, Jelke, *Intersecting Inequalities: Women and Social Policy in Peru, 1990–2000* (University Park, PA, 2010)

Borges, Jorge Luis, *Collected Fictions*, trans. Andrew Hurley (London, 1999)

Bowden, Mark, *Killing Pablo: The Hunt for the World's Greatest Outlaw* (New York, 2001)

Brading, David, *The First America: The Spanish Monarchy, Creole Patriots and the Liberal State, 1492–1867* (Cambridge, 1991)

Brewster, Claire, and Keith Brewster, *Representing the Nation: Sport and Spectacle in Post-Revolutionary Mexico* (London, 2010)

Brown, Matthew, *Adventuring through Spanish Colonies: Simón Bolívar, Foreign Mercenaries and the Birth of New Nations* (Liverpool, 2006)

——, ed., *Informal Empire in Latin America: Culture, Commerce and Capital* (Oxford, 2008)

——, ed. and trans., *Simón Bolívar: The Bolivarian Revolution, introduced by Hugo Chávez* (New York, 2009)

——, 'Inca, Sailor, Soldier, King: Gregor MacGregor and the Revolutionary Caribbean', *Bulletin of Latin American Research*, XXIV/1 (2005), pp. 44–70

——, *The Struggle for Power in Post-Independence Colombia and Venezuela* (London, 2012)

——, and Gloria Lanci, 'A Transnational Investigation of Football and Urban Heritage in São Paulo, 1890 to 1930', in *Global Play: Football between Region, Nation and the World in Latin American, African and European History*, ed. Stefan Rinke and Christina Peters (Stuttgart, 2014), pp. 17–40

——, and Gabriel B. Paquette, eds, *Connections after Colonialism: Europe and Latin America in the 1820s* (Tuscaloosa, AZ, 2013)

Bulmer-Thomas, Victor, *The Economic History of Latin America since Independence* (Cambridge, 1995)

——, Roberto Conde and John Coatsworth, *Cambridge Economic History of Latin America* (Cambridge, 2006)

Burns, Jimmy, *Hand of God: The Life of Diego Maradona*, revd edn (London, 2010)

Bushnell, David, ed., *El Libertador: Selected Writings of Simón Bolívar* (Oxford, 2004)

Cain, Peter, and Anthony Hopkins, *British Imperialism, 1688–2000* (London, 2001)

Calderón, María Teresa, and Clément Thibaud, *La majestad de los pueblos en la Nueva Granada y Venezuela (1780–1832)* (Bogotá, 2011)

Call, Wendy, *No Word for Welcome: The Mexican Village Faces the Global*

Economy (Lincoln, NE, 2011)

Carmagnani, Marcello, *The Other West: Latin America from Invasion to Globalization*, trans. Rosanna M. Giammanco Frongia (Berkeley, CA, 2011), first published in Italian in 2003

Carpentier, Alejo, *The Kingdom of this World* (Havana, 1949)

Carroll, Rory, 'Cadres or Caddies', *The Guardian*, 11 April 2008

Castañeda, Jorge, *The Life and Death of Che Guevara* (London, 1997)

Charge, Stephen, 'Great Britain and the War of the Triple Alliance', unpublished MA dissertation, University of Bristol (2010)

Chasteen, John Charles, 'The Pre-history of Samba: Carnival Dancing in Rio de Janeiro, 1840–1914', *Journal of Latin American Studies*, XXVIII/1 (1996), pp. 29–47

Chiaramonte, José Carlos, *Nation and State in Latin America: Political Language During Independence* (Buenos Aires, 2010)

Cicalo, André, 'From Racial Mixture to Black Nation: Racialising Discourses in Brazil's African Affairs', *Bulletin of Latin American Affairs*, XXXIII/1 (2004), pp. 16–30

Cieza, Daniel A., 'From Menem to Kirchner: National Autonomy and Social Movements in Argentina', in *Empire and Dissent: The United States and Latin America*, ed. Fred Rosen (London, 2008), pp. 188–204

Clark, Walter, 'What Makes Latin American Music "Latin"?: Some Personal Reflections', *Music Quarterly*, XCII/3–4 (2009), pp. 167–76

Cole Heinowitz, Rebecca, *Spanish America and British Romanticism, 1777–1826* (Edinburgh, 2010)

Collier, Simón, *The Life, Music and Times of Carlos Gardel* (Pittsburgh, PA, 1986)

Conaghan, Catherine M., *Fujimori's Peru: Deception in the Public Sphere* (Pittsburgh, PA, 2006)

Cordingly, David, *Cochrane the Dauntless: The Life and Adventures of Admiral Thomas Cochrane, 1775–1860* (London, 2007)

Coronil, Fernando, *The Magical State: Nature, Money and Modernity in Venezuela* (Chicago, IL, 1997)

Costeloe, Michael P., *Bonds and Bondholders: British Investors and Mexico's Foreign Debt, 1824–1888* (Westport, CT, 2003)

Cox Hall, Amy, 'Collecting a "Lost City" for Science: Huaquero Vision and the Yale Peruvian Expeditions to Machu Picchu, 1911, 1912, and 1914–15', *Ethnohistory*, LIX/2 (2012), pp. 293–321

Crow, Joanna, *The Mapuche in Modern Chile: A Cultural History* (Gainesville, FL, 2013)

Cushman, Gregory, *Guano and the Opening of the Pacific World* (Cambridge, 2013)

Darwin, Charles, *Journal of Researches into the Natural History and Geology of the Countries Visited during the Voyage of HMS Beagle, Round the World* (London, 1845)

Dawson, Alexander, *Latin America since Independence: A New Interpretation* (London, 2010)

Dawson, Frank Griffith, *The First Latin American Debt Crisis: The City of London and the 1822–1825 Loan Bubble* (London, 1990)

Dodds, Klaus, *Pink Ice: Britain and the South Atlantic Empire* (London, 2002)

Dunkerley, James, *Rebellion in the Veins: Political Struggle in Bolivia, 1952–1982* (London, 1984)

——, 'Evo Morales, the "Two Bolivias", and the Third Bolivian Revolution', *Journal of Latin American Studies*, XXXIX (2007), pp. 133–66

Dym, Jordana, *From Sovereign Villages to National States: City, State and Federation in Central America, 1759–1839* (Albuquerque, NM, 2006)

Earle, Rebecca, *The Return of the Native: Indians and Myth-making in Spanish America, 1810–1930* (Durham, NC, 2008)

——, '*Padres de la patria* and the Ancestral Past: Celebrations of Independence in Nineteenth-century Spanish America', *Journal of Latin American Studies*, XXXIV/4 (2002), pp. 775–805

Eastmond, Marita, 'Reconstructing Life: Chilean Refugee Women and the Dilemmas of Exile', in *Migrant Women: Crossing Boundaries and Changing Identities*, ed. Gina Buijs (Oxford, 1993), pp. 35–54

Ellis, R. Evan, *China in Latin America: The Whats and Wherefores* (Boulder, CO, 2009)

Elsey, Brenda, *Citizens and Sportsmen: Fútbol & Politics in 20th-century Chile* (Austin, TX, 2012)

Escalante Gonzalbo, Fernando, '¿Puede México ser Colombia? Violencia, narcotráfico y Estado', *Nueva sociedad*, 220 (2009), pp. 84–96

Evans, Richard J., 'Prologue: What is History – Now?', in *What is History Now?*, ed. David Cannadine (London, 2002), pp. 1–18

Farred, Grant, 'Fiaca and Veronismo: Race and Silence in Argentine Football', *Leisure Studies*, XXIII/1 (2004), pp. 47–61

Fausto, Boris, *A Concise History of Brazil* (Cambridge, 1999)

Feinstein, Adam, *Pablo Neruda: A Passion for Life* (London, 2004)

Ferguson, Niall, *Empire: How Britain Made the Modern World* (London, 2004)

——, *Civilization: The Six Killer Apps of Western Power* (London, 2011)

——, *Colossus: The Rise and Fall of the American Empire* (London, 2009)

Fernández-Armesto, Felipe, *The Americas: A Hemispheric History* (London, 2003)

Foot, John, *Calcio: A History of Italian Football* (London, 2006)

Formés, Gastón, and Alan Butt Philip, *The China–Latin America Axis: Emerging Markets and the Future of Globalisation* (New York, 2011)

Foster, Kevin, *Lost Worlds: Latin America and the Imagining of Empire* (London, 2009)

Fowler, Will, *Latin America since 1780* (London, 2002)

——, *Santa Anna of Mexico* (London, 2007)

——, 'The *Pronunciamiento* in Mexico', in Brown and Paquette, *Connections after Colonialism*, pp. 46–63

Franco, Jean, *The Decline and Fall of the Lettered City: Latin America in the Cold War* (London, 2002)

Freyre, Gilberto, *The Masters and the Slaves: A Study in the Development of Brazilian Civilization*, trans. Samuel Putnam (New York, 1964, first published in Portuguese in 1934)

Galeano, Eduardo, *Open Veins of Latin America: Five Centuries of the Pillage of a Continent* (London, 1973)

——, *El fútbol a sol y sombra* (Montevideo, 1998)

Gallegos, Rómulo, *Doña Bárbara* (Caracas, 1929)

Gallo, Klaus, *Great Britain and Argentina* (Basingstoke, 2001)

García Canclini, Nestor, *Hybrid Cultures: Strategies for Entering and Leaving Modernity* (Minneapolis, MN, 1995)

García Márquez, Gabriel, *One Hundred Years of Solitude*, trans. Edith Grossman (London, 1968, first published Mexico City, 1967)

Gardini, Gian Luca, *Latin America in the 21st Century: Nations, Regionalism, Globalization* (London, 2011)

Garner, Paul, *Porfirio Díaz* (New York, 2001)

Geggus, David, ed., *The Impact of the Haitian Revolution in the Atlantic World* (Columbia, SC, 2001)

Giulianotti, Richard, *Football: A Sociology of the Global Game* (London, 1999)

——, 'Football, South America and Globlisation: Conceptual Paths', in *Fútbol, Futebol, Soccer: Football in the Americas*, ed. Rory Miller and Liz Crolley (London, 2007)

Goebel, Michael, '*Gauchos, Gringos* and *Gallegos*: The Assimilation of Italian and Spanish Immigrants in the Making of Modern Uruguay, 1880–1930', *Past and Present*, XXVIII/1 (2010), pp. 191–229

Goldblatt, David, *The Ball is Round: A Global History of Football* (London, 2008)

Goodman, Jordan, *The Devil and Mr Casement: One Man's Struggle for Human Rights in South America's Heart of Darkness* (London, 2009)

Gott, Richard, *Cuba: A New History* (London, 2004)

Grandin, Greg, 'The Instruction of Great Catastrophe: Truth Commissions, National History, and State Formation in Argentina, Chile, and Guatemala', *American Historical Review*, C/1 (2005), pp. 46–67

——, *The Last Colonial Massacre: Latin America in the Cold War* (Chicago, IL, 2004)

——, *Fordlandia: The Rise and Fall of Henry Ford's Forgotten Jungle City* (New York, 2009)

Guardiola-Rivera, Oscar, *What if Latin America Ruled the World? How the South will Take the North into the 22nd Century* (London, 2011)

Guevara, Ernesto 'Che', *The Motorcycle Diaries: A Journey Around South America*, trans. Ann Wright (London, 1995)

Güiraldes, Ricardo, *Don Segundo Sombra* (Buenos Aires, 1926)

Gunder Frank, Andre, *Capitalism and Underdevelopment in Latin America: Historical Studies of Chile and Brazil* (New York, 1967)

Gutiérrez, Gustavo, *A Theology of Liberation* (London, 1988)

Hagedorn, Dan, *Conquistadors of the Sky: A History of Aviation in Latin America* (Miami, FL, 2010)

Hamilton, Adrian, *An Entirely Different Game: The British Influence in Brazilian*

Football (Edinburgh, 1998)

Hart-Dyke, Tom, and Paul Winder, *The Cloud Garden: A True Story of Adventure, Survival and Extreme Horticulture* (London, 2005)

Hennessey, Alistair, and John King, eds, *The Land that England Lost. Britain and Argentina, A Special Relationship* (London, 1992)

Heraud, Javier, *Poesias completas y cartas* (Lima, 1976)

Hiatt, Willie, 'Flying "Cholo": Incas, Airplanes and the Construction of Andean Modernity in 1920s Cuzco', *The Americas*, LXIII/3 (2007), pp. 327–58

Hitchens, Christopher, *The Trial of Henry Kissinger* (London, 2001)

Hulme, Peter, *Cuba's Wild East: A Literary Geography of Oriente* (Oxford, 2012)

——, and William Sherman, eds, *The Tempest and its Travels* (London, 2000)

Huntingdon, Samuel, *The Clash of Civilisations and the Remaking of World Order* (New York, 1996)

Hylton, Forrest, *Evil Hour in Colombia* (London, 2008)

Icaza, Jorge, *Huasipungo* (Quito, 1934)

Jackson, Jamie, 'The Journey Boys from Brazil', *The Observer*, 14 October 2012

Jara, Joan, *Victor: An Unfinished Song* (London, 1998)

Jobs, Richard Ivan, 'Youth Movements: Travel, Protest and Europe in 1968', *American Historical Review*, CXIV/2, (2009), pp. 376–404

Jones, Bart, *Hugo! The Hugo Chávez Story, from Mud Hut to Perpetual Revolution* (Hanover, NH, 2007)

Jones, Charles, *American Civilization* (London, 2007)

Joseph, Gilbert M., and Timothy J. Henderson, eds, *The Mexico Reader: History, Politics, Culture* (Durham, NC, 2003)

——, and Daniella Spenser, eds, *In From the Cold: Latin America's New Encounter with the Cold War* (Durham, NC, 2008)

Karush, Matthew B., *Culture of Class: Radio and Cinema in the Making of a Divided Argentina, 1920–1946* (Durham, NC, 2012)

Klein, Naomi, *The Shock Doctrine* (London, 2007)

Knight, Alan, 'The Mexican Revolution: Bourgeois? Nationalist? Or Was it Just a Great Rebellion?', *Bulletin of Latin American Research*, IV/2 (1985), pp. 1–17

——, 'Rethinking Informal Empire in Latin America (especially Argentina)', in *Informal Empire in Latin America: Culture, Commerce and Capital*, ed. Matthew Brown (Oxford, 2008), pp. 23–48

Kohli, Harinder S., Claudio M. Loser and Anil Sood, eds, *Latin America 2040* (New Delhi, 2010)

Kraay, Hendrick, *Race, State and Armed Forces in Independence-era Brazil, 1790s–1840s* (Stanford, CA, 2001)

Lambert, Peter, and Andrew Nickson, eds, *The Paraguay Reader* (Chapel Hill, NC, 2013)

Lazar, Sian, *El Alto, Rebel City: Self and Citizenship in Andean Bolivia* (Durham, NC, 2010)

Lesser, Jeffrey, *Immigration, Ethnicity and National Identity in Brazil* (Cambridge, 2012)

——, and Raanen Rein, eds, *Re-thinking Jewish Latin Americans* (Albuquerque, NM, 2008)

Lewis, Colin, 'Britain, the Argentine and Informal Empire', in *Informal Empire*, ed. Brown, pp. 99–123

Llorca-Jaña, Manuel, 'Of Shipwrecks, "Savages" and Seamen: British Consular Contacts with the Native People of Southern South America during the 1820s and 1830s', *International Journal of Maritime History*, XXIV/2 (2012), pp. 127–54

Logan, Joy, *Aconcagua: The Invention of Mountaineering on America's Highest Peak* (Tucson, AZ, 2011)

Luetchford, Peter, *Fair Trade and a Global Commodity: Coffee in Costa Rica* (London, 2011)

Lynch, John, *Simón Bolívar: A Life* (New Haven, CT, 2006)

——, 'British Policy and Spanish America, 1783–1808', *Journal of Latin American Studies*, I/1 (1969), pp. 1–30

——, *New Worlds: A Religious History of Latin America* (London, 2012)

McFarlane, Anthony, *War and Independence in Spanish America* (London, 2014)

McGuinness, Aims, *Path of Empire: Panama and the California Gold Rush* (New York, 2009)

Maradona, Diego, *Yo Soy El Diego* (Buenos Aires, 2000)

Martin, Gerald, *Journeys through the Labyrinth: Latin American Fiction in the Twentieth Century* (London, 1989)

Mascarenhas, G., 'Várzeas, Operários e Futebol: uma outra Geografia', *GEOgraphia*, IV/8 (2002), pp. 84–92

Maurer, Noel, and Carlos Yu, *The Big Ditch: How America Took, Built, Ran and Ultimately Gave Away the Panama Canal* (Princeton, NJ, 2010)

May, Robert E., *Manifest Destiny's Underworld: Filibustering in Antebellum America* (Durham, NC, 2002)

Meade, Teresa A., *A History of Modern Latin America, 1800 to the Present* (Oxford, 2010)

Medd, Rupert, 'Travel Writing and the Peruvian Environment: Testing Nature and Coloniality', unpublished PhD thesis, University of Bristol (2013)

Menchú, Rigoberta, with Elizabeth Burgos-Debray, *I, Rigoberta Menchú: An Indigenous Woman in Guatemala* (London, 1983)

Méndez, Cecilia, *The Plebian Republic: The Huanta Rebellion and the Making of the Peruvian State, 1820–1850* (Durham, NC, 2005)

Mignolo, Walter, *The Idea of Latin America* (Oxford, 2004)

Miller, Bonnie, M., *From Liberation to Conquest: The Visual and Popular Cultures of the Spanish–American War of 1898* (Amherst, MA, 2011)

Miller, Nicola, 'The Absolution of History: Uses of the Past in Castro's Cuba', *Journal of Contemporary History*, XXXVIII/1 (2003), pp. 147–62

——, 'Reassessing the Cuban Missile Crisis: The Post Cold War Historiography', in *War and Cold War in American Foreign Policy, 1942–1962*, ed. Dale Carter and Robin Clifton (London, 2001), pp. 211–39

Miller, Rory, *Britain and Latin America in the Nineteenth and Twentieth*

Centuries (London, 1994)

——, and Liz Crolley, eds, *Fútbol, Futebol, Soccer: Football in the Americas* (London, 2007)

Moraña, Mabel, Enrique Dussel and Carlos A. Jáuregui, eds, *Coloniality at Large: Latin America and the Postcolonial Debate* (Chapel Hill, NC, 2008)

Moya, José C., *Cousins and Strangers: Spanish Immigrants in Buenos Aires, 1850–1930* (Berkeley, CA, 1998)

——, ed., *Oxford Handbook of Latin American History* (Oxford, 2011)

Múnera, Alfonso, *El fracaso de la nación: Región, clase y raza en el caribe colombiano, 1717–1821* (Bogotá, 1998)

Myers, Gordon, *Banana Wars: The Price of Free Trade, A Caribbean Perspective* (London, 2004)

Neruda, Pablo, *Canto general* (Santiago, 1950)

Nieto-Phillips, John, 'Afterword: Echoes of Colonialism: Peninsulares, Wholesome Hispanics, Steamy Latins', in *Interpreting Spanish Colonialism: Empires, Nations and Legends*, ed. Nieto-Phillips and Christopher Schmidt-Nowara (Albuquerque, NM, 2005)

Ortiz, Fernando, *Contrapunteo cubano del tabaco y el azúcar* (Havana, 1940)

Panizza, Francisco, *Contemporary Latin America: Development and Democracy Beyond the Washington Consensus* (London, 2009)

Paquette, Gabriel B., 'The Brazilian Origins of the Portuguese Constitution', in *Connections after Colonialism*, ed. Brown and Paquette, pp. 108–38

Patenaude, Bertrand M., *Trotsky: Downfall of a Revolutionary* (New York, 2010)

Pearson, Andrew, Ben Jeffs, Annsofie Witkin and Helen MacQuarrie, *Infernal Traffic, Excavation of a Liberated African Graveyard in Rupert's Valley, St Helena* (London, 2012)

Pedraja, René de la, *Wars of Latin America, 1899–1941* (Jefferson, NC, 2006)

Perkins, John, *Confessions of an Economic Hit Man* (San Francisco, CA, 2004)

Pilcher, Jeffrey M., *Cantinflas and the Chaos of Mexican Modernity* (London, 2001)

Plotkin, Mariano Ben, *Mañana es San Perón: A Cultural History of Perón's Argentina* (London, 2002)

Posada-Carbó, Eduardo, 'Fiction as History: The Bananeras and Gabriel García Márquez's *One Hundred Years of Solitude*', *Journal of Latin American Studies*, XXX/2 (1998), pp. 395–414

Quijano, Aníbal, 'Coloniality of Power and Eurocentrism in Latin America', *International Sociology*, XV/2 (2000), pp. 215–32

Racine, Karen, '"This England, This Now": British Cultural and Intellectual Influence in Spanish America in the Independence-Era', *Hispanic American Historical Review*, XC/3 (2010), pp. 423–54

Reid Andrews, George, *Afro-Latin America, 1800–2000* (Oxford, 2004)

Rendell, Matt, *Kings of the Mountains: How Colombia's Cycling Heroes Changed their Nation's History* (London, 2002)

——, *A Significant Other* (London, 2003)

——, *Salsa for People who Probably Shouldn't* (London, 2010)

Rinke, Stefan, '¿La última pasión verdadera?: La historia del fútbol en América Latina en contexto global', *Iberoamericana*, VII/27 (2007), pp. 85–100

Rivera, José Eustacio, *La vorágine* (Bogotá, 1924)

Robson, Martin, *Britain, Portugal and South America in the Napoleonic Wars: Alliances and Diplomacy in Economic Maritime Conflict* (London, 2011)

Rock, David, *Argentina, 1516–1982* (London, 1986)

Safford, Frank, and Marco Palacios, *Colombia: Fragmented Land, Divided Society* (Oxford, 2002)

Santiso, Javier, *Latin America's Political Economy of the Possible: Beyond Good Revolutionaries and Free-Marketeers* (Boston, MA, 2007)

Sarmiento, Domingo, *Facundo: Civilization and Barbarism* [1845], ed. and trans. Kathleen Ross (Berkeley, CA, 2003)

Schoening, Max, and Sibylla Brodzinsky, eds, *Throwing Stones at the Moon: Narratives of Colombians Displaced by Conflict* (New York, 2012)

Schultz, Kirsten, *Tropical Versailles: Empire, Monarchy and the Portuguese Royal Court in Rio de Janeiro* (New York, 2001)

Seigel, Micol, *Uneven Encounters: Making Race and Nation in Brazil and the United States* (Chapel Hill, NC, 2009)

Sellers, Julie A., *Merengue and Dominican Identity: Music as National Unifier* (New York, 2004)

Sexton, Jay, *The Monroe Doctrine: Empire and Nation in Nineteenth-century America* (New York, 2011)

Simpson, Will, and Malcolm McMahon, *Freedom through Football: The Story of the Easton Cowboys and Cowgirls* (Bristol, 2012)

Skidmore, Thomas E., and Peter H. Smith, *Modern Latin America*, 3rd edn (Oxford, 1992)

Skinner, Joan Lee, 'Family Secrets: Incest in Jorge Isaacs' *Maria*', *Hispanic Review*, LXXVI/1 (2008), pp. 53–69

Sommer, Doris, *Foundational Fictions: National Romances of Latin America* (Berkeley, CA, 1992)

Spurling, Jon, *Death or Glory: The Dark History of the World Cup* (London, 2010)

Starn, Orin, Carlos Ivan Degregori and Robin Kirk, eds, *The Peru Reader: History, Culture, Politics* (Durham, NC, 2005), pp. 181–99

Stephenson, Charles, *The Admiral's Secret Weapon: Lord Dundonald and the Origins of Chemical Warfare* (Woodbridge, 2006)

Stern, Steve J., *Remembering Pinochet's Chile* (Durham, NC, 2004)

——, *Reckoning with Pinochet: The Memory Question in Democratic Chile, 1989–2006* (Durham, NC, 2006)

Taffet, Jeffrey, *Foreign Aid as Foreign Policy: The Alliance for Progress in Latin America* (London, 2007)

Taylor, Marcus, *From Pinochet to the 'Third Way'* (London, 2006)

The South American Handbook (London, 1927)

Thomas, Anne, 'Brazilian Footballer Lucio Offers All Glory to God', *Christianity Today*, 13 June 2006

Thomson, Guy, ed., *The European Revolutions of 1848 and the Americas* (London, 2001)

Thorp, Rosemary, *Progress, Poverty and Exclusion: An Economic History of Latin America* (Oxford, 2000)

Tinker Salas, Miguel, *The Enduring Legacy: Oil, Culture and Society in Venezuela* (Durham, NC, 2009)

Torres, Camilo, *Revolutionary Priest: His Complete Writings and Messages*, ed. J. Gerasi, trans. J. De C. Alcantara (London, 1973)

Tovar Pinzón, Hermes, 'Tras las huellas del soldado Pinzón', in *Memorias de un País en Guerra: Los Mil Días, 1899–1902*, ed. Gonzalo Sánchez and Mario Aguilera (Bogotá, 2001)

Vaamonde, Gustavo, *Oscuridad y confusión: el pueblo y la política venezolana del siglo XIX en las ideas de Antonio Guzmán Blanco* (Caracas, 2004)

Vale, Brian, *A War Betwixt Englishmen: Brazil against Argentina on the River Plate, 1825–1830* (London, 2001)

Vallejo, Jody Agius 'Latina Spaces: Middle-class Ethnic Capital and Professional Associations in the Latina Community', *City and Community*, VIII/2 (2009), pp. 129–54

Van Young, Eric, *The Other Rebellion: Popular Violence, Ideology and the Mexican Struggle for Independence, 1810–1821* (Stanford, CA, 2001)

Vargas Llosa, Mario, *The Dream of the Celt* (London, 2012)

——, *A Fish in the Water: A Memoir*, trans. Helen Lane (London, 1994)

Vásquez, Juan Gabriel, *The Informers*, trans. Anne McLean (London, 2009)

——, *The Sound of Things Falling*, trans. Anne McLean (London, 2012)

Waddell, D.A.G., 'British Neutrality and Spanish–American Independence: The Problem of Foreign Enlistment', *Journal of Latin American Studies*, XIX/1 (1987), pp. 1–18

Wade, Peter, *Race and Ethnicity in Latin America* (London, 2010)

Walvin, James, *Crossings: Africa, the Americas and the Atlantic Slave Trade* (London, 2013)

Watts, Jonathan, 'World's Conservation Hopes Rest on Ecuador's Revolutionary Yasuni Model', *The Guardian*, 3 September 2012

Whigham, Thomas, 'The Paraguayan War: A Catalyst for Nationalism in South America', in *I Die With My Country: Perspectives on the Paraguayan War, 1864–1870*, ed. Hendrick Kraay and Thomas Whigham (Lincoln, NE, 2004), pp. 179–98

Williamson, Edwin, *Borges: A Life* (London, 2004)

——, *Penguin History of Latin America* (London, 2009)

Winn, Peter, 'British Informal Empire in Uruguay', *Past and Present*, 73 (1976), pp. 100–126

Wisbeck, Dwayne R., and Robert M. Pike, *Communication and Empire: Media, Markets and Globalization, 1860–1930* (Durham, NC, 2007)

Wood, David, 'Playing by the Book: Football in Latin American Literature', *Sport and Society*, XII/1 (2011), pp. 27–41

Wright, Amaranta, *Ripped and Torn: Levi's, Latin America and The Blue Jean Dream* (London, 2006)

Wright, Winthrop, 'Foreign-owned Railways in Argentina: A Case Study of Economic Nationalism', *Business History Review*, XLI/1 (1967), pp. 62–93

ACKNOWLEDGEMENTS

I am most grateful to Michael Leaman for his forbearance and encouragement. Thanks to Jeremy Black for the original idea. Since 2005 I have taught a course to second-year undergraduates at the University of Bristol called 'From Frontiers to Football: Nations in Latin America since 1800'. The content of this book has grown out of the classes taught at Bristol, and in response to questions and scepticism from enthusiastic, intelligent and challenging students. In particular I would like to thank the class of 2012–13, who put up with me testing passages and interpretations on them with great grace. I am grateful to my colleagues Robert Bickers, Carmen Brauning, Jo Crow, Josie Mclellan, Paco Romero, Karen Tucker, Rossana Vanni and Caroline Williams, and to my parents Ann Brown and David Brown, for their support and inspiration. Working with Andrés Baeza, Barbara Castillo, Rupert Medd, Fernando Padilla and Alastair Wilson on their doctoral research projects has been a joyful and insightful process, for which I am most grateful. The material on early football in São Paulo draws directly on my work with Gloria Lanci, and I am grateful to her for permission to refer to it here, and for her constant demands for me to learn more. I also owe thanks to the managers and professors who advised me not to write this book, recommending me to focus on ever more esoteric and irrelevant subjects that might be considered cutting-edge by overworked and desperate reviewers. If I had not been so appalled by that advice, I may never have written this book.

I have written this book in the British Library and the University of Bristol, and am grateful to the custodians of the collections in those institutions who have provided me with books and assistance. My previous research projects have been financed by the British Academy, the Arts and Humanities Research Council, the Society for Latin American Studies, CONICYT and the Carnegie Trust for the Universities of Scotland. I thank Natasha, Calum, Keir, Morag and Mairi for their delightful distractions and multiple inspirations.

I thank Christopher Abel for always patiently suggesting that I try to situate the cultural history that interested me against the economic history that was important. I hope that he is not too disappointed with the broad range and general statements that litter the text. Kate Simpson and Jon Cassidy, this book has grown out of our long conversations in Villa María del Triunfo about how to talk with young Britons about Latin America. Conversations with Peter Wade, Peter

Brown, Nicola Foote, Michael Goebel and David Goldblatt helped me rethink key sections. I owe a debt to Edwin Williamson, who taught me as an undergraduate and whose *The Penguin History of Latin America* remains the standard reference work in English on many of the subjects discussed here. I am grateful to the many audiences who have challenged me on aspects of this subject in Latin America and Europe. All errors are mine alone. All translations from Spanish or Portuguese are my own unless otherwise stated.

The book is dedicated to the Latin Americans who first got me thinking about our interlinked histories, especially Francisco Correa, Marleny Silva, Paula Cruz, Katia Urteaga Villanueva, Sergio Meza, América Campoy de Cisneros, and in memory of my friend the wonderful poet Antonio Cisneros.

PHOTO ACKNOWLEDGEMENTS

The author and the publishers wish to express their thanks to the below sources of illustrative material and/or permission to reproduce it.

Agência Brasil (Department of Press and Media): pp. 189, 193, 198; Aurelio Escobar Castellanos Archive: p. 66; Library of Congress, Washington, DC: p. 73; Library of the National Congress of Chile: p. 152; MettaMomma: p. 137; Museo Che Guevara (Centro de Estudios Che Guevara, La Habana, Cuba): p. 120; Museum of the Argentine Bicentennial: p. 133; Neogeolegend: p. 165; Shutterstock: p. 181 (s_bukley); U.S. Central Intelligence Agency: p. 6; World Economic Forum: p. 149 (E.T. Studhalter).

INDEX